Understanding the community management of high risk offenders

CRIME AND JUSTICE
Series editor: Mike Maguire
Cardiff University and University of Glamorgan

Crime and Justice is a series of short introductory texts on central topics in criminology. The books in this series are written for students by internationally renowned authors. Each book tackles a key area within criminology, providing a concise and up-to-date overview of the principal concepts, theories, methods and findings relating to the area. Taken as whole, the *Crime and Justice* series will cover all the core components of an undergraduate criminology course.

Published titles

Understanding the community management of high risk offenders
Hazel Kemshall

Understanding modernisation in criminal justice
Paul Senior, Chris Crowther-Dowey and Matt Long

Understanding youth and crime
Sheila Brown

Understanding crime data
Clive Coleman and Jenny Moynihan

Understanding victims and restorative justice
James Dignan

Understanding white collar crime
Hazel Croall

Understanding justice 2nd edition
Barbara A. Hudson

Understanding crime prevention
Gordon Hughes

Understanding violent crime
Stephen Jones

Understanding risk in criminal justice
Hazel Kemshall

Understanding social control
Martin Innes

Understanding psychology and crime
James McGuire

Understanding drugs, alcohol and crime
Trevor Bennett and Katy Holloway

Understanding prisons
Andrew Coyle

Understanding public attitudes to criminal justice
Mike Hough and Julian Roberts

Understanding desistance from crime
Stephen Farrall and Adam Calverley

Understanding race and crime
Colin Webster

Understanding community penalties
Peter Raynor and Maurice Vanstone

Understanding criminology 3rd edition
Sandra Walklate

Understanding the community management of high risk offenders

Hazel Kemshall

Open University Press

Open University Press
McGraw-Hill Education
McGraw-Hill House
Shoppenhangers Road
Maidenhead
Berkshire
England
SL6 2QL

email: enquiries@openup.co.uk
world wide web: www.openup.co.uk

and Two Penn Plaza, New York, NY 10121-2289, USA

First published 2008

A catalogue record of this book is available from the British Library

ISBN13: 978–0–335–21998–8 (pb)   978–0–335–21999–5 (hb)
ISBN10: 0–335–21998–5 (pb)   0–335–21999–3 (hb)

Library of Congress Cataloging-in-Publication Data
CIP data applied for

Typeset by RefineCatch Limited, Bungay, Suffolk
Printed in the UK by Bell & Bain Ltd., Glasgow

The McGraw·Hill Companies

Contents

For
George Kemshall and Brian Williams
Sadly missed.

Series editor's foreword

This book is the latest in Open University Press' well established *Crime and Justice* series, which has been running since 1996. The core aim of the series is to produce short but intellectually challenging introductory texts in key areas of criminological debate, in order to give undergraduates and postgraduates, as well as interested practitioners or policy makers, both a solid grounding in academic debates and literature in the relevant area and a taste to explore them further. Although aimed primarily at students new to the field, and written as far as possible in plain language, the books are not oversimplified. All the authors set out to 'stretch' readers and to encourage them to approach criminological knowledge and theory in a critical and questioning frame of mind. Moreover, as with previous authors in the series, Hazel Kemshall has not only provided balanced summaries of previous literature, but has taken the debates further and put forward her own distinctive views and interpretations.

Professor Kemshall is well known nationally and internationally as a leading expert on the concept of risk as applied to issues in crime and criminal justice. She has written widely on related topics, particularly in relation to probation work and to the risk assessment and management of sexual and violent offenders. Her writing consistently combines depth of theoretical analysis, detailed knowledge of policy and practice, and the ability to present complex ideas in a straightforward and readily comprehensible manner. She is also forthright in advocating new policy directions if current approaches appear to be either ineffective or to lack respect for human rights. In this, her second contribution to the series, her focus is on key arguments and evidence relating to the 'community management' of (ex-)offenders assessed as posing a high risk to the public (or to particular individuals or social groups). She contrasts the 'community protection' model which has been adopted by many countries – that is, an approach based mainly on close surveillance and restrictions on the movement of such offenders – with alternative models which are gradually gaining support, built around re-integrative and restorative strategies and aimed at engaging both offenders' and local communities' co-operation in efforts to reduce the risks they pose. These include what she calls 'public health' approaches and the 'Good Lives' model. She frames the discussion within broader debates about the growth of risk-focused penal thinking and practice, the difficulties of defining and assessing 'dangerousness', and ethical dilemmas that arise in 'managing' people who are considered risky. She draws on a wealth of research, including her own, as well as the experiences of practitioners involved in this difficult work.

Other books previously published in the *Crime and Justice* series – all of whose titles begin with the word 'Understanding' – have covered criminological theory (Sandra Walklate), justice and penal theory (Barbara Hudson), crime data and statistics (Clive Coleman and Jenny Moynihan), youth and crime (Sheila Brown), crime prevention (Gordon Hughes), violent crime (Stephen Jones), community penalties (Peter Raynor and Maurice Vanstone), white collar crime (Hazel Croall), risk in criminal justice (Hazel Kemshall), social control (Martin Innes), psychology and crime (James McGuire), victims and restorative justice (James Dignan), drugs, alcohol and crime (Trevor Bennett and Katy Holloway), public attitudes to criminal justice (Julian Roberts and Mike Hough), desistance from crime (Stephen Farrell and Adam Calverley) prisons (Andrew Coyle), political violence (Vincenzo Ruggiero), race and crime (Colin Webster) and 'modernization' in criminal justice (Paul Senior, Chris Crowther and Matt Long). One (Walklate) is already in its third edition, four are in second editions, and other second editions as well as additional original texts are in preparation. All are on topics which are either already widely taught or are growing in prominence in university degree courses on crime and criminal justice, and each book should make an ideal foundation text for a relevant module. As an aid to understanding, clear summaries are provided at regular intervals, and a glossary of key terms and concepts is a feature of every book. In addition, to help students expand their knowledge, recommendations for further reading are given at the end of each chapter.

Mike Maguire
April 2008

Acknowledgements

I have experienced great kindness and generosity during my career researching risk and probation work. My thanks to all those who have given their time and interest during this period, and indeed who continue to generously do so.

Particular thanks go to Chris Neville for enduring the long years of 'risk' without complaint and providing support and encouragement during difficult periods. Thanks to my colleagues at De Montfort University who continue to support my work with unstinting generosity, in particular the late Brian Williams who was a prince among colleagues. Especial thanks must go to my colleague Jason Wood, a source of inspiration and enthusiasm during numerous projects cited in this book. I have also benefited from the advice, wisdom and hard work of Gill Mackenzie and Bernadette Wilkinson. Sincere thanks to Jane Banham for preparing the manuscript and for keeping me going. Warm thanks to Mike Maguire, series editor, who provided coaching, advice and support to write this book. My initial project on risk was sponsored by the Economic and Social Research Council's Risk and Human Behaviour programme grant number L211252018.

Finally thanks to my Father, my mentor and my friend.

List of acronyms

ACPO	Association of Chief Police Officers
CBT	cognitive behavioural therapy
CEOP	Child Exploitation and Online Protection Centre
CJA 2003	Criminal Justice Act 2003
CJCS 2000	Criminal Justice and Court Services Act 2000
CM	core member
COSA	Circles of Support and Accountability
DSPD	dangerous severe personality disorder
GLM	'Good Lives' model
GPS	Global Positioning System
IPPS	Indeterminate Public Protection Sentence
MAPPA	Multi-Agency Public Protection Arrangement
NPS	National Probation Service
NTE	night time economy
OASys	Offender Assessment System
OGRS	Offender Group Conviction Scale
OLR	Order for Lifelong Restriction
PHA	Public Health Approach
PPO	Prolific and Persistent Offender
RCT	randomized control trial
RMA	Risk Management Authority
ROC	Relative Operating Characteristic
RP	Relapse Prevention
SFO	Serious Further Offence
SIR	Serious Incident Report
SOPO	Sex Offender Prevention Order
SOSO	Sex Offender Supervision Order
SOTP	Sex Offender Treatment Programme
SP	sentence plan
TASC	Tackling Alcohol-related Street Crime
TDI	The Derwent Initiative

Introduction

The community management of high risk offenders has attracted extensive media, political and public attention, fuelled by blame and censure when 'things go wrong'. In this climate, attention has increasingly been focused on the policies, processes and practices required to regulate this group of offenders. In numerous jurisdictions (particularly among the Anglophone countries) this has resulted in the use of selective incarceration and 'dangerousness legislation' aimed at the tight regulation of such offenders in the community. This approach is commonly known as the 'community protection' model, with a heavy emphasis upon regulating the whereabouts and activities of offenders in the community (e.g., through satellite tracking, electronic monitoring) and restricting their access to potential victims (e.g., by using community notification).

More recently disillusionment with the community protection model has been expressed. In particular, concerns that community protection can weaken the engagement of offenders, undermine treatment compliance and erode rehabilitative objectives. Alternative risk management strategies have been proposed, largely rooted in re-integrative and restorative approaches to offenders. These include Public Health Approaches (PHA), focusing on early interventions, harm reduction and the risk management of risky environments (Laws 2000).

The book is divided into seven chapters. Chapter 1 reviews the contemporary context for the community management of high risk offenders, with particular attention to the 'community protection' model most commonly adopted in the Anglophone countries. The 'long view' is taken in Chapter 2, placing concerns about 'dangerous offenders' into a historical perspective. The chapter also highlights how some supposedly contemporary responses (e.g., sex offender registers) actually have a long history. The chapter also examines a range of perspectives and attendant responses on 'dangerousness', including psychological and sociological framings of the issue. In Chapter 3, the difficulties of risk assessment are discussed, including sources of error, flaws in decision making, and systemic faults in risk assessment processes. The growing emphasis upon public protection partnerships is discussed in Chapter 4. The chapter contrasts the community protection partnerships epitomized by the Multi-Agency Public Protection Arrangements with emerging partnerships rooted in re-integrative approaches to the management of offenders such as Circles of Support. Risk management strategies are the focus of Chapter 5. Community protection risk management has tended to emphasize cognitive-behavioural methods and restrictive conditions, combined with monitoring, surveillance and enforcement. Alternative approaches to risk management are also explored, including environmental management, public awareness and re-integrative approaches rooted in the Good Lives model. Chapter 6 reviews the key issues in risk work, particularly the tension between risks and rights; ethical dilemmas; disclosure and community notification; and the difficulties in evaluating effectiveness. The chapter concludes by asking whether community protection and re-integrative approaches can be 'blended' into 'protective re-integration' to offer more complementary risk management strategies. Chapter 7 concludes by pulling the threads together and re-examines the potential for a 'blended' protective re-integrative approach to the community management of high risk offenders.

chapter one

Framing the problem: contemporary responses to high risk offenders

Introduction

High risk offenders have come to dominate much of the contemporary penal policy agenda, creating political consternation and challenging both policy makers and practitioners alike. The pervasiveness of the 'risk agenda' can be measured by the volume of legislation (some seven major Acts in 12 years), and the extensive systems and processes designed for its management (Kemshall 2003; Nash 2006). The impact on key criminal justice agencies has also been significant. Within the UK, for example, this has resulted in a sea change in the role and responsibility of the Probation Service (and in Social Services in Scotland), and a tighter focus on risky offenders for the police (see Kemshall 2003 for a full review). 'Public protection' has become a major objective of penal policy, and all criminal justice agencies are enmeshed in it to some degree (Kemshall 2003).

Public protection is also a sensitive and contentious issue, attracting much media and political attention since its inception in the early 1990s (Kemshall 2003). Public protection and risk management failures elicit public scrutiny and blame, resulting in the dismissal of staff and most notably in the resignation of the Home Secretary, Charles Clarke, in 2006. It is also characterized by public anxiety, fear, distrust of experts and intense media scrutiny (Kitzinger 2004). Risk management failures provide a constant reminder that protection cannot be guaranteed and the failure to honour the promise brings into disrepute both policy makers and professionals tasked with its delivery. The erosion of public confidence and trust leads to further anxiety and greater demands for protection, and paradoxically more failure (Kitzinger 2004: 148–57).

One result of this risk spiral is an 'escalating vocabulary of punitive motives' (Welch et al. 1997: 486) in which ever harsher penal policies against the dangerous are advocated, a situation Sanders and Lyon (1995) have described as 'repetitive retribution'. This retribution has largely crystallized in the sex offender and most notably the paedophile (Kitzinger 2004; Thomas 2005), characterized as the 'monster in our midst' (Simon 1998). Increasingly incapacitation has been used for this group, with the use of longer prison terms including Indeterminate Public Protection Sentences (IPPS) on the grounds of public protection. Politically, incapacitation has been deployed both on the grounds of public protection and on the grounds of retribution, resulting in significant tensions between politicians and judiciary, and a growing prison population (discussed later in this chapter). There has been considerable seepage of this incapacitation strategy to other offenders and offence types, notably violent offenders, those deemed to have a 'dangerous severe personality disorder' and, following the Criminal Justice Act 2003, offenders convicted of acts of robbery. The net widening of public protection to encompass more offenders and offence types raises the important question, who exactly are high risk offenders?

This introductory chapter outlines the key issues presented in this book. Notably, difficulties in the identification of high risk offenders, key issues in their risk assessment and problems with risk prediction (see Chapter 3 for a full review). The legislative and policy context of community protection is reviewed, including the limits to community protection, differing perceptions of risk among criminal justice personnel and resistance to the risk agenda by workers. The chapter concludes by considering alternatives to the community protection approach, for example Circles of Support (fully discussed in Chapters 4 and 5).

Who are high risk offenders?

High risk offenders have been broadly defined in official discourse as those who have committed a violent or sexual offence, or who are assessed as likely to do so. This definition reflects an increasing preoccupation throughout the 1990s with those offenders likely to offend harmfully against the person, and those committing sexual offences resulting in physical harm or psychological trauma. In England and Wales this is encapsulated in the definition given in the Criminal Justice Act (CJA) 2003 where ' "serious harm" means death or serious personal injury, whether physical or psychological' (Section 224 (3)), and where 'the court is of the opinion that there is a significant risk to members of the public of serious harm occasioned by the commission by him of further specified offences' (Section 225 (1b)). Interestingly the CJA 2003 attempts to define the relevant offences, and produces a schedule of some 88 sexual and 65 violent offences (Schedule 15) for which the maximum penalty is between two and ten years (Taylor et al. 2004), and the offences range from 'actual bodily harm and exposure through to manslaughter and rape' (NPS 2003: 7). Such offences can attract an extended sentence of determinate length with the possibility of parole at the halfway point. In addition, violent offenders can be supervised after release from custody for up to five years, and sexual offenders for up to eight years (Taylor et al. 2004: 253). The Act also defines a 'serious offence' . . . as a specified sexual or violent offence which carries a maximum penalty of 10 years imprisonment or more, including life imprisonment (Section 224 (2); Taylor et al. 2004: 253–4).

The CJA 2003 attempts to set clear parameters for high risk offenders by defining and setting a high threshold for 'serious harm', defining the sexual and violent offenders that come within the remit of the Act, defining 'serious offences' and establishing criteria for judging both dangerousness and the risk of re-offending harmfully. The interaction of these parameters is, however, potentially complex, including characteristics of the individual offender, characteristics of the specified offences, judgements of seriousness, and judgements of the likelihood of repeat offending. Evidence and judgements from a number of sources, including probation and psychiatric reports, are used and, as recent Court of Appeal rulings indicate, sentencing decisions are by no means clear cut (Stone 2006a, b, c).

Defining and identifying high risk offenders is no easy task. Both perceptions and definitions of high risk are located in the context within which they are used (Rayner 1992; Kemshall 1996), and reflect the culture, ideology and values embedded within that context (Wynne 1982; Rayner 1992). Risk is not a value-neutral term and is inscribed with values and meanings by those who use it (Douglas 1992). These meanings can collide, for example between professional groups, when collaboratively assessing risk (Prins 1999), or between public and experts when debating acceptable risk (e.g., nuclear power; Wynne 1982). 'Risk' is never an undisputed given and is a source of much political conflict and tension (Douglas and Wildavsky 1982).

For the purposes of the present discussion it is possible to discern at least four 'contexts of use' for high risk offenders. In brief these are:

1 *Legislation*, for example the legal definitions provided by the Criminal Justice Act 2003 (Section 224(1), 224(2)). These definitions can change over time in response to public and political concerns, for example the CJA 2003 includes robbery as a violent offence. Legislation is also interpreted and the judiciary will be significant in deciding *how* the key definitions of the CJA 2003 are actually applied. The imposition of Indeterminate Public Protection Sentences (IPPS) under Section 225(1b) has already attracted considerable Court of Appeal review with the threshold for serious harm proving problematic and the criteria for 'dangerousness' difficult to operate in practice (see Stone 2004a, b, c). The key phrases of the Act – 'significant risk', 'serious harm' and 'dangerousness' – are open to considerable interpretation, the exact meaning of which is likely to be established by a combination of sentencing guidelines and Court of Appeal decisions (Taylor et al. 2004: 255).

2 *Policy*, for example key policy statements on penal priorities and objectives, national guidance and other official documents used to reshape the roles, responsibilities and tasks of criminal justice personnel. For example, guidance to the National Probation Service on the criteria for the imposition of IPPS (NPS 2003). While this follows the Act closely, there is an area of potential confusion between the definition of serious harm given by statute and that used by the Probation Service risk assessment tool Offender Assessment System (OASys), although the guidance claims they are 'comparable'. The OASys wording extends the criteria somewhat by stating: 'risk of serious harm can be defined as a risk which is life threatening and/or traumatic and from which recovery, whether physical or psychological, can be expected to be difficult or impossible' (NPS 2003: 15). The extent to which they actually are compatible and comparable will of course be a matter of investigation over time, and whether sentencing courts and the Appeal Court reject or accept probation assessments based on OASys. At times policy and its legislative expression can be at odds.

3 *The practice context* which produces practice-based definitions, interpretations and local agency concerns. These can include local policies and procedures, and the definitions of risk embedded within them, leading to considerable national inconsistencies (Kemshall 1998a). Definitions of high risk offenders can also differ across agencies with police definitions, for example, reflecting local policing priorities, and

prison definitions of high risk offenders including those most at risk of absconding. Such differing definitions can result in agency tensions within multi-agency settings and differing referral criteria (Maguire et al. 2001; Kemshall et al. 2005).

4 *The public and media context* often expressed through public campaigns (e.g., the *News of the World* campaign for Sarah's Law), and public action such as vigilantism and public protest. These campaigns can generate significant political anxiety and reaction. Kitzinger has examined the high levels of anxiety, public fear and stigmatization that accompanies sex offenders (2004), describing paedophiles as the 'ultimate neighbour from hell' (1999). This is the climate within which policy, legislation and practice take place, with a significant impact upon conceptualizations of sex offenders and responses to them (McCulloch and Kelly 2007).

The terms 'high risk' and 'dangerous(ness)' are used interchangeably in some contexts, most notably in policy and practice where a preoccupation with dangerous offenders has driven much of the multi-agency agenda (Kemshall and Maguire 2001; Maguire et al. 2001). In media coverage the term 'dangerous(ness)' predominates (Kitzinger 2004). In the legal context the terms 'high risk' and 'dangerous(ness)' tend to combine with the CJA 2003 attempting to define 'significant risk' and 'serious harm' but also addressing the 'assessment of dangerousness' and 'dangerous offenders' (Taylor et al. 2004). These four drivers also interact and influence each other, for example media coverage and public anxiety pressuring policy makers into particular penal options and legislative agendas, which in turn dictate the practice of criminal justice workers. This interaction is presented in Figure 1.1, and illustrates the minimal common understanding that may exist between these four important contexts.

In this book the term 'high risk' is the preferred term, reflecting more recent attempts in legislation, policy and practice to achieve greater precision and increased rigour in terminology and assessment. On occasion the term 'dangerous(ness)' will be used, reflecting original source material, historical context, and/or media and public framings of risk. However defined, the key question is, 'Can we know them'? This question is addressed in the next section.

Can we know them?

The identification of high risk offenders has been a perennial problem (Kemshall 2003). In brief, this is due to three major issues: designing and implementing a risk assessment tool capable of reliably and consistently identifying high risk offenders; differing interpretations of high risk among

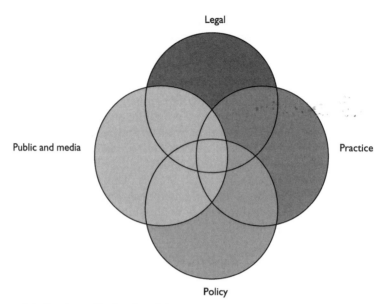

Figure 1.1 Framings of high risk and dangerousness

practitioners and sentencers; and establishing sufficiently robust criteria and evidence upon which to base judgements about the future.

Risk assessment tools

The history of the development of risk assessment tools has been characterized as an attempt to 'predict the unpredictable' (Kemshall 2003) and to literally 'tame uncertainty' (Hacking 1990). The 'problem of prediction' is well known (see Kemshall 2002a and 2003 for a full review), plagued by low base rates (that is, the rarity of the risky behaviour in the population as a whole), and by difficulties in transferring aggregate data about groups to the future behaviour of an individual. The rarer the behaviour the more difficult it is to accurately predict, although this is just the type of high risk behaviours that criminal justice personnel are tasked with predicting. Transferring aggregate data can be difficult – how do we know that this particular offender is not an exception to the rule? Sentencers in particular have resisted aggregated actuarial data, and to a lesser extent so have parole board members preferring instead to decide risk on a case by case clinical judgement (Hood and Shute 2000; see also Shute 2007).

The accuracy of risk assessment tools has also proved difficult, both in terms of maintaining long-term reliability and because claims for risk of reconviction scores and risk of harm scores are often confused. The two main probation tools can operate at around the 70 per cent mark (e.g., OGRS at 71.4 and OASys at 69.2 in Clark 2002; and more recently

OASys has achieved an 'Area Under the Curve (AUC)' score of 0.764 out of 1.0, 'a good measure of predictive accuracy' in Howard 2006; see also Howard et al. 2006). However, this is only for predicting the risk of reconviction and no such claims have been made for the prediction of risk of harm (indeed this is seen as an area requiring improvement, see Moore et al. 2007). In addition, these scores can be difficult to maintain over time due to lack of integrity in the completion of the tool and poor inter-rater reliability (Kemshall 2003). In the second evaluation of OASys 'OASys scores were found to be a good predictor of reconviction. 26% of those rated as low likelihood of reconviction were reconvicted within 24 months, compared with 58% rated as medium likelihood and 87% rated as high likelihood' (Howard 2006: 1). While this means that OASys out predicts a number of clinical tools it does not out predict OGRS (Offender Group Reconviction Scale) (Copas and Marshall 1998).

The development of 'third generation' risk assessment tools (Bonta 1996) combine actuarial and dynamic risk factors, and the development of increasingly specialized tools for sexual and violent offending has also increased the accuracy of many tools (see Kemshall 2001; Kemshall 2003: ch. 3). 'Structured risk assessment tools' utilize both actuarial methods and structured interviewing techniques by practitioners. The actuarial component assists in establishing basic probability information on likely risks, and the structured interviewing aids practitioners in focusing on the right dynamic factors to both refine prediction but also to assist with the formulation of risk management plans, treatment and intervention choices (Raynor 1999). Increasingly these tools adopt a multifactorial approach and practitioners are encouraged to consider a range of risks, the potential impacts and consequences of such risks, and the likely outcome of any risk management plans – commonly labelled 'fourth generation tools' (Bonta and Wormith 2007; see Stalans et al. 2004 on classification trees). The approach draws extensively on decision theory and attempts to encourage practitioners to consider a range of possible options in a systematic and evidenced way. This technique has potentially much to offer in the complex world of child protection, and particularly where practitioners must balance vulnerability and harm, risks and rights (see Munro 2002: ch. 7 for a full discussion). Decision trees allow workers to speculate more rigorously about the outcomes of their decisions on users and others, and to weigh more transparently and empirically the decision choices available to them. These issues will be further reviewed in Chapter 3.

The problem of risk prediction

Prediction has been a perennial issue in risk assessment (Kemshall 2003), not least in being sure which risk factors have the most predictive utility and why. This is due in large part to the difficulty in establishing the relationship between risk factor(s) and subsequent offending; in essence, demonstrating causal relationships and establishing the relative causal weight of differing risk factors. For example, causal relationships may only be correlations, and it is difficult to attribute weight to different factors when causes may be multifactorial, and risk 'scores' are not merely additive (Farrington 2000: 7). For an offender it may be the range and interaction of risk factors that is important, and not just their presence or absence. Risk factors can have a differential impact, what impacts on one offender does not necessarily impact on another.

Prediction is also plagued by the 'statistical fallacy', the limits of meta-analysis, and low base rates (for a full review see Kemshall 2002a). In brief, the statistical or 'ecological' fallacy describes the difficulty in transferring aggregated data from groups (such as white male prisoners) to the prediction of risk in an individual case. In such cases the risk prediction (usually the risk of reconviction) is expressed in terms of statistical probability, for example a 60 per cent likelihood of re-offending. However, a 60 per cent score of reconviction after sentence for an offender only means that that particular offender has a six in ten chance of reconvicting, not whether that individual actually will. It still remains a matter of case by case judgement to determine whether the offender is likely to be in the 60 per cent reconviction group, or the 40 per cent non-offending group. Most predictive scores cluster at around the 40–60 mark and where chances are almost even. This does not greatly assist practitioners tasked with making difficult decisions about issues relating to liberty, quality of life, risk of harm or child protection.

Many statistically-based tools are derived from a technique known as meta-analysis. This is a statistically-based technique that analyses the outcomes of a large body of primary research studies. These outcomes are then aggregated to produce the core factors that have statistical significance for risk prediction (McGuire 1997). However, this approach has been criticized for its inability to appropriately distinguish between factors and impacts, and a failure to appropriately examine and account for multivariant effects (Copas 1995; Mair 1997).

Low base rates have also proved problematic, particularly for tools designed for the prediction of the risk of harm (Kemshall 2001). Low base rates refer to the low incidence of an event or behaviour in the population as a whole (e.g., homicide), making them low probability events and therefore difficult to predict. If something doesn't happen very often it is difficult to know if and when it might happen in the future, although the consequences of it happening could be very high. This is the key difficulty in predicting catastrophic events (e.g., 'natural disasters' such as Hurricane Catriona) – they are low probability but high consequence and are often the sort of events we particularly want to accurately predict and manage. Similar difficulties apply to the prediction of 'grave crimes' such as murder. In recent years statistical methodologies have developed to incorporate something called the ROC (Relative Operating Characteristic) adjusted score – in effect, an actuarial prediction free from base rate limitations (Mossman 1994). This has improved the predictive scores of recent assessment tools for violence and sexual offenders (see Kemshall 2001 for a full review), and enables better comparison between the various risk assessment tools.

Differing interpretations of risk

Judgements of risk are notoriously open to bias, stereotypical framing and interpretation (Slovic 1987; Royal Society Study Group 1992), with professionals engaging in subjective decision making as well as the public (Kemshall 1998a). The influences on risk perception have been well documented (see the seminal work by Slovic 1992). Within the criminal justice system these differences in risk perception impact on how differing professional groups define and assess risk (including high risk offenders) (Maguire et al. 2001; Kemshall et al. 2005). Differences in assessment can also exist *within* agencies resulting in poor inter-rater reliability when risk assessment tools are used (Kemshall 1998a; Robinson 1999).

Sentencers, including the judiciary, also interpret risk. For example, homicide as a result of domestic violence has traditionally aroused less risk-based concerns, resulting in more lenient sentencing (Nash 2006). These crimes are often framed as 'one-offs', being provoked and exceptions to the norm, although as Nash demonstrates they are often premeditated and steeped in long histories of repeat victimization. Many victims (usually women) have been subject to much systematic abuse and injury prior to their death (Nash 2006). However, the distinction between domestic and stranger homicide remains, but the grounds upon which this distinction is made are often subjective and questionable (Nash 2006). Nevertheless, this distinction frames perceptions of risk. Interestingly, formalized risk assessment tools are helping to combat this issue, for example the Spousal Assault Risk Assessment (SARA) Guide. This is a structured, 20-item checklist for the risk assessment of males for spousal abuse and is used to determine treatment programmes and group work attendance as well as risk prediction. The tool can identify those likely to go on to commit further spousal abuse (Kropp 2004; Kropp et al. 2004). The tool has helped to give domestic violence and the likelihood of serious injury and death arising from it greater prominence, and a key technique for practitioners (particularly within Multi-Agency Public Protection Arrangements (MAPPA)) to evidence their concerns (Robinson 2005; Robinson and Tregidga 2005).[1]

Kitzinger (1999, 2004) notes the distinction made in media coverage and in resulting policy and legislation between intrafamilial sex offending and 'stranger danger'. This framing has resulted in an excessive focus on the 'men in dirty macs' and less focus on the danger present in many families (Kitzinger 2004: 129), an emphasis that is repeated in court. The paedophile is always defined as an 'outsider' (Cross 2005: 290) – a rather more comfortable thought for those on the inside. Most policy and procedures are geared towards detecting and controlling this outsider, resulting in overwhelming shock and blame when children are harmed by those charged with their care (e.g., Victoria Climbié in Laming 2003). In addition to framings of the victim, Melossi (2000) has examined how differing representations of the offender can impact upon both sentencing and policy responses to perpetrators, not least those of gender, class and ethnicity.

Criteria and evidence

In England and Wales the criteria and evidence for 'dangerousness' are set out in Sections 229(2) and 229(3) of the CJA 2003, and the court is required to consider a number of aspects in deciding whether the offender presents a 'significant risk'. Interestingly, there is a distinction between offenders who have no previous convictions or who are under 18 and those who have previous convictions or who are over 18. In the case of the former, the Court:

- must take into account all such information as is available to it about the nature and circumstances of the offences;
- may take into account any information which is before it about any pattern of behaviour of which the offence forms a part;
- may take into account any information about the offender which is before it.

(Section 229(2); Taylor et al. 2004: 257)

In essence, the Court needs to be persuaded of the risk by the information presented. The Court will rely on information about the nature of the offence as presented in Court, probation pre-sentence reports and, where appropriate, psychiatric reports.

For the latter offenders,

'the court must assume that the offender poses a "significant risk" ' unless after taking into account

- all such information is available to it about the nature and circumstances each of the offences,
- where appropriate, any information which is before it about any pattern of behaviour of which any of the offences forms part, and
- any information about the offender which is before it

the court considers that it would be unreasonable to conclude that there is such a risk.

(Section 229(3); Taylor et al. 2004: 257–8)

In this case there is a presumption of significant risk unless the presenting information disproves it. The differing procedures and presumptions of risk carry different approaches to the criteria and evidence for risk – in case one risk is to be actively proved. In case two it is to be actively disproved. While it is speculative, presumably it will be harder to disprove risk than to prove it.

Other difficulties are likely to occur. For example, is information accurate (Taylor et al. 2004) and are crucial facts of the case disputed? Facts are also open to interpretation. When is a fact(s) evidence of a pattern of behaviour? What constitutes a pattern of behaviour? What types of behaviour(s) are indicative of future risk? Recent Appeal Court cases on the use of indeterminate sentencing under the CJA 2003 have grappled with these difficult issues. In brief (see Stone 2006a, b, c for a full review), recent Appeal Court judgments have indicated that while offenders may have previous convictions, these do not necessarily indicate a pattern predictive of further offending of serious harm; robbery while covered by the CJA 2003 may be considered to be 'serious', it is not necessarily resulting in 'significant risk' of 'serious harm'; previous convictions may indicate that an offender is a persistent or prolific offender but this does not necessarily mean that the offending is or will be harmful in the sense laid out by the Act. Stone concludes that to date 'the Court of Appeal has . . . taken a relatively restricted interpretation of the threshold test in respect of serious harm' (2006b: 299). This reiterates a point made by Scott some 20 years earlier that, 'the legal category, even murder, arson and rape, is not very useful in determining dangerousness' (1977: 129), and that rather complex judgments based upon the interaction of offender, circumstances and victim, combined with in-depth knowledge of behaviour, attitudes and motivation is required (Kemshall et al. 2006).

While there are a number of significant issues in 'knowing' high risk or dangerous offenders, policy, legislation and practice are all conducted *as if* we can know them. As Nash points out, 'the "pool" of potentially dangerous offenders is enormous' (2006: 21) comprising anyone who has the *capacity* to act harmfully. The trick is to discern with a reasonable degree of accuracy and consistency who might. In Home Office parlance this is the 'critical few' (Home Office 2004a, 2007a; Ministry of Justice 2007). Issues in risk assessment, and particularly identifying the critical few, will be explored in Chapter 3. The next section will consider the rise of community protection as the dominant model for dealing with high risk offenders.

The rise of community protection

Connelly and Williamson (2000) reviewed the sentencing of dangerous offenders (including civil commitment and the management of severe personality disorder) across a number of jurisdictions in Anglophone countries and Western Europe. They present three models (summarized from Connelly and Williamson 2000):

- *Community protection.* This approach prioritizes public protection and is characterized by the use of restriction, surveillance, monitoring and control, compulsory treatment and the prioritization of victim/community rights over those of offenders. Sentencing can be disproportionate to current crime and based upon assessments of future risk, and selective incarceration is used for those deemed high risk. Upon release special measures such as licence conditions, tagging, exclusions, registers are all extensively used (Kemshall 2003; Kemshall et al. 2005). The USA and Canada are the main exponents of this approach, with England and Wales pursuing an increasingly community protection approach and with Scotland beginning to follow suit. Community protection can include compulsory mental health treatment and civil commitment.
- *Clinical treatment.* This approach sees problematic behaviours as the product of illness, with treatment having a 'therapeutic emphasis' and based on voluntary commitment where possible. The increasing use of compulsory commitment and treatment in recent years has begun to move mental health provision into the community protection model, to the consternation of many mental health professionals (see Royal College of Psychiatrists 1996, 2004).
- *Justice model.* This approach sees the offender as a rational actor deserving punishment and sentencing contains elements of retribution and deterrence. Despite the deterrent element, proportionality is the cornerstone of this approach – if the 'punishment fits the crime' then the rational choice offender will make an informed choice to desist.

The late 1980s and 1990s saw a penal policy shift from rehabilitative to retributive sentencing, epitomized by the 'just deserts' approach of the CJA 1991 (Wasik and Taylor 1991). The demise of the rehabilitative ideal has been reviewed elsewhere (see for example Garland 1985, 1990, 2001), and the rejection of treatment, particularly for demonized offenders such as sex offenders, was acute by the end of the 1980s (Simon 1998). However, the justice model in turn was soon perceived to be equally ineffective in terms of lowering crime rates and preventing high risk crime, and arguments for special measures for the 'dangerous' gained pace in the 1990s particularly in the USA and latterly in the UK (La Fond 1992; Petrunik 1993, 1994; Clarkson 1997; Dingwall 1998; Kemshall 2003). While recidivism and persistent offenders had long tasked penal policy makers (Pratt 1997), Connelly and Williamson insightfully comment that: 'The maturation of the concept of dangerousness from persistence to physical and psychological harm, necessitated a transition from habitual offender legislation to dangerous offender legislation' (Connelly and Williamson 2000: 85).

This shift has continued throughout the 1990s and into the twenty-first century, predominantly in the Anglophone countries and to a lesser extent in Western Europe (see for example Carpenter 1998; Frenken 1999). Nash (2006: ch. 6) has helpfully reviewed the development of 'dangerousness legislation' in England and Wales, and Connelly and Williamson have provided a useful overview across a number of jurisdictions. Given these excellent reviews, it will suffice here to summarize briefly the key legislation in England and Wales:

- Criminal Justice Act 1991. While an Act predicated largely on proportionality, the Act also introduced the concept of risk-based sentencing. Notably, Section 1(2) (b) which introduced custodial sentencing to protect the public; and Section 2 (2) (b) which introduced longer sentences in order to protect the public from the risk of harm presented by an individual offender (see Wasik and Taylor 1991; Von Hirsh and Ashworth 1996; www.opsi.gov.uk/ACTS/acts1991/Ukpga_1991053_en_1.htm).
- Crime (Sentences) Act 1997. The Act introduced mandatory life sentences for the commission of a number of second-time violent and sexual offences (see www.opsi.gov.uk/ACTS/acts1997/19910037.htm).
- The Sex Offenders Act 1997. This Act established the Sex Offender Register and set out registration requirements for sex offenders. As Nash (2006) points out 'loopholes' were quickly discovered; the effectiveness of the register was challenged (Hebenton and Thomas 1996); and issues in the practical implementation of the register caused concern for the Association of Chief Police Officers (ACPO), including no right of entry and no effective means of carrying out community surveillance (see www.opsi.gov.uk/ACTS/acts1997/1997051.htm).
- The Crime and Disorder Act 1998. This Act established Sex Offender Supervision Orders (SOSOs), extended licences for violent and sexual crimes (Section 58), and in Section 115 it established that agencies could exchange confidential information in order to prevent crime. As such it closed the 'loopholes' of the Sex Offender Register, continued selective incarceration for sexual and violent offenders and enabled agencies to exchange information. Sex Offender Orders were aimed at offenders whose behaviours warranted more intrusive measures and negative prohibitions such as restricting access to victims. While only requiring civil standards of proof they carried up to a five year custodial sentence for breach. The Act removed registration anomalies and brought approximately 100,000 offenders under registration procedures (see www.opsi.gov.uk/ACTS/acts1998/19980037.htm).
- The Criminal Justice and Court Services Act 2000. This Act formally established Multi-Agency Public Protection Arrangements (MAPPA) in Sections 67 and 68 to assess and manage high risk offenders. The Act

also amended the registration arrangements by reducing the notification period for sex offenders to register from 14 days to 72 hours, and
includes a requirement to notify of foreign travel and provisions for
photographs and fingerprints from sex offenders (see www.opsi.gov.uk/
acts/acts20000043.htm).

- The Sexual Offences Act 2003. This Act extended the definition of
  sexual offences, tightened the law on paedophiles, established Sex
  Offender Prevention Orders (SOPOs) to replace SOSOs, and tightened
  notification requirements (see www.opsit.gov.uk/ACTS/acts2003/
  20030042.htm and Shute 2004).
- The Criminal Justice Act 2003. This Act has a clear public protection
  focus and provides not only extended sentences but also Indeterminate
  Public Protection Sentences (IPPS) for those assessed as dangerous
  (Section 225 (1b)). The Act defines 'serious harm', 'significant risk' and
  'serious offence', and attempts to establish the criteria and evidence
  base for dangerousness (Section 229). Interestingly the Act also focuses
  on violent offending (specifying some 65 violent offences) in response to growing concerns about the risks posed by violent offenders
  (see www.opsi.gov.uk/ACTS/acts2003/2003004.htm and Taylor et al.
  2004).

This period has also seen an unprecedented amount of official guidance to
criminal justice agencies on the assessment and management of high risk
offenders. Nash (2006) identifies 12 Probation Circulars on this issue in
2005, and 2006 saw six and a *Risk of Harm Guidance and Training
Resource* (Kemshall et al. 2006), with a significant upturn following the
publication of the Serious Further Offence reports on Hanson and White,
and Anthony Rice (HMIP 2006a, b). In brief, Hanson was mis-assessed as
medium risk and, while under parole supervision, murdered John Monckton
during the commission of a burglary with White. Anthony Rice, while under
parole supervision and the management of the local MAPPA, befriended and
killed Naomi Bryant. The HMIP reports highlighted both practice and process deficiencies in the assessment and management of high risk offenders,
tensions between rights and protection, and served to sharpen the debate
about public protection, culminating in the departure of the then Home
Secretary, Charles Clarke.

The incoming Home Secretary, John Reid, summed these cases up by
stating that: 'Reasonable people would view the decision to release someone
that appears to emphasize the rights of a convicted murderer over the rights
of his potential victims as tragically and disastrously mistaken' (Home
Secretary 2006: 1). The Home Secretary continued this theme by stating
that: 'The public has the right to expect that everything possible will be done
to minimise the risk from serious violent and dangerous offenders' (Home
Secretary 2006: 1). This expectation was quickly translated into a 'dramatic

overhaul of public protection arrangements' and a rebalancing of justice between offenders and victims (Home Office 2006a; Home Secretary 2006). In respect of parole, the Home Secretary announced proposals to enhance the public protection focus of the Parole Board including unanimous verdicts on serious offenders; the use of 'public protection advocates' to represent victims' and society's views, and to review whether parole supervision and the whole process were sufficiently 'joined up' (Home Secretary 2006: 1–5).

While it is difficult to measure the erosion of public trust in the criminal justice system and public protection measures, there is little doubt that the political response to restore public confidence was swift (Home Secretary 2006; Home Office 2006c; Home Office 2006d). This has included proposals to 're-balance' the criminal justice system 'in favour of the law abiding majority' (Home Office 2006a), proposals which refer to 'shocking recent incidents in which offenders who were under our supervision have committed serious crimes' (p. 34), and outline the 'decisive action' required to improve the management of 'serious, violent and dangerous offenders following release from custody' (p. 34). Violent Offender Orders to impose additional conditions of residency, and restricting who offenders can associate with or visit, with a breach penalty of five years imprisonment, have also been made (Home Office 2006a, b, c). This, coupled with the provisions of the CJA 2003, has in effect widened the concept of 'dangerous offenders' from sex offenders to encompass violent offenders also.

The focus on public protection has been unrelenting, with substantial political pressure on criminal justice agencies to make protection of the public their main focus (Home Office 2006b), including a 'restructuring' of the Probation Service to reduce re-offending (Home Office 2005a), and an increased emphasis upon multi-agency work (Home Office 2004a). Key drivers in this restructuring have been the political emphasis upon reduction of re-offending, modernization of criminal justice and within this Probation, and a greater focus on value for money (see Kemshall 2003: ch. 4 for a full review; for legislative and policy developments in the 1980s and 1990s see Dunbar and Langdon 1998; Cavadino et al. 2000; Senior et al. 2007).

A key driver for this has been public and media disquiet with sex offenders, resulting in sex offenders being chosen for what is in effect a second-time punishment. Having completed their lawful detention they are then subjected to potentially indefinite detention in civil mental health establishments. In essence, they are being detained for what they might do in the future, the same rationale for imposing protective sentences in court. These forms of civil detention act almost as a second strike sentence where offenders will be punished again, not for what they have done but for tendencies they show (Nash 2006: 118; for similar developments in Canada and the USA see Petrunik 2002).

It is important to remember that sexual offending actually constitutes

0.9 per cent of all police recorded crime, and that serious sexual crime, such as rape, forms about one-quarter of that 0.9 per cent (Dodd et al. 2004). The number of children abducted, sexually assaulted and subsequently killed by a stranger has remained fairly constant since the 1940s at about six to eight children per year (Soothill 2003), although media coverage and public perception of this risk would suggest otherwise (Kitzinger 2004; Thomas 2005).

Limits to the community protection model

Interestingly, Connelly and Williamson in their review described the English and Welsh approach to high risk offenders as a 'hybrid' between community protection and clinical models. They base this claim on the contention that there is still a 'strong clinical focus in England and Wales on the management of mentally disordered offenders' (2000: 85). However, they acknowledge that proposals for dangerous severe personality disorder (DSPD) persons who may not yet have committed an offence 'indicate that a community protection model is increasingly preferred in the management of dangerous persons' (2000: 86). This transition in mental health services was given added impetus by the case of Michael Stone and the murder of Lin and Megan Russell, and the recognition that some patients should be subject to indeterminate containment, and some to preventative civil commitment on the grounds of actual or potential dangerousness. Further criticisms of the risk management provided by psychiatric services took place following the temporary discharge and absconsion of John Barrett who subsequently stabbed to death Denis Finnegan in 2004 ('Killer psychiatric care panned' www.news.bbc.co.uk, accessed 9 March 2007). The subsequent independent inquiry report concluded that 'interventions did not give sufficient weight to the risk John Barrett could pose to the public' and 'there was a tendency to emphasise unduly the desirability of engaging John Barrett rather than intervening against his wishes to reduce risk' (NHS London 2006: 9). The report highlights a number of tensions between public protection and patient rights, with at times an overemphasis upon maintaining the therapeutic relationship at the cost of adequately managing risk.

While community protection has gained pace since Connelly and Williamson's review, their point on hybridization does indicate a significant tension between criminal justice and mental health approaches to 'dangerous offenders'. This is evidenced by difficulties in fully integrating mental health services into the Multi-Agency Public Protection Arrangements (Kemshall et al. 2005), and the resistance of the Royal College of Psychiatrists (1996) to the DSPD proposals (see also Farnham and James 2001; Feeney 2003). It is also possible to discern a significant commitment to the 'therapeutic ideal' among mental health practitioners somewhat at odds with the community protection model of management prevalent in criminal justice (see for example Craissati 2004). This tension also highlights significant ideological and cultural differences between health and criminal justice, although the extent to which this functions as a check on the inexorable rise of community protection is more difficult to discern.

However, key stakeholders within the community protection 'system' do exercise resistance, not least the judiciary (Freiberg 2000; Nash 2006). As Freiberg expresses it: 'In the same way that judges over the centuries have found ways to subvert the operation of mandatory penalties . . . they have resisted governmental attempts to remove or shape their discretion in relation to the dangerous' (2000: 56).

Freiberg describes 'the range of techniques' or 'guerilla tactics' deployed, although he warns against interpreting such actions as concerted, necessarily planned or as enjoying the support and consensus of all the judiciary. He also notes that 'resistance' can differ across jurisdictions, with the Australian judiciary, for example, displaying more resistance than sentencers in the USA. He notes the sources of resistance as: 'nineteenth century liberalism', notions of proportionality, a commitment to 'due process', difficulties in evidencing future risk sufficiently well, and in some jurisdictions the constraints of international law (e.g., the European Convention on Human Rights (ECHR 1998) in Western European jurisdictions). Commitment to the independence of the judiciary from the executive in jurisdictions such as England and Wales should not be underestimated, and judicial resistance to the erosion of discretion has been well documented (Nash 2006: 108–11; Silverman 2006). Increased use of mandatory sentences in most Anglophone countries has reduced discretion, although as Frieberg puts it: the guerrilla warfare continues, and it may be that the dangerous, now defined to include the judiciary as well as offenders, are no longer governed, but subdued (2000: 68).

Resources can also constrain public protection sentencing, not least the shortage of prison places. Despite a policy emphasis on 'bifurcated' or twin-track sentencing[2] intended to reserve custody for the most risky (Bottoms 1977, 1995; Home Office 2005, 2006a), the use of custody has continued to outstrip prison places (*The Sunday Times* 2006: 16).[3] In January 2007 the Home Secretary, John Reid, urged the judiciary to 'limit jail sentences' (www.news.bbc.co.uk accessed 8 March 2007), resulting in an outcry when a paedophile was sentenced to a six-month suspended jail term ('Child porn sentence is condemned', www.news.bbc.co.uk accessed 8 March 2007; and 'Full jails change child porn term' www.news.bbc.co.uk accessed 8 March 2007). This led to a perception that custodial sentences were based upon availability of prison places and not the riskiness of the offender or the seriousness of the crime. Bifurcated sentencing struggles to operate in pure form in the face of finite prison places, executive instructions, judicial interpretation and public opinion. The 'leniency debate' during 2006, sparked by the sentencing of Carl Sweeney for the abduction and sexual assault of a 3-year-old girl, illustrates media, public and executive pressure on the judiciary. While Sweeney was given a life sentence, his minimum tariff term (that is the earliest date at which he could be considered for release) was set at five years, provoking media comment, public disquiet and comment from the Attorney General ('Call for stiffer sentence for attacker of girl, 3', www.news.bbc.co.uk accessed 8 March 2007). Attempts to reduce lenient sentencing through the extension of mandatory life sentences for murder under the CJA 2003 have also been criticized, most notably by the Lord Chief Justice Lord Phillips who commented that: 'murderers are spending too long in jail' and that 'government guidelines on the length of time murderers should spend in prison had the effect of "ratcheting up" sentences' ('Some murderers in jail "too long" ' www.news.bbc.co.uk accessed 9 March 2006).

The sentencing and subsequent management of high risk offenders can also be constrained by international law, in particular the European Convention on Human Rights (ECHR 1998). The decision of Mr Justice Sullivan to give nine Afghans who had hijacked a Boeing 747 in 2000 discretionary leave to remain in the UK on the basis of human rights legislation was subsequently described by Prime Minister Tony Blair as 'an abuse of commonsense' ('Reid loses Afghan hijack ruling' www.news.bbc.co.uk accessed 9 March 2007). Perceptions of risks and rights have continued to clash (see for example the Chief Inspector of Probation's comments on the community management of Anthony Rice in HMIP 2006b), and debate has focused on whether registration and extended supervision post-custody constitute 'cruel and unusual punishment', the legality of disclosure to third parties, rights to privacy and rights to free association (see Power 2003; Kemshall and Wood 2007a, 2008). These issues will be discussed in greater detail in Chapter 6.

Practitioners themselves can also act as a 'firewall' to the inexorable rise of risk and public protection (Kemshall 2003; O'Malley 2004a, b). Policies are mediated by the workforces tasked with implementing them (Maynard-Moody et al. 1990). Workers bring their own values and ideologies to bear on policy interpretation and delivery, and in the area of community protection present 'firewalls' to the direct impact of current policies by prioritizing 'therapeutic relationships', failing to complete or act on risk assessment tools (Kemshall 1998a, 2003; Robinson 2002, 2003) and prioritizing rehabilitation over risk management (Wood and Kemshall 2007). However, the centre responds to such 'intransigence' and the history of probation over the last ten years can be characterized by the centre's pursuit of worker compliance with the public protection and crime reduction agendas (Kemshall 2003; Nash 2006).

While there are some limits to the community protection model, the approach now dominates criminal justice and is currently reshaping mental services. The pace since the completion of Connelly and Williamson's review has been swift, and their claim for hybridization may require re-appraisal following the CJA 2003.

Protection or punishment?

The distinction between a retributive and risk-based penality has also been disputed (see for example O'Malley 1999, 2001), with some commentators arguing that public protection has acted as something of a 'veneer' for increasingly retributive and emotive sentencing (Pratt 2000a, b), particularly for sex offenders (Thomas 2004a). Under the guise of public protection, retributive principles still operate, with sexual and (to a lesser extent) violent offenders singled out for particularly harsh sentencing and intrusive measures upon release (Nash 2006). This has been led by the taboo about 'sex crime' and paedophilia in particular (Silverman and Wilson 2002), but has extended to other crimes where the media and public perception is that the 'punishment should fit the crime', not always the same as the punishment should fit the risk. This tension was evidenced in the media response to the Lord Chief Justice's comments that some murderers do not need to serve 'life' and that judges should be allowed more discretion in the setting of tariff terms. The tabloid reaction was somewhat predictable, with headlines such as: 'So much for justice: free killers earlier says top judge' (*Daily Mail*, 10 March 2007: 12); and 'Let killers out: they're clogging up jails' (*Sun*, 10 March 2007: 2). Retribution can literally outweigh risk, with selective incarceration extended beyond the highest risk offenders. One result is a burgeoning prison population with more prisoners serving longer terms. Bifurcated sentencing tends to fail in the face of retribution and a vocal punitive populism that has gained momentum since the murder of Jamie Bulger (Goldson 2005). The demonization of sex offenders has been particularly acute (Simon 1998; Pratt 2000a, b; Garland 2001), and is an area where protection and punishment merge (Pratt 2000b). The community's protection is in effect the sex offender's punishment. The harsh penal climate of the 1990s saw the combination of proportionality and protection increasingly strained (Pratt 1997; Kemshall 2003). It is possible to conclude that the intervening years have seen penal policy driven as much by media campaigning and public disquiet as by risk (Sparks 2000, 2001a, b; Thomas 2005).

Exclusionary or integrative? Alternative approaches to risky offenders

While exclusionary and punitive approaches to risky offenders (and particularly sex offenders) have predominated, this has not been at the exclusion of other approaches to managing high risk offenders. As O'Malley and colleagues have argued, penal forms and processes are rarely 'univocal' and predetermined, but are often 'multivocal', contested and contradictory (O'Malley et al. 1997: 513; O'Malley 2004a, b). Within this space of contradiction, alternative approaches to the management of high risk offenders have emerged. The most significant of these is the Public Health Approach (PHA) (Laws 1996, 2000). The approach has its roots in the 'new public health' (Petersen and Lupton 1996; Petersen 1997) which emphasizes health promotion and disease prevention, and is an example of what Dean (1999) has called an 'epidemiological' approach to risk, which includes techniques like mass immunization (e.g., MMR), drug needle exchanges, and crime prevention strategies like the use of closed circuit TV (CCTV) (O'Malley 2004b: 22). The major aim is harm reduction, and through the management of general risk categories (e.g., sex offenders) rather than through individuals, although individuals often benefit from experiencing these risk management strategies (e.g., reducing their sex offending or their dependence on drugs). PHA is increasingly combined with re-integrative methods with its roots in restorative justice approaches to offenders (see McAlinden 2006 for a full review), and aimed at harm reduction, offender resettlement, re-integration and rehabilitation.

While the community protection model's construction of the demonized 'predatory paedophile' creates a distance between offender and society, literally the spectre of an invisible yet monstrous stranger in our midst (Simon 1998; Wilczynski and Sinclair 1999), the public health approach seeks to achieve integration and social regulation via the community (Kemshall and Wood 2007b). One such integrative approach is 'Circles of Support and Accountability' (Thames Valley Circles of Support and Accountability 2005). Originating in Canada and Quaker faith-based communities, Circles of Support develops small circles of volunteers around a sex offender following release from prison. The Circles provide support, vigilance and assistance to a crime-free life. Piloted in the UK in Hampshire and Thames Valley, at time of writing there were some 25 circles operating in the Thames Valley with 105 volunteers working with high risk offenders (Thames Valley Circles of Support and Accountability 2005). These 'paedo-pals' as they have been dubbed are also effective. Some 60 per cent of sex offenders can be expected to re-offend, while within the Circles of Support pilots in the Thames Valley no one has (although one offender in the Thames Valley has been reconvicted for breach of a SOPO). In addition, Circles of Support are effective in maintaining contact with offenders, whereas police forces have lost contact with some 322 convicted sex offenders on the register (Roberts 2007). Circles also hold offenders to account for their behaviour. The Thames Valley evaluation (Bates 2005: 21) highlighted three offenders recalled to prison on breach of parole licence, and four who received intensive MAPPA supervision because of concerns about recidivist behaviours. Interestingly, Circles of Support has had limited media coverage, and limited financial support, although it does receive Home Office funding and the support of local criminal justice agencies. Although re-integrative approaches are limited (McAlinden 2006), they are developing and this book will examine other initiatives such as, Stop It Now! UK and Ireland, Leisurewatch and the work of the Derwent Initiative (see Chapter 5).

In an article entitled, 'The prison trick' (*Guardian*, 17 June 2006), David Wilson argues that 'the idea that locking up paedophiles for longer will solve the problem of dangerous offenders is an illusion. The real solution lies in the community'. This book will explore community strategies for the management of high risk offenders, comparing and contrasting differing approaches. This is not just about comparisons of effectiveness. Rather it raises issues about the differing conceptualizations of the offender embedded in these differing approaches, and the differing relationships between offender and society, and offender and local communities framed by these management strategies. At its most basic it is also about 'how we want to solve the problem of risk – either as an exclusive society or as an inclusive one' (Kemshall and Wood 2007b).

Notes

1 MAPPA were created in England and Wales by the Criminal Justice and Court Services Act (CJCS) 2000, Sections 67 and 68. These are statutory multi-agency bodies for the assessment and management of high risk offenders. They are discussed in detail in Chapter 4, this volume.
2 This is a sentencing policy in which longer sentences should be reserved for harmful offences against the person and high risk offenders; and shorter sentences are used for less harmful offences and less risky offenders. In practice this is difficult to operate, not least due to public and sentencer views on offences and their particular risk, for example burglary where the divide between property crime and personal harm is difficult to draw. Bifurcation is also affected by media and public disquiet over particular crimes, reactions to crime trends and differing perceptions of harm.
3 By February 2007 the prison population in England and Wales stood at 80,002, the highest per capita population in Western Europe at 143 people per 100,000 (and was continuing to grow) (World prison populations, www.news.bbc.co.uk accessed 8 March 2007). The Carter Review of Prisons proposed a 'large modern "Titan" prison' to deal with overcrowding (Carter Review of Prisons 2007: 2).

Further reading

Kemshall, H. (2003) *Understanding Risk in Criminal Justice*. Maidenhead: Open University Press.
Nash, M. (2006) *Public Protection and the Criminal Justice Process*. Oxford: Oxford University Press.

Useful websites and key sources

CJA03 National Guide on new sentences for public protection, Edition 1 (v1) June
     2005.
National Probation Service Briefing (2003) *Issue 16 2003 – Criminal Justice Act
     2003*. London: Home Office.
www.homeoffice.gov.uk/
www.inspectorates.homeoffice.gov.uk/
www.justice.gov.uk/

chapter two

Differing perspectives on an old problem: how do we know the dangerous?

Introduction

Chapter 1 explored some contemporary framings and responses to high risk offenders, and those deemed to be dangerous. In this chapter the themes of 'framing', 'characterizing', and 'categorizing' risk, high risk and dangerousness are continued. The chapter begins with a brief historical overview of characterizations of 'the dangerous' and reviews the techniques for their social regulation and the penal strategies that have evolved to manage them. The chapter then continues by examining three disciplinary knowledge bases that have made a significant contribution to how risk and dangerousness are currently understood. The examination of these differing knowledge constructions of the 'problem of dangerousness' highlight how different framings, conceptualizations and characterizations of the issue can impact upon societal and penal policy responses and reveals conflicts and tensions at policy and practice levels. The chapter begins with a historical overview. While 'periodizing' change can be problematic (Rigakos and Hadden 2001; Kemshall 2003), retrospective views can help one to understand the present and, in the spirit of risk, to anticipate the future.

The long view

Like the poor, the dangerous have always been with us (Kemshall 1997). How to identify, assess and manage the dangerous has been a perennial problem (Pratt 1997), with some commentators suggesting that the 'spectre of the individual dangerous person ... first appears as nomadic figures which could threaten communities anywhere' as early as the 1600s (see Thomas 2005: 41). The first identifiable embodiment of the 'dangerous person' is the 'vagrant'. As Thomas puts it: 'A figure that blends in with mythical tales of demons, werewolves and those, like the "raggle-taggle gypsies", who would steal your children' (p. 41).

By the 1700s this characterization had extended to the 'mentally disordered person' (Vagrancy Act 1714 cited in Thomas 2005) and began to extend to adults and children destined for the workhouse. Throughout the 1700s the definition extended to the poor, homeless, immigrants (usually Irish), 'mad', orphaned youth and included petty criminals and those deemed to be 'feckless'. Interestingly, the notions of 'community protection', regulation and exclusion were implanted early. Protection of communities from those seen to pose a moral threat, potential public disorder, physical harm or crime was embedded in the Vagrancy Acts of 1714 and 1744 (Radzinowicz 1948; Thomas 2005), a situation which has resonance with present day public protection policies. As part of the regulation of the dangerous, a register was suggested as early as 1748 (Radzinowicz 1948; Thomas 2005) and both employment and police registers were mooted throughout the 1700s. As Thomas concludes: 'The idea of a sex offender register in 1997 has a long pedigree' (2005: 42). Registers would label dangerous persons and store personal information useful for their effective management or exclusion.

This period also saw increasing transportation to Australia and New Zealand of the 'dangerous classes' (Pratt 1997), a very literal exclusion. The Transportation Act 1718 was 'for the more severe and effectual punishment of atrocious and daring offenders' (Melbourne Immigration Museum, Australia, September 2005). Transportation to Tasmania stopped in 1853 and by 1857 the census showed that 50 per cent of all Tasmanians and 60 per cent of all males were convicts or ex-convicts, yet the Tasmanian prison rate was lower than for any similar sized colony. The suggested explanation for this was the development of charitable institutions and government spending on 'social services' that was on average three times higher than that in Victoria or New South Wales, posing the intriguing question as to whether Tasmania had a successful record in the reformation of habitual criminals or in the creation of the social conditions for successful desistance (Melbourne Immigration Museum, Australia). The 1700s saw the habitual criminal increasingly demarcated as dangerous resulting in a burgeoning prison population. The Hulks Act 1776 created, as a 'temporary measure', facility to accommodate convicts on ships (ex-navy 'hulks'). The conditions on board the hulks were appalling with mortality rates of around 30 per cent of those transported, some 2000 deaths out of 6000 between 1776 and 1795 (Melbourne Immigration Museum, Australia).

The 1800s saw the Poor Laws become more punitive, with vagrants, the destitute and orphans increasingly institutionalized in the workhouse. The County Asylum Act in 1808 established the large lunatic asylums that persisted into the twentieth century and housed the 'mad' and the criminally insane. This began an institutionalization of 'the dangerous' that has persisted to the present day.

By the Victorian era the habitual, dangerous classes could no longer be dealt with by prison hulks or by transportation. As Pratt puts it, this presented society with the problem of 'non-capital repeat offenders', in essence the 'dangerous' in the community (1997: 2). The seeds of the twentieth century's preoccupation with the 'monster in our midst' were sown (Simon 1998). The prison population grew during the Victorian period as did prison building and techniques of population control and surveillance within prison (Foucault 1977). However, the threat posed by released prisoners took hold of the public imagination (Bartrip 1981; Thomas 2005) and the Penal Servitude Act of 1853 created an early forerunner of the parole system by creating 'ticket of leave' men discharged under licence and required to report to the police. The system failed to work adequately and failed to retain public confidence. Reporting problems, failures to comply and failures to adequately track licensed offenders have a stark resonance with contemporary failings of parole supervision and MAPPA (HMIP 2006a, b). The Habitual Criminals Act of 1869 attempted to rectify these inadequacies through a national register and repealed the ticket of leave arrangements (Thomas 2005).

By the end of the nineteenth century recidivism was seen as an intractable problem. Longer prison terms were largely ineffective as a deterrent and criminals were not only seen as recidivists but also as intransigent. Crime was seen as a matter of personal choice and not as driven by 'desperation' or need, and the 'professional' criminal was seen as morally degenerate and beyond the rest of society. The habitual offender driven by desperate social conditions was transformed into the professional recidivist committing crime with impunity. As Pratt (1997) argues, a number of factors coalesced in framing the recidivist as dangerous. Most notably, developments in technical knowledge such as finger printing and databases that literally made the recidivists more 'knowable'; a perception of their growing numbers; their increased mobility around the country and conversely the perception that they were congregating in urban areas; and the ineffectiveness of penal sanctions were all important. This period also prioritized property crime (indeed violent crime levels were reasonably low) and persistent property offenders were seen as a particular threat – crystallizing in a particular fearfulness of burglary. This threat was insidious, any person's property could be under threat and thus the crime risk of the dangerous was transferred from the State to the individual citizen (Loader and Sparks 2002).

However, the twentieth century saw the State assume a growing responsibility for the management of dangerousness, particularly through the general regulation of the population by 'welfarism' and through extensive penal strategies such as indeterminate sentencing, post-custodial supervision and moral re-engineering through treatment (Garland 1985, 2001). The 'psy' disciplines (predominantly psychiatry) played a significant part in responding to dangerousness, particularly after the Second World War (Foucault 1965, 1973, 1977, 1978), with the identification and treatment of madness, including compulsory detention, playing a significant role in dealing with 'moral degenerates' and 'incorrigibles'. This social engineering had reintegration and rehabilitation as its aims (Donzelot 1980), but recidivism continued to be problematic.

By the 1970s the 'rehabilitative ideal' was in disrepute, and the State's management of 'dangerousness' through welfarism was dogged by perceptions of failure (especially of treatment), the high costs of welfare and a burgeoning prison population on both sides of the Atlantic (Martinson 1974; Folkard et al. 1976; Flynn 1978; Garland 1985). The post-1970s period saw considerable American penal imperialism in which England and Wales (but also other Anglophone jurisdictions) were subject to a growing colonization of criminological ideas and penal strategies: 'boot camps', 'three strikes and you're out' sentencing, indeterminate sentencing, mandatory life sentences, cognitive behavioural programmes and actuarial risk assessment, to name a few. This colonization was aided by personal links between political leaders, shared political ideologies, email communication between research communities and rapid dissemination of penal strategies and evaluations through the Internet.

The period from the late 1970s onwards also saw a retreat from traditional liberalism and particularly from State and social responsibility for risk (see Kemshall 2003: ch. 2 for a full review; Rose 1996a, b, 2000). This has been characterized as a shift in risk management from the State to the individual, characterized by self-regulation and the requirement for individuals to predict and manage their own risks (Rose 1996b, 2004). Perversely, this has resulted in heightened anxiety about risk and increased perceptions about personal vulnerability (Hope and Sparks 2000). In effect, a constant state of risk anxiety in which risk is perceived to be potentially everywhere (Beck 1992, 2005; Denney 2005). As James and Raine contend, anxiety and fear breed the conditions 'under which both government and public become eager participants in a tough stance on crime' (1998: 30). This crime threat was, however, complex containing both the spectre of pervasive and perpetual property crime and the possibility of a serious one-off personal crime fuelled by high profile crimes against children (e.g., Jamie Bulger; Holly Wells and Jessica Chapman; Sarah Payne in the UK; and Megan Kanka, Christopher Stephenson and Jacob Wetterling in the USA and Canada).[1]

The complexity of this crime threat was reflected in an increasingly bifurcated penal policy from the late 1970s onwards which had gained significant momentum by the late 1990s (Bottoms 1995). The long-standing prioritization of offences relating to property was partially challenged by a preoccupation with offences against the person. The Floud Report (Floud and Young 1981) proposed preventative sentencing for 'dangerous offenders' based not merely on the type of crime but on the potential impact of the crime, and selective incarceration was mooted as a protective measure for high risk offenders. In the USA similar proposals were made and preventative measures were seen as justifiable against the harmful recidivist (Greenwood and Abrahamse 1982).

Fuelled by the feminist movement and increasing attention on women as both the victims and perpetrators of crime, the 1980s saw the discovery of sexual offending against women (Worrall 1997) and subsequent concerns with the prevalence and impact of sexual offending against children (Grubin 1998). By the 1990s legislation had begun to harden this bifurcation into crimes of serious harm of a sexual or violent nature; paralleled by concerns with 'persistent and prolific offenders' (PPOs) engaged in high levels of property crime to fund drug abuse. However, recidivism and harm did not become entirely unlinked. The concept of the harmful recidivist and notably the persistent predatory paedophile came to dominate the penal agenda (Kemshall 2003). Rather than merely separating habituation and harm, these were actually meshed. As Thomas puts it: 'The spectre of the invisible sex offender moving around at will took up the mantle of the dangerous vagrant' (2005: 54).

Penal strategies by the end of the twentieth century were not merely retributive, but also preventative. Punishment was required to fit the poten-tial risk as well as fit the crime. This meant sentences followed individual risk targeted at individuals rather than mere offence types. However, this risk is often assessed using formal risk assessment tools based upon aggre-gated group data derived from similar offence and offending types. The individual is ascribed their risk status through the lens of group data.

By the beginning of the twenty-first century the 'monster in our midst' is the sex offender, to a lesser extent the violent offender and more recently the terrorist (Furedi 2005; Mythen and Walklate 2006). The period is characterized by a preoccupation with the technologies of risk, information and surveillance of risk, acute public accountability and public blame for failure and a deep-seated politicization of risk. This situation applies to most of the Anglophone countries (see Pratt 1997 on Australia and Pratt 2006 on New Zealand; Garland 2001 on the USA), but also to other Western democracies including countries often presented as among the most liberal (see Van Swaaningen 1997, 2000 on the Netherlands;[2] see also Albrecht 1997 on dangerousness legislation in Germany; and Ray and Craze 1991 on provisions in Denmark), and further afield (see Kim and Lee 2001 on Korea for example).

At the start of the twenty-first century the term 'dangerous offender' is a more heterogeneous term than ever before, but has crystallized around the sexual and violent offender and notably those offenders committing sexually violent and predatory crimes against children. The category is, however, almost endlessly flexible, encapsulating potential terrorists, asylum seekers, 'problem youth', the socially excluded, as well as a wide range of sexual and violent offences of varying degrees of gravity. 'Dangerous' has also elided into the more ubiquitous term 'risk'. Every offender is deemed to present some risk (HMIP 2006a), the key is to determine the level of risk and match responses accordingly.

Framing risk and dangerousness

The 'long view' reminds us that dangerousness has had various incarnations and various classes of persons and individuals have been considered dangerous at different points in time. Theoretical approaches to dangerousness have also changed over time.

This section will examine a number of contemporary theoretical approaches to dangerousness rooted in the disciplines of sociology, criminology and psychology. The approaches presented are not intended to be exhaustive, but rather illustrative of different understandings of, and responses to, dangerousness.

Criminological and legal approaches to risk and dangerousness

In an examination of contemporary penal practices across the Anglophone countries Brown highlights the contradictory conceptions and use of 'risk' concluding that:

> Risks presented by an offender are frequently calculated in different and often contradictory ways and these differing conceptions of risk are used to justify a set of equally disparate and conflicting responses to the supposedly dangerous individual. It is on the grounds of these different

conceptions of risk, therefore, that the penal strategies as diverse as 'three-strikes' law, intensive therapeutic programmes and indefinite sentences find their justification.

(Brown 2000: 93)

An examination of criminological and legal approaches to risk and dangerous offenders reveals an emphasis upon a technical understanding of risk within which risk and dangerousness are framed as objectively knowable phenomena if only the correct measures and tools can be designed (see Kemshall 2003: ch. 3 for a full review). This artefact framing of risk has seen an ever developing pursuit of reliable risk assessment tools to identify 'dangerous offenders', 'the critical few' or high risk offenders. The accurate 'capture' of risk is seen as a matter of tool design and integrity of use (Bonta 1996; Bonta and Wormith 2007). Work of this type has been largely uncritical of the rationalities underlying the new penology and has been presented in value neutral terms as 'administrative criminology' concerned with effectiveness and efficiency in the administration of penal strategies (Nelken 1994).

The tension between tool development and subsequent use by practitioners and sentencers has also received attention (see Kemshall 1998a, b; Robinson 1999; Lynch 2000; O'Malley 2006). From the administrative criminology view point this is usually expressed as the ill-informed resistance, irrationality or bias of tool users which should be corrected by training, instruction and enforcement (see the following probation circulars on risk practice for example: PC 53/2004, PC 49/2005, PC 82/2005, PC 15/2006, PC 22/2006, PC 36/2006). However, research informed by other perspectives, such as social constructivism, has identified other issues affecting the use and implementation of risk assessment tools, including flaws built into the systems and processes of assessment themselves (Kemshall 2007); clashes of ideology and professional values (Robinson 1999, 2002); and practitioner and judicial resistance based upon legitimacy and human rights issues (Freiberg 2000).

Tensions in tool use can also be understood as arising from differing conceptualizations of risk rather than as necessarily due to practitioners' lack of compliance. In essence, risk assessment tools see the riskiness of an offender as rooted in the behaviour(s) and circumstances of that individual. Brown (2000) describes such an understanding of risk as 'fluid', changeable along a behavioural continuum of low to high risk, and triggered by specific circumstances. Such risks are knowable and calculable if behaviours and triggers can be measured against known risk profiles produced by the aggregated data on risky populations – in essence this is the job that most risk assessment tools do and numerous actuarial, clinical and combined structured tools exist for the assessment of such risk (see Chapter 3, this volume). Behaviours and triggers are also seen as changeable to some degree, and hence such tools target offenders for interventions and behavioural programmes as well as for custodial sentences, and a number can measure the impact of interventions over time.

In contrast, Brown identifies categorical risk, most often seen in legal definitions of risk and danger. For example, offence-based categories of risk (particularly high risk), such as those offences used in the CJA 2003 which qualify for an Indeterminate Public Protection Sentence (IPPS), or in the Scottish Order for Lifelong Restriction (OLR). Offence-based categorizations are not dependent upon the characteristics or behaviours of the offender. The categorization is defined by the type of offence, its gravity and seriousness. This can produce two problems for risk-based sentencing. The first is epitomized in the USA by three strikes legislation in which the third offence could be far less serious and still trigger a life sentence (e.g, the famous 'pizza incident' in which the third offence of stealing a pizza triggered a life sentence) (Brown 2000). In this example the legal definition alone counts, not the behaviour or circumstances of the offender or offence.

The second problem is in the operation of bifurcated sentencing based upon dividing offences into risky and non-risky. The very separation of offence from offender in the categorical approach to risk makes bifurcation difficult to operate. Burglary is an important case in point where decisions about risk and seriousness cannot be made on offence type alone, but where consideration of behavioural patterns, motivation and the key circumstances of the commission of the offence (e.g., whether targeted at lone females) are all essential to understanding the risk. In such decisions categorical and fluid definitions of risk have to be balanced but often conflict. Probation officers may find that categorical offence-based definitions under pitch risk when they 'find out' further behavioural or circumstantial information about an offender and then, for example, seek to redefine risk levels under the Multi-Agency Public Protection Arrangements. Sentencers may in turn be restricted by legal definitions when sentencing and are subsequently accused of lenient sentencing (see News BBC 2006, 'Call for stiffer sentence for attacker of girl, 3', www.news.bbc.co.uk accessed 8 March 2007). Fluid and categorical risk are also conflated in legislation, for example legislation creating indeterminate preventative risk-based sentencing, such as the CJA 2003. This legislation utilizes both offence categories (some 88 sexual and 65 violent), but also provides a threshold for serious harm which requires risk assessment based on behaviours, triggers and offence circumstances as set out in Sections 229(2) and 229(3). This has already created significant difficulties and appeal court challenges (see Stone 2004a, b and c; Taylor et al. 2004; Chapter 1, this volume).

In a study of 42 judges in the USA, Bumby and Maddox (1999) found that judges hold varying views about sexual offending, risk factors and behaviours: 'Of particular interest is the finding that, compared to other cases, sexual offense cases were rated by judges as more difficult over which to preside from a legal and technical standpoint, a personal and emotional viewpoint, and a public scrutiny and public pressure standpoint' (Bumby and Maddox 1999: 305).

Practitioners such as probation officers often experience tensions between fluid and categorical risk (Kemshall 2000). Probation officers will assess offenders using fluid risk but may find these assessments conflict with or are overruled by categorical definitions of risk, for example when they refer to MAPPA and find that their referral does not meet the risk levels or MAPPA categories – they 'intuitively feel' the offender is dangerous, but the person does not meet the criteria for an intervention. In addition, probation officers in pre-sentence reports can assess potential risk of serious harm based on behaviours and patterns, but the Court of Appeal has not always accepted that offenders meet the criteria for an IPP sentence, including cases over-turned because a pattern of behaviour had not been sufficiently established (see Stone 2004a, b and c).

Criminological and legal approaches have also tended to individualize risk, centring upon the individual rational actor characterized as a 'free-willed actor who engages in crime in a calculative, utilitarian way and is therefore responsive to deterrent' (Garland 1997: 11). In practice, assess-ments will often be concerned with levels of culpability and blame, whether offenders were in control and acting rationally or were mentally ill, and the extent to which their rational choice might have been constrained (for example, were they provoked?). While the rational actor has been a core feature of much criminological research on risk (see Kemshall 2006a), this actor is more difficult to discern in practice. Interestingly, while the offender is cast as a risk-informed rational actor, the dangerous or high risk offender is often recast as irrational, incapable of making informed decisions (for example, to lower their risk or to comply with treatment), they are then deemed to be more dangerous and in need of greater restriction and con-trol (Janus 2000). In some jurisdictions this has legitimated civil/mental health containment post-custody, especially for sex offenders (Connelly and Williamson 2000; Janus 2000).

Criminological and legal approaches to risk and dangerousness have con-tributed risk assessment tools to the justice system and thus a degree of consistency and rigour to risk assessment (although the extent of this is hotly disputed; see Kemshall 2003). Legal definitions in particular have attempted to draw high thresholds for risk, particularly in respect of preventative sen-tencing although how this works in practice is still under review. In addition, administrative criminology has also focused attention on crime opportun-ities, crime prevention and crime reduction, and introduced a prevention paradigm into some areas of crime management. This has characterized the offender, including the persistent and dangerous offender, as a rational actor capable of free will and choice who can be managed, if not changed (see Kemshall 2006a for a full review).

Limits to criminological and legal approaches to dangerousness

Criminological research and theorizing about risk and dangerousness has been criticized on the grounds of its discipline insularity and lack of engagement with social theory in particular (Brown and Pratt 2000). In addition, criminology has been seen as increasingly policy driven, with research serving policy initiatives and skewed towards evaluative rather than discovery research (Maguire 2004). Brown and Pratt argue that this results in an administrative and positivist bias in criminology, with an emphasis upon empirical research on processes, systems and techniques of risk predominating:

> Thus, the vast bulk of criminological writing on dangerous offenders over the past three decades has concerned itself with either the quest for prospective identification of serious offenders (usually invoking the concept of reoffending risk) or with efforts to develop technical or principled responses to the dangerous individual in the realms of policy and sentencing practice.
>
> (Brown and Pratt 2000: 3–4)

There has been rather less engagement with 'disciplinary assumptions' and underlying penal rationalities, although more recently the seminal works of Pratt (1997, 2000a, b, 2006) and Garland (2001) have challenged this. The growing interaction of criminology and social theory, particularly with governmentality theory (discussed below), has facilitated a growing critique of administrative criminology and risk-based penology.

The notion of the rational actor has also been much criticized, notably for its lack of attention to the social factors that may restrict the exercise of rational choice (see Kemshall 2006a for a full review). The introduction of social theory into criminological research has addressed this to some extent by providing useful empirical research on how choices are actually made, how risks are perceived and responded to, and how offenders actually desist from offending (Maruna 2001; Farrall 2002; McNeill and Maruna 2007).

Psychological framing of high risk offenders and dangerousness

The 'psy' disciplines (particularly psychiatry) were dominant between the 1930s and the 1950s (Foucault 1977, 1988), and following a decline post-1970s they are currently gaining in significance. This approach frames risk and dangerousness as the individual, inherent traits of the offender. In essence, risk factors are understood as those factors predisposing the individual towards sexual or violent offending. These factors may be within the personality of the individual, a result of mental illness or located within childhood experiences or family functioning. While risk and dangerous behaviours are thus individualized, it is usually in terms of abnormality from the norm and linked to assessments or diagnoses designed to reveal the reasons for such abnormality. Such assessments are used not only to determine culpability but also to determine treatability. In considering a psychological approach to high risk sex offenders, Craissati states that:

> Essentially, sex offenders are understood in terms of their internal emotional and cognitive lives, their relationship to particular others (including past and potential victims) and their perception of their place in the wider world. These constructs are likely to be shaped, to a greater or lesser degree, by experiences across the life span interacting with individual inherent characteristics.
>
> (2004: 203)

In her work Craissati reviews the main risk assessment tools used in the psychological risk assessment of high risk sex offenders, and how these inform treatment responses. The main treatment response has been the Sex Offender Treatment Programme (SOTP) provided and evaluated initially in prison (see Beckett et al. 1994; Beech et al. 1999) and transferred to community provision in the late 1990s (for a full review see Beech and Fisher 2004). Programmes have tended to be characterized by cognitive behavioural therapy (CBT) treatment (see Beech and Fisher 2004 for a review; and Chapter 5, this volume) – although psychodynamic therapies and systemic family therapy for incest cases are also pursued (see Craissati 2004 for a review). CBT is based on the premise that patterns of thinking, emotions and perceptions of the world are learnt and become habituated. These patterns can become distorted (e.g., sex offending with children is normal and unproblematic), justified by the perpetrator and are key triggers in offending (Beech and Fisher 2004; Fisher and Beech 2004). Increasingly these programmes are accredited and run by Prison and Probation Services, often as compulsory programmes on parole licence or community supervision. Treatment programmes are also often supported by relapse prevention programmes and intensive one-to-one work (e.g., the Northumbria Sex Offender Treatment Programme).

Psychiatric assessments and treatment often run parallel to psychological approaches, targeted at those high risk offenders deemed to have a mental illness. Psychiatry has attempted to provide typologies of dangerous offenders, for example typologies of serial killers (Holmes and Holmes 1998), and in the USA a psychiatrist has established a '22 level gradation of evil' to assist courts in determining culpability and punishment (M. Stone 2005 cited in D'Cruze et al. 2006: 24). Psychiatry focuses in part on the unconscious mind, and in addition to issues of treatability will also focus on the level of control and intentionality of the offender. In a sense, psychiatry assists in the forensic function of apportioning blame – did the offender know what they were doing or not? While lack of blame may diminish punishment, mental health diagnoses for high risk offenders can result in compulsory detainment and treatment in secure units, and the mental health field has been increasingly characterized by a preoccupation with risk prevention and compulsory intrusive measures on the grounds of public protection (Connelly and Williamson 2000). Mental health services in the community have become preoccupied with 'risky thinking' as clinical judgement about care and treatment is replaced by risk management and control as patients are displaced from long-term hospitals into the community (Rose 1998; Moon 2000). 'Care in the community' has become 'control in the community'.

The 'psy' disciplines have a long history in the regulation of populations and the moral re-engineering of deviant populations (Foucault 1965, 1973, 1977, 1988; Pratt 1997). 'Psy-knowledge' played a significant part in the normalization programme of the welfare state, that is, in the identification and moral re-engineering of those deviants who could be rescued from their deviancy (see Pratt 1997; and Garland 2001 for a full review). Interventions were case based and predicated on a unique relationship between therapist/worker and client. The second half of the twentieth century saw social work and probation dominated by this case-based treatment paradigm (McWilliams 1986).

The 'psy' disciplines and the 'psy' knowledge they are based on began to diminish in influence in the 1970s. This was in part due to lack of effectiveness in both assessment and diagnosis of 'dangerousness', resulting in an unethical overprediction; overintrusive and unjustified treatments (often inequitable when compared to pure punishment); stigmatization and bias against particular groups in the population including minority groups; and a growing lack of credibility with sentencers, politicians and the public alike (Garland 2001). The challenge presented to 'psy' knowledge by actuarial, statistically-based risk methods has been well documented (see Pratt 1997; Garland 2001; Rose 2001, 2004; Kemshall 2003), although the 'psy' disciplines have not been entirely eclipsed by actuarialism. Those disciplines and agencies with historical roots in welfarism (e.g., psychiatry, probation and social work) tend to have a hybridized approach to risk, comprising clinical case-based assessments with actuarially-based formal risk tools. Indeed many of the statistical methods and risk factors are informed by psychological concepts, and the renaissance of psychological approaches to risk owes much to its use in risk assessing prisoners, and in informing actuarial risk tools (see Bonta 1996). Formal risk tools and the 'psy' disciplines have been increasingly meshed, and the revival of psychological approaches to risk has been driven by its use and power in the risk agenda.

In practice, this mixed economy of aggregated risk factors and profiles combined with case-based individualized assessments (Dean 1997) produces tensions and conflicts in the process of risk assessment. Workers struggle to translate aggregated data to individual assessments, resist the application of formal tools in a case work setting, and struggle to justify risk-based interventions when individual offenders present as 'exceptions to the rule'.

The limits of 'psy' framings of dangerousness

The 'psy' disciplines made a major contribution to the framing and understanding of dangerous offenders, particularly in the twentieth century. They played a key role in the articulation of problematic behaviours, mental disorders, predisposing factors and triggers, and in the development of increasingly effective treatments for sexual and violent offenders. In terms of prison and probation interventions with sexual and violent offenders, psychological approaches have tended to predominate (Kemshall and McIvor 2004). However, the 'psy' approach has attracted criticism on the grounds of stigmatization and net widening (Canton 2005); discrimination against key groups (Hudson and Bramhall 2005; Fitzgibbon 2007); and ineffectiveness (for example, the famous Folkard et al. study of 1976; and Martinson 1974). More recently criticism has centred on the lack of attention to the cultural, social and structural context within which dangerous behaviours take place. For example, the role of masculinity and patriarchal power in male violence and sexual abuse of women and children has been seen as a key oversight in psychological approaches to abuse (Smart 1989; Stanko 1990; Kitzinger 2004). The 'psy' disciplines have also been subject to increasing hybridization with other approaches. For example, assessment and diagnosis has been influenced by formal, structured actuarial tools particularly when distinguishing high risk offenders from others and in deciding the risk of serious harm for courts, for example the use of the Offender Assessment System (OASys) in pre-sentence court reports in England and Wales. Interventions have been influenced by survivor and feminist perspectives and these are incorporated into CBT programmes challenging sexual abuse and violence with male perpetrators (Kitzinger 2004).

Sociological understandings of risk and dangerousness

Sociological understandings of risk and dangerousness are eclectic, drawing on a range of theoretical approaches within the broader discipline of sociology.

This section explores arguably the most influential: cultural theory, governmentality theory and social construction approaches.

Cultural theory

Cultural theory examines how some dangers are chosen for attention while others are not (for example, the attention to 'stranger-danger' in child sexual abuse and the relative neglect of sexual abusing within families, see Kitzinger 2004). Such work pays attention to the symbolic and cultural meanings carried by risk and danger (Douglas 1992), and the political rationalities and strategies that underpin them (Sparks 2001b). In essence, dangers are not morally neutral but always carry a political and morally infused message (O'Malley 2004a, b, 2006). Cultural theory attempts to 'unpick' such underlying rationalities, and is most often associated with the work of Mary Douglas (1992).

In her work, *Risk and Blame* (1992), Douglas explored the forensic function of risk and danger, in essence how risk and danger function to allocate blame, re-enforce both social and moral orders, and marginalize threatening 'others'. As Lupton puts it: 'in a climate where political dangers dog one's every action and choice, the risks that receive most attention in a particular culture are those that are connected with legitimating moral principles' (1999: 45).

Hence, Thomas's 'mad, bad and vagrant' continue to attract attention, albeit in slightly different forms. This is what Douglas has called the 'forensic function of risk':

> Above all, its forensic uses fit the tool to the task of building a culture that supports a modern industrial society. Of the different types of blaming system that we can find in tribal society; the one we are in now is almost ready to treat every death as chargeable to someone's account, every accident as caused by someone's negligence, every sickness a threatened prosecution. Whose fault? is the first question.
>
> (1992: 15–16)

Risks have to be accounted for and blamed on someone. Risk is a 'rhetoric of retribution and accusation against a specific individual' (Lupton 1999: 47) – and increasingly against specific groups (Young 1999). In essence, the blaming process (and the accountability that always accompanies it) establishes and maintains the group's norms and boundaries.

Garland (2001) has extended this into a 'criminology of the Other' and describes it as a:

> criminology that trades in images, archetypes, and anxieties, rather than in careful analyses and research findings. In its deliberate echoing of public concerns and media biases, and its focus on the most worrisome threats, it is, in effect, a politicised discourse of the collective unconscious, though it claims to be altogether realist and 'commonsensical' in contrast to 'academic theories'. In its standard tropes and rhetorical invocations, this political discourse relies upon an archaic criminology of the criminal type, the alien other. Sometimes explicitly, more often in coded references, the problem is traced to the wanton, amoral behaviour of dangerous offenders, who typically belong to racial and cultural groups bearing little resemblance to 'us'.
>
> (2001: 135; see also Boutellier 2000; Matravers 2005)

Bottoms (1977) in a seminal article on the 'renaissance of dangerousness' argued that as the State loses its power to maintain social cohesion the 'criminological other' fulfils an important function in maintaining a collective conscience.

Some key examples of 'Others' are Pratt's (2000) 'wheel barrow men' of the nineteenth century; the ticket of leave men (Pratt 1997); and more recently black offenders (Fitzgibbon 2007; see also Hudson and Bramhall on 'assessing the Other' 2005); paedophiles (Ashenden 1996, 2002); and immigrants (Tulloch and Lupton 2003). Other contemporary images include 'hoodies', paedophiles and various 'monsters in our midst' (Simon 1998).

The spectre of the 'Other' justifies increasingly anticipatory measures. That is, early identification of risk and preventative measures to prevent those risks occurring. At the extreme, this can mean preventative sentencing for high risk offenders such as Indeterminate Public Protection Sentences, or the use of measures against offenders such as Sexual Offender Prevention Orders (SOPOs) requiring only civil standards of proof. Anticipatory measures are increasingly expressed against groups within the population and membership of such groups can trigger the marker dangerous (Fitzgibbon 2007). For example, powerful images merge race and crime (Garland 2001: 136), the underclass (Murray 1990) and, more recently, the rather sanitized term 'the socially excluded' (Social Exclusion Unit 2002).

The limits of cultural theory

Cultural theory has been criticized for being too broad and too deterministic (Denney 2005), and for failing to recognize that cultural forms can be mediated by the actions of individuals and groups (Seidel and Vidal 1997), we are not 'mere cultural dupes' (Giddens 1984). It has also been criticized for conflating high impact risks and dangers with the risks of the everyday – not everything is catastrophic and many dangers are pervasive but small. While this may contribute to a general feeling of anxiety it does not necessarily mean we see dangers everywhere or necessarily demonize those who are not quite like us (McGuigan 2006). Coping with anxiety and uncertainty, while disconcerting, does not necessarily result in a constant 'policing' of potential dangers. Such 'demons' are not necessarily new either, and in taking the long view we can see that the traditional signifiers of race, class and indeed gender have and still do play a major role (Pratt 1997; Young 1999; Furlong and Cartmel 2006).

The major contribution of cultural theory has been in the articulation of the rationalities of risk and danger – for example, their framing and use in the debate about global warming and climate change, and how they are inevitably politicized (McGuigan 2006). It has also been important in alerting us to the 'culturally rooted and pervasive' nature of risk and danger, a sense of 'uncertainty and chance' in addition to fears of catastrophic risk (McGuigan 2006: 215). In essence, the risks and dangers embedded in everyday life (Lupton 1999; Sparks 2001a, b; Tulloch and Lupton 2003).

Governance: surveillance, social sorting and social regulation

The insecurity of everyday life is readily discerned in the arena of crime management (Kemshall 2003; Denney 2005): 'The risk of crime is presented as a form of social malignancy by governments globally, which, if not checked, will spread, eating away at the core of social order' (Denney 2005: 122).

Managing social order and social regulation in advanced liberal society has been a growing theme of contemporary social theory (see for example Rose 2000, 2004). In effect, how to provide security and effective crime management in societies characterized by diversity, fragmentation and a shrinking State (Rose 2000; Stenson 2001; Stenson and Edwards 2001; Stenson and Sullivan 2001). Such analyses focus on how populations are regulated and managed, how risks are distributed, and how the allocation of responsibility for their effective management is distributed between communities and the State (see Ashenden 2002 on the governance of paedophilia). In essence, the major danger is the threat to social order and social regulation itself.

Governmentality theorists in particular 'explore risk in the context of surveillance, discipline, and regulation of populations, and how concepts of risk construct particular norms of behaviour which are used to encourage individuals to engage voluntarily in self-regulation in response to these norms' (Lupton 1999: 25). This is what Rose has called responsibilization (1996a, b, 2000): in effect a mechanism of social regulation in which individuals are made responsible for their own actions, including their own risks, and for their own self-risk management (Kemshall 2003: 148, 2006a: 84). Rose has described this as governance at the 'molecular level' in which the active, prudent citizen is required to self-regulate towards the preset norms of society (see Draper and Green 2002 for an example relating to food choices). Those who fail to exercise the prudent choice are excluded, marginalized and demonized (Kemshall 2006a, b). Offenders are, of course, a case in point. Those deemed amenable to treatment and moral re-engineering are selected for reintegration largely through compulsory programmes (e.g., Probation Service cognitive behavioural groups); those who are not are submitted to containment through custody and intensive programmes of monitoring and surveillance (Kemshall and Maguire 2001; Kemshall 2002b). In effect, a risk-based segregation, with surveillance in criminal justice itself bifurcated with intensive surveillance for the 'hardcore of persistent or problematic offenders' (Norris 2007: 139).

New techniques of surveillance (most often electronic) have been increasingly linked by governmentality theorists to social regulation (D. Wood

2006). Most obvious examples are the electronic tagging and satellite tracking of offenders; the use of car number plate recognition systems in speed and CCTV cameras to monitor the movement of paedophiles and so forth (Kemshall et al. 2005; Norris 2006, 2007). However, such surveillance is not necessarily restricted to offenders, for example speed and CCTV cameras are numerous and cover us all. Other techniques of surveillance can be more insidious, with tracking via credit and debit cards, store cards and so on (Lianos with Douglas 2000). How we spend our money, leisure time, habits and personal preferences can all readily be surveilled, with some commentators now speculating that we are living in a 'surveillance society' (Lyon 2003). In this sense, surveillance is more than mere watching but is defined as: 'Where we find purposeful, routine, systematic and focused attention paid to personal details for the sake of control, entitlement, management, influence or protection, we are looking at surveillance' (D. Wood 2006: 4).

Such surveillance is, of course, critical for pre-emptive strategies: for example, who to target for health campaigns (Petersen and Lupton 1996); targeted policing (Johnston 2000); or children for early intervention measures (Armstrong 2004; Payne 2004; Hall et al. 2007). Kemshall and Maguire summarize this as a world:

> in which an all-consuming desire to eliminate threats to safety produces ever more sophisticated technologies of information-gathering, classification, surveillance, control and exclusion: in which attention shifts from the individual to the aggregate 'risk group'; and in which concepts such as individual justice, rights and accountability lose their meaning.
>
> (2001: 238)

While Rigakos and Hadden (2001) point out that social regulation and panoptical (all seeing) surveillance have a long history (dating back at least to the seventeenth century), there is a distinction between traditional approaches and contemporary postmodern regulation. In brief, the former is seen as focused on normalization and reintegration (Donzelot 1980), in other words with integrating people back into society. The latter is concerned with exclusion and social sorting, literally with sorting people *out* (Gandy 1993; Lyon 2003). Lyon has summarized these developments thus: 'today's surveillance systems sort these ordinary people into categories, assigning worth or risk, in ways that have real effects on their life-chances. Deep discrimination occurs, thus making surveillance not merely a matter of personal privacy, but of social justice' (2003: 1).

So what are the implications of such social sorting? The most obvious is the objectification of the offender. Traditionally dangerousness was considered to be an inherent quality of the offender (often closely allied to notions of evil), discoverable by in-depth clinical and highly individualized assessments (Pratt 1997; Aas 2005). Contemporary understandings of the dangerous are more complex, with traditional conceptions continuing in the area of psychiatry for example, but risk factors and formal risk assessment tools have enabled a more abstract notion of dangerousness to develop in which offenders are profiled against an aggregate understanding of dangerous behaviour through the use of electronically-based risk assessment tools such as MATRIX 2000. As Aas puts it: 'what intervention policies address are no longer individuals but factors, statistical correlations of risk. In fact, individuals may not even need to be present' (2005: 127). One key example of this is the English and Welsh Parole Board's policy of not interviewing prisoners as part of the Board's assessment process, informed by research which indicated that risk assessment tools and board papers alone could provide assessments more accurate than face-to-face interviews (Hood and Shute 2000).

A further implication is the compounding of existing inequalities in which already disadvantaged groups lack the resources to self-risk manage or to take the required prudential choices (for example, to eat healthily, see Petersen and Lupton 1996). Crime victims restrained by poverty, structural inequality, and lack of geographical mobility are not always in a position to exercise the 'right choice' about risk avoidance (Walklate 1997, 1998; Hope 2001). The British Crime Survey, for example, now plots differential exposure to risk across different segments of the population and records higher levels for British Minority Ethnic (BME) groups (Budd et al. 2005). Interestingly such groups are also differentially risk marked as dangerous (Fitzgibbon 2007), and again social structural constraints on an offender's capacity to 'desist' or 'change' may be significant (Farrall 2002).

The limits of governmentality, surveillance and social sorting

While surveillance studies are growing in volume and influence (Lyon 2003), the evidence that we are living in a surveillance society is patchy (Lips et al. 2007). Surveillance technologies are indeed growing but the evidence that we are living in a panoptical society is far from clear cut (Lips et al. 2007). In addition, surveillance is not a new phenomenon, populations have long been subject to scrutiny in some form (Thomas 2005), although contemporary techniques are more sophisticated and electronically-based. Social sorting also has a long history. The welfare state operated by social sorting, for example the deserving from the non-deserving poor, and as Pratt's seminal study indicates we have long sorted the 'mad, bad, and poor' (1997). Are we actually identifying any new groups or merely recycling the usual groups into new categorizations of risk?

However, governmentality theses do usefully identify a number of interesting trends. The increasing use of actuarially-based risk profiling as opposed to individualized diagnoses of risk is one, although in those professions characterized by individualized case assessment and management such as psychiatry and probation a 'mixed economy' of actuarial and clinical techniques continues (Dean 1997, 1999a, b; Kemshall 2003). Another key trend is the use of risk profiles to justify preventative strategies, commonly referred to as the 'risk prevention paradigm' (Farrington 2000), in which early interventions are justified on the basis of preventing risk (for example, early interventions with juveniles 'at risk' of crime). Governmentality analyses have increasingly scrutinized such policies and practices and provide an important critique on the growing political response to governance issues and risk.

The social construction of risk and the role of the media

Social construction approaches to risk and danger argue that 'a risk is never fully objective or knowable outside of belief systems and moral positions: what we measure, identify and manage as risk are always constituted via pre-existing knowledges and discourses' (Lupton 1999: 29). This is not to say that risks and dangers are not real, but that perceptions of risk and how risks and dangers are chosen for importance and attention is significant. A key example is the contrast between the media, political and public attention given to children abducted and killed by strangers (around six to eight per year) and the 150 to 200 children killed per year by a parent (NSPCC 1992; Kitzinger 2004; Hughes et al. 2006).

This was exemplified in May 2007 by the disappearance of Madeleine McCann in Portugal, and the subsequent spawning of dozens of websites dedicated to expressing sympathy for the plight of child and family. By 19 May 2007 there were 90 different Madeleine related groups on the social networking site Facebook alone, (*Guardian Unlimited*, 19 May 2007), and the official website had registered 60 million hits within days of set up. As Kitzinger has eloquently argued, our current framing of child sexual abuse is of 'stranger-danger', the loner and the outcast from society who is a 'monster in our midst' preying on our children (2004: 157), yet ongoing research by Gallagher indicates that only 9 per cent of assaults involve stranger abduction and sexual assault (Gallagher 2007). This deflects attention from the extensive abuse occurring within families and that 'most paedophiles in the community are undetected and probably well integrated into their neighbourhood' (Kitzinger 2004: 156). Paedophiles are our neighbours – an uncomfortable thought.

Kitzinger's work is an excellent exposition of the media framings of 'danger' and the complex relationship between media coverage and audience response. As such it will suffice to merely summarize the key points here. Kitzinger examines one of the key contemporary risks of our time, child sexual abuse. She plots the 'discovery' of child sexual abuse in the 1980s, particularly the discovery of the paedophile (a point supported by the research of Soothill and Walby 1991; Grover and Soothill 1995; Thomas 2005), and the volume of media coverage epitomized by the 'satanic abuse' cases of Cleveland and Orkney (Butler-Schloss 1988).[3] Drawing upon both media analysis and audience reception and response research, Kitzinger examines the complex relationship between media stories, influence and audience reaction. She concludes that audiences are not mere 'sponges' or receptors of media messages. However, she also concludes that:

> Nevertheless, my research reveals that in spite of, and sometimes because of this, the media are a crucial resource in constructing our sense of the world around us. The mass media can help to define what counts as a public issue, impact upon our understandings of individual cases, shape suspicions and beliefs, and resources memories and conversations. The media also influence how we think about ourselves and each other, impacting on how we relate to family, friends and 'outsiders'. They can even help us to interpret the most intensely private experience and influence our hopes and fears for the future.
>
> (2004: 180)

The media shape issues, place them on the public and political agenda, and provide a frame of reference against which we measure our own experiences. Media can 'champion' causes (e.g., Sarah's Law), validate causes and experiences, demonize particular groups and popularize new fears, risk and dangers. Importantly media can also help to frame solutions (or indeed inhibit them), mobilize activists and enable or prompt policy makers into action (again the *News of the World* campaign on Sarah's Law is a case in point). Audiences mediate stories through mechanisms such as reinterpretation, disbelief and cynicism, and avoidance; and framings of key risks and dangers are evaluated against personal experience and the lived reality of the immediate locale. In particular audiences draw on the following when responding to media messages (Kitzinger 2004: 186):

- their own sense of identity and group loyalties;
- political frameworks for opposition;
- information from trusted professionals;
- 'gossip' and community networks;
- work experience around the issue; and
- direct personal experience.

She concludes by arguing for a more 'nuanced' understanding of media influence and audience responses.

Interestingly Kitzinger also examines how the media 'discover' a social problem, in this case child sexual abuse. She points out that the phenomenon was by no means new when media coverage 'took off' in the 1980s.

Campaigners 100 years earlier in the 1880s had highlighted the issue of child prostitution (Kitzinger 2004; Thomas 2005) leading to the formation of the National Society for the Prevention of Cruelty to Children (NSPCC). Investigative reporting during the 1880s by William Stead and his series of articles in the *Pall Mall Gazette* (see Kitzinger 2004; and Thomas 2005 for a full review) also provided political pressure. Within days of publication the law on consent was raised to 16. In contrast the twentieth century largely ignored child sexual abuse and incest (Kitzinger 2004; Thomas 2005). So what changed in the 1980s? For Kitzinger there were a number of key components, not least the impact of feminist movements highlighting sexual abuse of women and children within families; the inception of Childwatch and Childline enabling children to disclose abuse and seek help; subsequent media coverage of the 'Childline phenomenon' ('Childine received 50,000 calls on its opening day and calls continued at a rate of 8,000 to 10,000 per day after that' (2004: 35)); the rise and influence of survivor groups; and the interest of professionals such as social workers and probation officers. As Kitzinger puts it: 'The mass media discovery of sexual violence against children facilitated, and may have been a prerequisite, for its transition from a shameful, individual secret to becoming a public issue' (Kitzinger 2004: 46).

The limits to social constructionist and media framings of dangerousness and risk
These have been well expressed by a number of research studies (notably Tulloch and Lupton 2003; Kitzinger 2004; Hughes et al. 2006). Media influence cannot simplistically be understood as a 'simple "hyperdermic" effect on our perceptions' (Hughes et al. 2006: 260). Our perceptions of media messages are mediated by who we are, where we are, our personal and social location, and who we interact with (Tulloch and Lupton 2001). The process of influence is subtle albeit significant, and as the above example of 'discovering child sexual abuse' indicates it is also interactive – in this case with survivor groups and with professionals. As Hughes et al. express it, there are many sources of knowledge about threat:

> The circulation of everyday knowledge in routine conversation between friends and acquaintances is also key in supporting the focus on some sources of threat, and not others. The 'social currency' of different types of risk knowledge (the extent to which it is publicly shared or not) may also play a role in shaping everyday understandings of risk. When an unknown man behaves suspiciously around children (e.g. hanging around outside a school offering sweets) this becomes a matter for public knowledge. The head teacher may send out letters of warning and parents will exchange their concerns around the school gate. By contrast, when a child is discovered to have been sexually abused within a family this is usually a closely guarded secret.
>
> (2006: 262)

Informal communication can be as significant as media messages, and local experiences of threat are mediated by and often consolidate national media images. The mixture of local experience, distrust of professionals and high anxiety coupled with media presentations of 'predatory paedophiles' proved a powerful concoction in the vigilante action in Paulsgrove (Nash 2006). The key message in all of this is to understand audiences as active (and sometimes interactive) consumers of media, and policy makers should beware of treating the public as 'mere media dupes'.

The impact of mass media, and particularly television, has had more subtle effects and has contributed to what Garland has called a collective and institutionalized crime consciousness. Experience of crime and victimization is an everyday social fact, indeed it is an expectation of our everyday life which contributes to our anxiety and fear of crime (2001: 157–65). We are constantly aware of crime risks, take precautions against them and yet we perversely feel less safe.

Conclusion

This chapter has reminded us that 'risk' and 'dangerousness' are elusive terms with long histories. The 'long view' highlights those groups who have been demarcated as 'Other' and the varied techniques for their identification and regulation. Penal strategies continue to adapt and develop in order to capture 'the dangerous'; and in the early twenty-first century surveillance techniques have become more ubiquitous and insidious. Paralleling this historical view, we can also discern three key knowledge/discipline approaches to risk and dangerousness: criminological and legal, psychological and sociological. These disciplinary approaches provide differing conceptualizations and characterizations of risk and dangerousness, and characterize both the dangerous and societal responses to them differently. It is important for practitioners, managers and policy makers to understand these different framings and responses, not merely to understand where they and others are 'coming from', but to understand the potential sources of tension and conflict (e.g., between practitioners and judiciary, policy makers and implementers), but also to provide some critical reflection on current policy developments and penal strategies.

Notes

1 Jamie Bulger, a toddler, was abducted from a shopping centre and killed by two older children. The other children in this list were assaulted and killed either by known sex offenders or, in the case of Ian Huntley, the killer of Holly Wells and Jessica Chapman, by a person known to the police but not adequately vetted for

his employment as a school caretaker. These cases all led to public outrage about the inappropriate regulation of sex offenders in the community and resulted in changes in policy, practice and law. Legal changes in the community regulation of sex offenders, particularly in the USA, are often emotively named after child victims.

2 Note that in the Netherlands around 90% of 'dangerous offenders' under dangerousness legislation are violent offenders (Kinzig 1997).

3 These cases became notorious for the investigation of 'satanic abuse' following identification of child sexual abuse within a number of families. The cases sparked a preoccupation with the identification of networks of abuse, although subsequently the accusations were found to be incorrect. The investigation processes were later examined by the Butler-Schloss inquiry. Both Cleveland and Orkney were the subject of extensive and, at times, excessive media coverage (Kitzinger 2004).

Further reading

Garland, D. (2001) *The Culture of Crime Control: Crime and Social Order in Contemporary Society*. Oxford: Oxford University Press.

Kitzinger, J. (2004) *Framing Abuse: Media Influence and Public Understanding of Sexual Violence Against Children*. London: Pluto Press.

Lupton, D. (1999) *Risk*. London: Routledge.

Thomas, T. (2005) *Sex Crime: Sex offending and society*, 2nd edn. Cullumpton: Willan Publishing.

chapter three

Risk assessment: difficulties and dilemmas

Decision making on risk: the key issues

Rigorous risk assessment is crucial to the effective identification and management of high risk offenders (Kemshall et al. 2005). However, this is an area prone to difficulty and failure, and this chapter will explore the key dilemmas and difficulties experienced both in individual practice and multi-agency settings. The chapter will not review individual risk assessment tools, as this has been extensively done elsewhere (Kemshall 2001, 2003; Kemshall et al. 2006). Rather, the focus will be on the faults and difficulties routinely encountered in risk assessment, with some suggestions for how they can be reduced in practice. The issues chosen are by no means exhaustive, but are those most commonly experienced in the field, namely how to categorize risk and operate clear thresholds of risk; the systemic faults in risk assessment, particularly across agencies and at the interface of those agencies required to work together; individual sources of error and bias in the assessment process; and the views of offenders on risk assessment.

Categories and thresholds of risk

It is important to recognize that a category is not a definition, although it is often treated in practice as if it is. For example, the risk under scrutiny may be the risk of harm (rather than the risk of reconviction) and may be divided into the categories of low, medium, high and very high. Such categories are essentially about the *degree* of risk and are used to create thresholds to govern the level of service delivery and resources for individual cases. Categories and thresholds are thus inextricably linked, demonstrated by the almost inevitable extension of the 'threshold ladder' from high to very high risk once the volume of cases in the high category outstrips the available resources to manage them appropriately. The Probation Service risk assessment tool OASys has been revised over time from three to four categories (PC36/2006)[1]; the MAPPA categories have also been similarly revised as have the risk categories used in the sex offender assessment tool MATRIX 2000 (MAPPA are discussed in Chapter 4).

Categories and thresholds are, however, difficult to operate in practice. In brief, to work properly a category needs at least the following:

- clear criteria regarding inclusion and exclusion;
- a clear boundary indicating what is in the category and what is outside it;
- to be easily understandable and useable by those required to apply it;
- consensus on the category and how it will operate;
- integrity and rigour in its use.

Clear criteria for inclusion and exclusion are essential for the boundary between categories to operate. In this case offenders need to be clearly assigned to a category, they cannot belong to more than one if the resource allocation system is to work. However, boundaries are permeable and can elide, and categorization is no easy task. Categorization can be influenced by a number of factors, not least the 'precautionary principle' defined by the Rio Declaration on Environment and Development (1992) as: 'Where there are threats of serious or irreversible environmental damage, lack of full scientific certainty shall not be used as a reason for postponing cost effective measures to prevent environmental degradation'. The UK Interdepartmental Liaison Group on Risk Assessment summed it up as: ' "Absence of evidence of risk" should never be confused with, or taken as, "evidence of absence of risk" ' (ILGRA 2002: 5). The precautionary principle tends to dominate when defensive practice and management cultures develop as a response to blame, fear and censure. The drop in parole release during the first quarter of 2007 following the publication of the Hanson and White Serious Further Offence (SFO) report (HMIP 2006a; see www.paroleboard.gov.uk; accessed 8 August 2007) is one example. In these circumstances practitioners tend to eschew the low risk category in favour of the safety of medium. Where practitioners are struggling to access resources for lower risk cases they can be tempted to redefine cases as high risk (Kemshall et al. 2005).

Confusion and lack of consensus about the criteria for establishing the degree of risk can also be problematic. Such criteria are increasingly complex and make significant demands on the skills, knowledge and competence of risk assessors. The criteria used by the Risk Management Authority (RMA) in Scotland to categorize offenders as low, medium, and high[2] require extensive knowledge of the following:

- likelihood;
- impact and scale of harm, sometimes referred to as 'seriousness';
- absence/presence of protective factors;
- the offender's motivation to change risky behaviours;
- the offender's ability to self-risk manage.

The complex interplay of these criteria to determine a particular risk level are presented in Table 3.1:

Table 3.1 Assessment of risk to public and known adults

Risk category	Seriousness	Absence/prevention of protective barriers	Imminence
High	Presents an ongoing risk of committing an offence causing serious harm.	Pervasive risk and a lack of protective factors to mitigate that risk.	More than likely to happen imminently. Requires long-term risk management to contain the risk (including long-term treatment). Will happen if controls are absent.
Medium	Capable of causing serious harm *but* . . . (see next column).	There are sufficient protective factors to mitigate that risk. The offender evidences a capacity to engage with risk management strategies and/or comply with treatment. Some capacity to self-risk manage.	May present a risk if protective factors 'fail', are absent or diminish. Protective factors require maintenance and support.

Low	May have caused serious harm in the past, but a repeat of such behaviour is not probable.	Will cooperate with risk management strategies and/or comply with treatment. Some capacity to self-risk manage with appropriate support. Presence of protective factors.	Not imminent and a repeat offence is 'on the balance of probability' deemed unlikely.

This table draws on the RMA Guidelines (2006: 40) and from Kemshall, Mackenzie, Miller and Wilkinson (2007). See also RMA (2007).

These are difficult criteria to combine and operate with consistency and rigour. Essentially we are asking staff to make informed, evidenced and careful judgements about:

• the capacity of an offender to commit an offence causing serious harm;
• the pervasiveness of risk factors in the future;
• the presence or absence of protective factors in the future; and
• the need for ongoing risk management including treatment to mitigate risk.
        (List adapted from the RMA 2006: 27; and Kemshall et al. 2007.)

While Table 3.1 attempts to present relatively clear criteria it is a synthesis of a number of guidelines from official sources, which require high levels of skill and knowledge to apply (acknowledged by the guidance and the standards set for risk assessment in Scotland). Practitioners do not necessarily have the luxury of accessing, reading, and synthesizing such material into a useable format. Email communication can exacerbate such problems, allowing for rapid distribution of policy and procedures, but inadvertently creating an 'explanation gap'. Policies and procedures do not speak for themselves, and in the case of risk categories and criteria, they can be open to subjective interpretation of meanings and applied against existing practices and beliefs (Kemshall 1998a; Robinson 1999, 2001, 2002; Kemshall 2000). Categories and thresholds are also contestable, both within and between agencies. A case in point is the difference in categorizing risk levels between the RMA and MAPPA in Scotland, with the former initially using three levels with a firmer rooting in Scottish legislation and the historical context of the MacLean report (2000), and the latter following the English four level categorization which includes 'very high risk' (see Home Office 2004a). With responsibility for policy and procedures targeted at the same offender groups, this was a potential source of conflict and confusion happily resolved by debate and subsequent refinement of the RMA levels. However, consensus about the meaning and use of categories or the criteria underpinning them cannot be assumed, and MAPPA, for example, have had to use extensive briefing and training to achieve this across its participating agencies (Kemshall et al. 2005; Wood et al. 2007). In addition, risk categories and their attendant levels do not necessarily predict future risk. Ansbro, (2006) in an examination of 90 Serious Incident Reports (SIRs) in the London Probation Area between 2002 and 2003, noted that: 'offenders assessed as high risk generated a disproportionate high number of SIRs . . . equally serious incidents across all risk bands' (2006: 57). This point was supported by the National Probation Service (NPS 2005) analysis of serious incidents (see also J. Wood 2006 for a profile of 136 high risk cases).

Integrity and rigour in the use of categories is essential, but this can be compromised in a number of ways, for example when staff or agencies seek to access or withhold resources by recategorizing offenders. This was common in the early days of the MAPPA. For example, categorization as high risk would provide quicker and easier access to housing or supervised accommodation (Maguire et al. 2001). Similarly, staff may recategorize in order to manage fear and/or anxiety about a case (e.g., avoiding low risk because they fear subsequent censure in the light of a failure; or downgrading high risk cases because they fear the increased intensity of work with a difficult/frightening offender). Turner and Columbo (2004: 34) noted that: 'Practitioners appeared more concerned with spreading the burden of responsibility, than on making risk assessments about offender dangerousness'. Sharing responsibility for a case/offender is common if a worker doubts their own competence, or where an agency is unused to working with risky offenders (see Kemshall et al. 2005 on the workings of MAPPA). Categorization downwards enables workers to avoid taking uncomfortable actions, for example challenging difficult offenders about their behaviour, enforcing orders or recalling offenders on licence (see HMIP 2006a). Fragmented responsibility for a case can also impact upon the integrity of categorization. Police and probation can differ in their categorizations of sex offenders on the Sex Offender Register (Kemshall et al. 2005); and probation, prisons and the Parole Board may differ in their views of risk in pre-release planning (see for example the Hanson and White SFO report (HMIP 2006a) as discussed in Chapter 1, this volume). The interface between the Parole Board and MAPPA has also been a cause for concern (see Kemshall 2007 for a full discussion).

Timmermans and Gabe (2003) describe these difficulties as 'agency misalignment', expressed by differences in objectives, goals, values and language surrounding risk and rooted in 'contrasting professional backgrounds, training and experiences' (Turner and Columbo 2004: 34; Columbo et al. 2003). Such misalignment is pronounced between criminal justice and mental health agencies (Turner and Columbo 2005), particularly regarding information sharing, although Kemshall et al. (2005: 23) found some mechanisms to integrate forensic mental health teams into MAPPA more effectively and to overcome some of these difficulties.

These issues (and they are by no means exhaustive) can undermine the effectiveness of risk categorization. They can also combine and compound one another, resulting in systemic faults in risk procedures and leading to what has been called a 'catalogue of failures' in individual cases (see HMIP 2006a). These systemic faults are the subject of the next section.

Systemic faults in risk assessment

'It's the doers wot get the blame' (Kemshall 1998b): risk management failures are most often attributed to the incompetence, negligence or poor practice of individual workers (e.g., Climbié in Laming 2003). However, on further inspection many risk management failures have their roots in the systemic faults inherent in the complex systems set up to deal with risk (Hood and Jones 1996), and in essence failures have been created and 'incubated' within the risk management system itself (Perrow 1984). Research into complex risk management systems from a number of fields including the nuclear industry, the oil industry, railways, health, social work and social care, and probation indicates a number of systemic threats to effective risk management. In brief, these can be understood as historical, contextual and organizational sources of failure.

Sources of failure can include the origins of the agency and its historical base that can become significantly 'at odds' with more recently imposed risk management tasks. Nowhere has this been more evident than in the English and Welsh Probation Service with its roots in police court missionary work and meeting the welfare needs of offenders (McWilliams 1987). The transition from 'need' to 'risk' has been arduous and troubled (see Kemshall 2003: ch. 4 for a full review; Robinson 1999, 2001, 2002), resulting in contentious debates about the value and purpose of probation (Priestley and Vanstone 2006; Robinson and Raynor 2006), and the legitimacy of 'doing risk' (Robinson 1999, 2001, 2002; Tuddenham 2000). Workers and managers interpret risk policies and procedures against their existing value bases and existing work-based cultures, and this can result in significant mediation of such policies as they are applied in practice (Hood and Jones 1996; Horlick-Jones 1998; Kemshall 1998a, 2000). The influence of personal experience, social and work-based networks, and the context within which the risk worker is operating can be extensive (Macgill 1989; Lupton 1999). In addition, perceiving risk can be mediated by the worker's preferred value base and can be deployed strategically to achieve particular outcomes, like risk or blame avoidance, or passing responsibility for the risk onto others (Lipsky 1980; Maynard-Moody et al. 1990; Kemshall 1998a). Central policy makers and senior managers in their 'rush to risk' have often underestimated the pervasiveness of these historical influences, finding subsequent lack of compliance in the workforce increasingly irksome (Lawrie 1997). Value debates can be controversial and painful but often very necessary as a prerequisite for doing risk well (Douglas 1986; Kemshall 2000).

Within the work context the routinization of tasks can be a significant bar to change, and to the necessary vigilance and alertness to doing risk well. Workers tend to routinize complex tasks over time, particularly in the face of high volume and professional stress (Satayamurti 1981; Lynch 2000), and risk is no exception (Kemshall 1998a). Worker compliance with risk procedures can be mistaken for ownership, and without vigorous and repeated enforcement it can fall. Hence procedural compliance declines over the long term as shown by numerous 'disaster' inquiries (Fennell 1988; Health and Safety Executive 1988; Hidden 1989; Cullen 1990). An investigative stance is lost (Prins 1999) and judgement is weakened. The consequences of this can be severe. For example, workers may fail to see signs of escalation (as in the case of Hanson in HMIP 2006a), or indeed they may operate contrary to risk procedures in order to 'get the job done' as in the Piper Alpha fire (Cullen 1990); the Challenger Shuttle disaster (Presidential Commission 1986; Starbuck and Milliken 1988; see also Runciman 1993 for examples in health care) and of course the Chernobyl nuclear disaster (USSR State Committee on the Utilization of Atomic Energy 1986). The case of Anthony Rice illustrates how once a decision (in this case to release) has gained momentum it is difficult to undo, even in the face of significant risk information (HMIP 2006b). Indeed the Chief Inspector noted that the Parole Board gave: 'insufficient weight to the underlying nature of his Risk of Harm to others' and that this happened for a number of reasons including (unreal) optimism, lack of information, a momentum towards release and prioritizing offender rights over risk to the public (HMIP 2006b: 5, para. 1.3).

Organizationally there can be difficulties with inadequate resourcing and competing priorities, leaving staff unsure as to where time and energy should be focused, and juggling competing risks within large caseloads. The fragmentation of work across specialisms and high risk teams common in many health, social work and criminal justice agencies can exacerbate this problem leaving staff working in functional silos and failing to take a joined up approach to risk. This can also result in a fragmentation of responsibility for risk management, a known source of risk management failure particularly where responsibility is divorced from accountability (Cullen 1990; Adams 1995). The early history of child protection and case conferencing is characterized by such failures (Parton 1986 on Jasmine Beckford; Reder and Duncan 1999), and mental health case management has been prone to similar failures (Blom-Cooper et al. 1995; Sheppard 1996; John Barrett Report in NHS 2006). Multidisciplinary and group decision making can be particularly prone to 'problematic processes' (Peay 2003). The most significant flaws are the failure to exchange critical information, the failure to communicate changes in risk status, divisions between those who risk assess and those who risk manage resulting in a failure of risk management delivery as intended, and a lack of accountability for decisions made and subsequent failures to act. The case of Hanson, for example, illustrates failures to communicate between prison, home area and Parole Board, and within the London probation area (HMIP 2006a); and the case of Anthony Rice illustrates the misperception about appropriate responsibilities and accountability within a complex system of risk management (HMIP 2006b – see for example paras. 6.9.6, 10.3.1, 10.3.17; and Kemshall 2007 for a full discussion).

Complex risk management systems require proactive and strategic management in order to function well (Kemshall 2007). Recent case management failures and serious incidents have alerted us to these potential flaws and it is time to think about strategic management of the system as well as the censure of individual practitioners (Kemshall 2007: 214). In effect: 'To function effectively, a system of this complexity needs information and decision making to be recorded, stored, maintained, updated, communicated and acted upon throughout contact with the offender'.

To achieve this, organizations must ensure that (Wilkinson in Kemshall et al. 2006):

- appropriate resources including assessment tools and programmes of intervention are available, and that they are used to best effect by staff with the appropriate skills, working within clear and realistic priorities;
- responsibility for the assessment and management of risk is clear throughout, particularly at points of transfer from one part of the system to another;
- shared understandings and, if necessary, protocols are in place to guide interagency communication and decision making.

The next section will consider the sources of individual error and strategies for combating them.

Individual sources of error

In an ideal world practitioners would always have enough information available upon which to make their risk decisions. However, practice with offenders does not take place in ideal conditions, and practitioners often have to make decisions based on incomplete information and in a climate of blame, censure and increased accountability. In essence, this describes 'decision-making under conditions of uncertainty' (Ruszczyski and Greengard 2002). Paradoxically, while uncertainty presents anxiety and risk to practitioners and is seen as largely undesirable, a degree of uncertainty about future outcomes and the ability to consider alternative risk management strategies is also seen as desirable (Munro 2002). In essence, if X happens I will do Y, but if A happens I may need to do B. This paradox and uncertainty itself presents risk decision makers with severe challenges and can have a number of possible outcomes for decisions (see Figure 3.1).

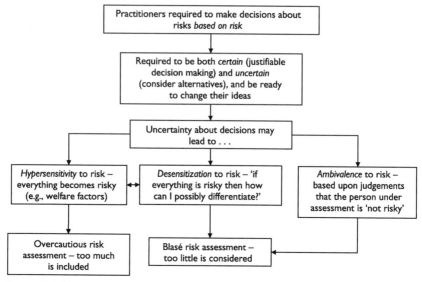

Figure 3.1 Uncertainty and risk assessment outcomes

Source: With the kind permission of Alex Sutherland, Centre for Criminology, Oxford University.

Practitioners deal with uncertainty in a number of ways, but most notably through the use of heuristics, that is, established thinking patterns rooted in bias, stereotypes and commonsense: in effect cognitive short cuts. This section will briefly review the most common heuristics and the types of error they can result in, and make some suggestions for how to avoid their use in practice. These are:

- confirmation bias;
- representational bias;
- availability bias;
- hindsight bias.

Confirmation bias occurs when we only pay attention to information that confirms our existing judgement, and/or validates the actions already taken or planned. Eileen Munro, in an important study of child protection workers, found that workers were reluctant to change initial assessments and their initial views of parents, even in the light of significant contradicting information (1996, 1999, 2002). This was also a significant flaw in the management of the Jasmine Beckford case, where 'unreal optimism' played a role in preventing the child's removal into care (Parton 1986). The Cleveland Inquiry into the notorious ritual abuse cases found that evidence to confirm abuse and the existing assessments of workers was actively sought, and little weight was given to contradictory evidence (Cleveland Inquiry 1988). The confirmatory bias played a role in the Damien Hanson SFO, where because parole had been agreed it was allowed to continue even in the face of changing circumstances and risk levels (HMIP 2006a). Unreal optimism can justify actions that are indefensible with hindsight, but more importantly it can justify inaction in the face of deteriorating behaviour and escalating risk. Intuitive reasoning is also flawed by discriminatory beliefs and values, and by the personal experiences of the worker (Munro 2002). While intuitive reasoning may positively assist 'practice wisdom' (Schon 1983), it is important that this does not result in short cut, 'lazy' thinking (Kemshall 1998a), but that the thinking is made explicit and well grounded in the evidence (Munro 2002). In the event of a risk management failure, how well a practitioner can account for their earlier reasoning will be central to the defensibility of the decision.

Representational bias occurs when we assume that one instance or case is generally representative of a number of others because they superficially appear similar or share some common characteristics. Strachan and Tallant give a good example of such bias:

> For instance, our initial perception of the immediate dangers or risks presented by a known violent offender during an unplanned home visit are often assessed not in reference to that person's actual record of violent offending (or to the wider statistical occurrences of such behaviour), but by comparing that person's similarity to one's own stereotype of how we would expect a 'dangerous person' to look or act.
> (1997: 20)

This bias can be particularly influential in case management and in initial risk assessments where hard-pressed workers will be tempted to think in stereotypes in order to complete assessments within short time frames.

Availability bias takes place when risks are assessed based on available information only and not on a thorough review of the necessary data, and where vivid events skew our view of risk. Catastrophic events are a case in point, for example when dramatic events such as a plane crash skews public perception, leading people to expect further similar events, when in fact statistically air travel is proven to be one of the safest forms of transport (Strachan and Tallant 1997). As Cowie puts it: 'By far the most dangerous part of your annual holiday to Tenerife is the car journey to the airport' (2007: 24). This can result in an inflated perception of low risk events, and a failure to give appropriate attention to more likely risks. Slovic (1992) has demonstrated how involuntary, taboo and vivid risks inflate our perceptions of both probability and impact, and can result in an overreaction to low frequency risks. This plays a key role in inflating 'stranger-danger' sex offending risks to children while underplaying sexual abuse risks within families (Kitzinger 2004).

In case work, this can result in lower risk cases treated as if they were higher risk, based on vividness or fear of a 'catastrophic event'. Murderers released on life licence are one example: many are referred to MAPPA at levels two or three although statistically most murderers do not murder again (Kemshall 2003). Such practice can weaken the notion of the 'critical few' and divert resources from more pressing, albeit less vivid, cases. The availability bias can also lead to 'illusory correlations' (Bazerman 1994). Because I see A and B together I assume that A has caused B. This can be particularly pertinent when case workers see particular social factors such as unemployment, homelessness and drug use present in the lives of offenders. While accepted as important criminogenic risks in re-offending, it is important that workers establish the causal weight of such factors and do not merely assume that they have, for example, caused violent offending. They may exacerbate some risky offending but they do not necessarily cause it. These 'illusory correlations' can be compounded by hindsight bias.

Hindsight bias is also an important source of error in which knowledge of an outcome leads to a gross overestimation of a prior probability (Fischoff 1975). This type of reasoning suggests that because this is outcome X it must have been produced by factor Y, although direct evidence or observation to demonstrate this argument may be lacking. This imputes a causal connection that may not in fact be present, and has been referred to as 'creeping determinism' (Fischoff 1975; Bazerman 1994). This type of cognitive bias may result in false risk predictions, as these imputed causal connections are used to calculate the probability of future events.

A further key fault in risk assessment and risk management is a misunderstanding about the relationship between cause and effect. Einhorn (1986) has described clinical assessment in particular as a narrative, account of past behaviour and events. In the production of a coherent narrative, causal connections and correlations are imputed literally to make sense of what has happened. This sense making is highly dependent upon the theoretical views of practitioners, their biases, previous practice experience and heuristic devices to aid decision making (Strachan and Tallant 1997).

This can result in the following errors:

- incomplete understanding of the behaviour in question, and moving to solutions before finding out the range of causes and connections;
- assuming something is the cause of offending when it is not;
- competing solutions that undermine each other's effectiveness;
- when something isn't working, doing more of the same, i.e., 'turning up the volume';

- using confusion or disagreement about cause and effect to avoid doing what needs to be done – poor problem definition becomes an excuse for inactivity.

(adapted from Wilkinson in Kemshall et al. 2006)

Solutions for reducing error

There are numerous sources of error. However, errors can be reduced by improved methods, increased rigour and professionalism by workers, and good management practice by the agencies involved (see Kemshall 1998a, b; Munro 1996, 2002). Workers can combat individual error by improving their understanding of probability calculations; their understanding of base rates; avoiding anecdotal information; checking for stereotyping; and checking their own judgemental processes. Monahan (1981) and Moore (1996) have both argued that risk assessors are rarely experts in probabilistic calculations of risk. Thinking actuarially, that is using statistical data to calculate the likelihood of risk, is not a natural process, we tend to think in individual terms rooted in the commonsense biases outlined above (Moore 1996). However, workers can improve their actuarial thinking by using actuarially-based formal risk assessment tools, and by improving their understanding of the base rate for the offence, behaviour or risk of concern. The base rate is the statistical frequency at which the behaviour or risk occurs in the population as a whole, and within the population of concern (e.g., offenders). It provides the basis for an actuarial prediction of behaviours in similar cases. For behaviours with low base rates, such as child abuse or sexual offending, predictions made without reference to the relevant base rate can lead to error: usually to overprediction of a risk due to the availability heuristic (Kemshall 2001).

More recent statistical developments in actuarial research have compensated for this effect through the application of a technique known as Relative Operating Characteristic (ROC) (Mossman 1994; Rice and Harris 1995). In short, this technique enables actuarial evaluations of violence prediction free from base rate limitations and clinical 'biases for or against Type 1 and Type 2 prediction errors[3] Mossman 1994: 783). In a re-evaluation of 58 data sets from 44 published studies using the ROC technique, Mossman demonstrated that mental health practitioners' predictions of violence were substantially more accurate than chance, that short-term predictions were no more accurate than long-term ones, and that past behaviour was the best predictor of future behaviour (1994: 783).

In addition, practitioners should acquire knowledge about the types of offences and offenders they are required to risk assess. For example, the difference between instrumental and emotional violent offending can be crucial to judging escalating risk (HMIP 2006a); and the differences in victim type and motivation between men who kill and women who kill is important to both assessment and risk management (Kemshall 2004).

Risk assessors can also overrely on anecdotal information and opinions that are not sufficiently rooted in the evidence. Kemshall et al. (2005) observed this during multi-agency public protection panel meetings. This could result in risk assessment based upon shared anecdotes rather than on well evidenced risk factors. To combat this, MAPPA coordinators had begun to introduce structured agendas; assessment formats to assist panel members to focus on key risk factors; a minute format to record the evidence provided and sought; mechanisms to quality assure decision making and to evaluate subsequent outcomes (PC 2004b; Kemshall et al. 2005). In a climate of legal challenge and judicial review it is essential that risk assessments are grounded in the evidence.

The Parole Board is another arena where an evidential approach is crucial, both to ensure robust decision making in the face of judicial review and to withstand public scrutiny when 'things go wrong'. The Chief Inspector of Probation has stated that: 'the public is entitled to expect that the authorities will do their job properly, i.e. take all reasonable action to keep risk to a minimum' (HMIP 2006a: 4):

> a position reiterated by the then Home Secretary, John Reid. To ensure this, Probation Circular 82/2005 (PC 2005b) poses the following questions as being essential to quality risk practice:
>
> - Is there *sufficient* assessment and planning in the sentence plan (SP) and risk management plan to address the risk of the offender's causing serious harm to the *victim(s)* of the offence?
> - Is there *sufficient* assessment and planning in the SP and risk management plan to address the risk of the offender's causing serious harm to the *public*?
> - Is there *sufficient* assessment and planning in the SP and risk management plan to address the risk of the offender causing serious harm to *staff*?
>
> A further overall question is posed:
>
> - Overall, is there sufficient evidence in the case file that throughout the period of supervision the risks of harm have been identified and assessed to the required standard and all reasonable actions have been taken to keep the offender's risk of harm to a minimum (i.e., would the case would pass a Serious Further Offence management review)?
>
> (PC 2005b)

This could usefully be translated into minimum standards for a release decision. Such standards would be more challenging than achieving a unanimous decision (it is, of course, possible to have a consensus that is wrong as well as a consensus that is right). In essence, this would create criteria against which the decision is tested and recorded, in addition to the current case summaries presented at panels. The criteria might cover:

- a review and checklist of the evidence presented;
- the panel's view on its adequacy and quality, e.g., what is missing, what it is based on (offender interviews, MAPPA risk assessment, etc.);
- actuarial risk tool used and score;
- identification of key risk factors;
- if appropriate, whether a referral has been made to MAPPA and information received from MAPPA, including a risk management plan;
- adequacy of the risk management plan – whether it meets the risk factors identified, how it will reduce the risk, how it will be delivered, how it will be reviewed and how it will be enforced;
- identification of contingency plans for a risk management failure;
- recommendation of the Board including use of conditions and licence requirements.

(Summarized from Kemshall 2007: 212–13)

The Parole Board chair could be tasked with ensuring that this proforma is used and completed, providing a focus, test and record for defensibility.

Stereotypes can also play a role in risk assessment and can distort the gathering, processing and analysis of information (Moore 1996). In essence, the assessor is an important filter of information and processing short cuts are often rooted in stereotypes. These can take various forms from common views of sex offenders as lone men in 'dirty macs' (Kitzinger 2004) to the over-association of mental disorder with violent offending (Taylor and Gunn 1999; Morgan 2004). Such stereotypes are often reinforced by the representative bias. Practitioners need to check out their stereotypical assumptions against evidenced risk factors and base rate levels. We cannot necessarily trust our judgemental processes and it is important that practitioners can self-check and quality assure their own decision-making processes and that staff supervision enables them to do so.

At an organizational level, broader strategies for reducing error will need to be pursued. These include:

- consistency of language, concepts and understandings;
- critical and reflexive practice rooted in the evidence and encouraged through proactive supervision of staff (Schon 1983; Tuddenham 2000);
- increased skills, knowledge and competence of the workforce including the managers;

- appropriate line management responsibility for risk, and appropriate use of supervision and appraisal to monitor and improve performance;
- commitment and professionalism of staff;
- common objectives and goals, and shared values and beliefs.

What do offenders think about risk assessment?

The two studies used here present views from 60 high risk prisoners serving custodial sentences for sexual offences (Attrill and Liell 2007) and 15 offenders convicted of a sexual offence against children, subject to MAPPA supervision at level two or three (four of them in custody and 11 in the community). While they do not necessarily represent all dangerous or high risk offenders, they do represent offenders at the highest level of risk both within prison and the community, and as such their views are interesting and important. Both studies are small scale but used in-depth interviews rather than surveys to gather detailed data on offender perceptions of risk assessment, supervision, interventions and risk management. The studies have some of the usual limitations associated with research of this type, notably: size and scale; the status of the self-report of the participants; and the potential 'halo' effect of the interviewers, particularly where they were prison service employees. However, the employees did not work directly with the prisoners and had no impact on their day-to-day life or progression through the prison system and their anonymity was preserved. The studies chosen are not meant to be exhaustive, but merely illustrative of the range and type of views held by high risk offenders.

When asked about the purpose of risk assessment, the prisoners in Attrill and Liell's (2007: 193) study described it thus:

> Looking at the risk of you reoffending and how much harm you might cause, helps decisions on how much support you need and how much monitoring.

> To see if an offender is a risk to society and if at risk of committing the same offence. See if they are doing anything which contributed to the offence or whether they've done work to address the behaviours which contributed to the offence.

As Attrill and Liell comment, offenders reflect the professional preoccupation with predicting and qualifying the likelihood of re-offending, and whether or not an individual prisoner, if released, would harm anyone (2007: 193). They recognized that a number of factors would be considered, including severity, harm and imminence; and while some felt actively engaged in the process, for the most part it was experienced as something imposed upon them. Interestingly, they were able to identify most of the accepted crimino-genic risk factors and social factors associated with offending, although the paradox of risk assessment, particularly for prisoners, was noted: in effect, how can prisoners prove their reduced risk without being released? And without demonstrating reduced risk they cannot achieve parole.

Comments were also obtained about accuracy and fairness. Not surprisingly, some offenders were concerned about the accuracy of written information about them and that decisions could be made on out-of-date information. Other important factors cited were the knowledge, skill and competence of the risk assessor; the time taken to 'get to know them'; the level of their inclusion in the assessment; whether they were given sufficient credit for change; and whether negative factors were balanced with positive ones (Attrill and Liell 2007: 195–9). Media and political influences were seen as particularly problematic, potentially distorting the objectivity of assessors and the Parole Board, and with exceptional high-profile cases having a disproportionate impact on the risk assessment of others.

Attrill and Liell (2007: 201) conclude that:

The views and comments made by the offenders we met were not unreasonable, unrealistic or naïve. What they often wanted was probably much the same as we do, as professionals involved in risk assessment and decision-making. They wanted accuracy, fairness and a chance to be in involved decisions about their future. In this, and many other things, we have common ground.

Wood and Kemshall (2007) in their study found that high risk offenders subject to MAPPA were more likely to comply and engage with supervision if they had been informed and engaged in risk assessment by supervising officers. The practice of fully explaining the meaning of MAPPA and the consequences for the offender increased the offenders' understanding and compliance, and many saw MAPPA as having a legitimate role in helping them to avoid future offending and in being reintegrated into society. Staff also echoed the importance of strong but non-collusive relationships with offenders, promoting a 'readiness to disclose' in offenders and increased benefit from interventions. This echoed existing work on prosocial supervision promoted by Trotter (1993, 1999, 2000); Rex (1999); and McNeill and Batchelor (2002) among others. Offenders were able to articulate the techniques helpful in changing behaviours and these included:

- self-risk management including the use of 'contracts' and self-reporting to police or probation if an offender believed they were about to offend;
- clear articulation of victim issues, including the recognition of the impact of sexual offending upon children;

- the use of 'distraction techniques' to avoid inappropriate sexual thoughts when seeing children.

(Wood and Kemshall 2007: 14)

From these small-scale studies it is possible to conclude that offenders do understand and accept the purpose of risk assessment and management, and a focus on risk is accepted as both legitimate and sensible. Interestingly, as Attrill and Liell remind us there is often more common ground between workers and offenders than we may imagine, with offenders valuing the good practice aspects of professional practice, including prosocial supervision, and responding accordingly.

Summary

This chapter has reviewed the key issues in risk assessment and the main faults in decision making: both individual and systemic. Maintaining the integrity of risk decisions, particularly around levels and thresholds is problematic and is exacerbated in multi-agency settings. Practitioners are working in a wider context of decision making, in which the difficulties facing them are significant. Improving and maintaining the integrity of decisions in this context is essential, and various solutions at both the individual and organizational level were outlined. Perhaps the most significant of these is attention to systemic as well as individual sources of error. The chapter has also reviewed the views of offenders on risk assessment, and reminded us that these may be more commensurate with those of practitioners than commonly believed. The next chapter will explore the development of partnership in the effective management of dangerous offenders. In brief, two types of partnership can be discerned – those based on the community protection model and dominated by criminal justice agencies and those based on PHA, led largely by the voluntary sector or faith-based organizations. The key issues in the development and maintenance of partnerships will be explored.

Notes

1 See Moore et al. 2007 for a discussion on current work to improve the risk of harm section of OASys and to improve the integrity of OASys use.
2 This ranking was subsequently extended to very high in a later version, to make the risk levels commensurate with those adopted by Scottish MAPPA. This is a further example of the mutability of risk levels over time.
3 A Type 1 prediction error is a false positive prediction, i.e., a prediction of a risk that does not happen; a Type 2 prediction error is a false negative prediction, a risk that is not predicted but does happen.

Further reading

Kemshall, H. (2003) *Understanding Risk in Criminal Justice.* Maidenhead: Open University Press / McGraw-Hill.

RMA (Risk Management Authority) (2006) *Standards and Guidelines for Risk Assessment (Version 1 April 2006).* RMA: Paisley. Available at: www.RMAScotland.gov.uk

RMA (Risk Management Authority) (2007) *Standards and Guidelines for Risk Management (Version 1).* RMA: Paisley. Available at: www.RMAScotland.gov.uk

Protection through partnership

Partnership has been a growing theme in public protection since the early 1990s, although such partnerships have taken various forms, and have been located in both the statutory and voluntary sectors. Differing approaches to the management and regulation of (particularly) sex offenders and violent offenders has resulted in differing types of partnerships between agencies, and between the statutory and voluntary sectors. The key distinction has been between *community protection* and *public health approaches*, the latter including reintegrative strategies rooted in restorative justice approaches. Generally speaking, community protection has been delivered through statutory partnerships, with public health approaches delivered by the voluntary sector – although, as this chapter will argue, this distinction is now getting blurred. This chapter will begin with a focus on the types of partnership involved in both community protection and public health approaches, before considering how these approaches are beginning to complement each other in the community management of high risk offenders. Chapter 5 subsequently explores the types of risk management strategies utilized by each of these approaches and the range of risk management interventions used by these differing types of partnerships.

MAPPA: the statutory approach to public protection

Formal partnerships for protection emerged early within the public protection agenda, most notably in West Yorkshire with police and probation exchanging information in the early 1990s on high risk offenders (see Kemshall and Maguire 2001; Maguire et al. 2001; Wood and Kemshall 2008). Such partnerships gained momentum and legislative force in the Criminal Justice and Court Services Act (CJCS) 2000; Criminal Justice Act (CJA) 2003; and official guidance (Home Office 2004a, b); and quickly became embedded within the main agencies and processes of criminal justice (Kemshall 2003). These partnerships were concerned largely (although not exclusively) with the statutory supervision of high risk offenders in the community and with the oversight of high risk offenders upon release from prison. These partnerships have crystallized into the formal Multi-Agency Public Protection Arrangements (MAPPA), firmly rooted in the community protection approach to risk management (Connelly and Williamson 2000). An evaluation of these emerging arrangements found inconsistency and poor quality in some practices, most notably:

- Differences in terminlogy, representation on panels, chairing arrangements, referral procedures and case management responses. This resulted in a lack of national consistency, particularly in structural differences across areas and whether a one-tier or two-tier panel system was adopted.
- Partnership arrangements between police and probation also differed, with well developed interagency partnerships in some areas. There were also examples of more 'one-sided' arrangements (usually police dominated) and with other agencies playing a more marginal role.
- Difficulties with information exchange and disclosure were also noted. Information exchange was largely limited to offenders on the Sex Offender Register although panels covering other categories of offender were exchanging information between police and probation and making routine child protection checks with social services. Respondents identified the systematic recording of actions and risk management plans as an area for development.
- Risk management varied and there was inconsistency in the use of risk categorizations (low, medium, high and very high) to allocate risk management resources.
- Systems of accountability and oversight also varied, with a lack of genuine multi-agency structures. The management and accountability of the system 'tended to depend too much upon informal processes and informal networks' (Maguire et al. 2001: 50).
- The work was seen as an 'add-on' to existing workloads and was not subject to appropriate financial planning and review. Dedicated clerical

resources and a central coordinator were recommended as best practice developments.

(Maguire et al. 2001; Wood and Kemshall 2008)

In response to Maguire et al.'s (2001) research, the partnership arrangements were given new statutory force and clarity with the implementation of the Criminal Justice and Court Services Act (2000) that placed a responsibility on police and probation to:

Establish arrangements for the purpose of assessing and managing risks posed in that area by:

(a)   relevant sexual and violent offenders, and
(b)   other persons, who, by reason of offences committed by them (wherever committed), are considered by the responsible authority to be persons who may cause serious harm to the public.

(CJCS 2000: Section 67(2))

Further prescriptive statutory guidance followed (e.g., Home Office 2004a; Ministry of Justice 2007), which attempted to ensure areas were adopting similar practices and standards for risk assessment decision making and risk management planning. A further evaluation (Kemshall et al. 2005) found that MAPPA had become more consistent, adopting a tiered approach to risk management and allocating offenders across three levels of risk management as enshrined in the guidance (see Figure 4.1). A range of agencies made contributions to risk assessment and risk management as active partners. These arrangements were given further statutory force by the Criminal Justice Act 2003 which placed a statutory duty on the Prison Service to become a 'Responsible Authority' alongside police and probation; and a range of other agencies (such as education services, housing and social services) were given a 'duty to cooperate'. Thus the partnership became truly multi-agency and was given legislative force and a statutory footing for its existence and operation (for a full review see Kemshall et al. 2005; Kemshall and Wood 2007a; and Wood and Kemshall 2008).

The workload projections arising from the Sexual Offences Act 2003 and the Criminal Justice Act 2003 have been estimated at a maximum of 100 sex offenders per year for the new sex offences; and 500 cases by 2006–07; 1000 cases for 2007–08; and 1500 for 2008–09 for the Dangerous Offender Sentences. There will be a cumulative effect on MAPPA as these offenders will remain on statutory supervision for long periods and many will remain at level three (NPS 2004). In these circumstances MAPPA have been urged to concentrate on the 'critical few'. The critical few is an operational term and relates to very high risk offenders (as defined by OASys) and those requiring very intensive risk management at level three of MAPPA.

- **Level 1 - ordinary risk management:** Where the agency responsible for the offender can manage risk without the significant involvement of other agencies. This level of management is only appropriate for category 1 and 2 offenders who are assessed as presenting a low or medium risk.
- **Level 2 - local inter-agency risk management:** Where there is active involvement of more than one agency in risk management plans, either because of a higher level or risk or because of the complexity of managing the offender. It is common for Level 3 cases to be 'referred down' to Level 2 when risk of harm deflates. The permanent membership of Level 2 should comprise those agencies that have an involvement in risk management. Responsible Authorities should decide the frequency of meetings and also the representation, taking an active role in the convening of meetings and quality assurance of risk management.
- **Level 3 - Multi Agency Public Protection Panel (MAPPP):** For those defined as the 'critical few', the MAPPP is responsible for risk management drawing together key active partners who will take joint responsibility for the community management of the offender. An offender who should be referred to this level of management is defined as someone who:

  (i) is assessed under OASys as being a high or very high risk of causing serious harm; **AND**
  (ii) presents risks that can only be managed by a plan which requires close co-operation at a senior level due to the complexity of the case and/or because of the unusual resource commitments it requires; **OR**
  (iii) although not assessed as a high or very high risk, the case is exceptional because the likelihood of media scrutiny and/or public interest in the management of the case is very high and there is a need to ensure that public confidence in the criminal justice system is sustained.

Figure 4.1 Risk management: the tiered approach

Source: MAPPA guidance 2004: para. 116 – subject to revision by Ministry of Justice 2007.

While there is much emphasis upon the critical few, the range of offenders covered in total by the MAPPA is far wider. In brief, these are: Category 1: registered sex offenders; Category 2: violent and other sex offenders; Category 3: other offenders (see Home Office 2004a: 16–17, paras. 52–7). Given the numbers involved and the resources required for community management, it is essential that precious resources are targeted at the critical few, following the principle that 'cases should be managed at the lowest level consistent with providing a defensible risk management plan' (Home Office 2004a: 34, para. 109). The 2004 guidance refined the definition and criteria for the critical few, and recognized that inconsistency of definition had been a problem (see DoH 2002), and added the following:

Although not assessed as high or very high risk, the case is exceptional because the likelihood of media scrutiny and/or public interest in the management of the case is very high and there is a need to ensure that public confidence in the criminal justice system is sustained.

An offender on discharge from detention under a hospital order.

An offender returning from overseas (whether immediately following their release from custody or not).

An offender having been managed as medium or even a low risk in the community . . . comes to present a high or very high risk as the result of a significant change of circumstances.
(Home Office 2004a: 36, paras. 116–17)

However, there have been significant difficulties with operating these tiers and levels of risk, most notably: the differing interpretations of risk across the differing agencies; a 'precautionary principle' from referring practitioners and panel members; and difficulties in consistently using the criteria for the different levels (see Chapter 3, this volume; and Kemshall et al. 2005 for a full discussion). The formal risk assessment tool, OASys, has been used to try to achieve greater consistency across probation and MAPPA risk assessments. OASys attempts to capture the gradation of risk by using the following risk categories:

1 *Low*: no significant current indicators of risk of harm.
2 *Medium*: there are identifiable indicators of risk of harm. The offender has the potential to cause harm but is unlikely to do so unless there is a change in circumstances, for example, failure to take medication, loss of accommodation, relationship breakdown, drug or alcohol misuse.
3 *High*: there are identifiable indicators of risk of serious harm. The potential event could happen at any time and the impact would be serious.
4 *Very high*: there is an imminent risk of serious harm. The potential event is more likely than not to happen imminently and the impact would be serious.
(From the Probation Service OASys tool, see Home Office 2007a)

It is likely that offenders in the high and very high risk categories will be subject to further assessments using more specific tools like MATRIX 2000 for sex offenders, and the HCR-20 for violent offenders (see Kemshall 2001; and Kemshall et al. 2006 for a full review). These tools are tailored to both offence and offender type and use risk factors generated from these offender populations. Such tools combine both actuarial and dynamic factors and provide risk scores that can categorize offenders and can discriminate between low, medium and high risk. However, such tools can inadvertently generate more high risk cases than available resources can manage (Kemshall and Maguire 2001), and categories can be revised by subjective judgements as both practitioners and managers pursue 'occupational survival' (Satyamurti 1981) in the face of high demand and low resource. Tools can be circumvented, used without integrity and manipulated by assessors who ignore those risk factors that do not resonate with their own value base and practice-held beliefs (see Chapter 3, this volume for a full discussion).

Effective risk assessment, particularly of the critical few, requires at least the following: the use of the correct risk assessment tool appropriate for the offence and offender type. This requires tools relevant to the population being assessed and a more careful distinction between those tools that screen for potentially high risk of harm (OASys) and those that provide in-depth assessments and problem definition for interventions (e.g., HCR-20 for violent offenders and MATRIX 2000 for sex offenders). Reliable risk assessment is also dependent upon effective information exchange across relevant agencies with specific attention to at least the following information:

- Victims – who has been a victim in the past? Who is likely to be in the future? How are they targeted and groomed – what are the circumstances under which the offender gains access, proximity and trust?
- Under what conditions and circumstances has this risk occurred in the past and under what conditions and circumstances might it occur in the future?
- Consideration of imminence – is there an opportunity to re-offend? Is an opportunity being created? Is there a lack of internal controls on behaviour(s) or are external controls to prevent re-offending breaking down?
- Level of motivation to offend and level of motivation to comply with risk management plan. What is the evidence of compliance and self-risk management? What is the offender's view of his/her risk?
- Are risks escalating? Is (will) the risk management plan (be) capable of containing the risk or not? What has worked in the past and what has failed in the past?

(From Kemshall and Wood 2007a: 389)

Key issues in statutory partnerships

At their most simple, partnerships are intended to avoid functional silos; provide joined up services (in this case risk management); improve service delivery and enhance the coordination of services; and provide multidisciplinary expertise (Newman 2001; Prins 2002; Kemshall and Wood 2007a). The first MAPPA evaluation found significant hurdles to the effective functioning of partnership, most notably: value clashes; ideological disputes; inadequate resourcing and preciousness over agency services; lack of coordination; and an absence of a multidisciplinary approach (Kemshall and

Maguire 2001; Maguire et al. 2001). The subsequent evaluation (Kemshall et al. 2005) found significant improvements, but a number of key issues remained. While agency-based value disputes are now relatively less common, boundaries between the MAPPA agencies have become increasingly permeable, resulting in what Nash has famously called a 'polibation officer' (Nash 1999a, b): with the roles and responsibilities of police and probation merged. It is crucial that permeable boundaries do not become 'fuzzy boundaries', particularly in respect of statutory duties, such as enforcement of orders or enforcement of the Sex Offender Register. Role and boundary confusion has been significant in previous risk management failures and inquiries (Sheppard 1996). There is also evidence that MAPPA remains underresourced and that the public protection commitment of the relevant agencies has not been sufficiently costed (Kemshall et al. 2005). This has led to subsequent problems in delivering costly interventions, such as long-term community surveillance or intensive treatment programmes. In addition, the multidisciplinary expertise of MAPPA is presently undermined by the lack of cooperation from health services (particularly from forensic mental health and psychological services). Where they are making a local contribution, both the risk assessments and risk management plans are improved, and access to relevant services is enhanced (Kemshall et al. 2005).

MAPPA processes and systems have improved since its inception, although difficulties remain in operating strictly the risk tiering (see Chapter 3, this volume), and in identifying accurately those most likely to present the most risk (see Kemshall et al. 2005). However, a Home Office (2007b) report, *MAPPA – The First Five Years*, notes that the number of serious further offences committed by offenders managed at levels two and three in 2005–06 was only 0.44 per cent. The biggest impact was at level three, 'and such a low serious re-offending rate for this particular group of offenders is to be welcomed and supports the view that MAPPA is making a real contribution to the management of dangerousness in the community' (Home Office 2007b: 6–7). Enforcement and breach of parole licences and court orders have also risen for levels two and three, in effect, taking action to prevent further offending based upon problematic behaviours or breach of conditions. Action to enforce the Sex Offender Register requirements also increased by 30 per cent (through cautions and further convictions) and affected some 1295 offenders, '4.3% of the total registered in the community' (Home Office 2007b: 7). The year 2005–06 also saw the use of 973 Sex Offender Prevention Orders under the Sexual Offences Act 2003. This evidence of impact mitigates the critique of commentators like Lieb (2003) who contend that MAPPA is little more than 'joined-up worrying'.

However, MAPPA's lack of accountability to the public and lack of transparency about its operation leaves it potentially isolated from local communities, and the distance between experts and the public is problematic in the long-term management of taboo risks (Lupton 1999). While MAPPA has a legal obligation to publish annual reports, these represent a very limited communication strategy with local communities, and public engagement about the work of MAPPA is low key. This can result in low trust and low credibility for the MAPPA system, and a public intolerance of sex offenders 'in our midst', which results in the pursuit of largely exclusionary rather than inclusionary strategies of risk management. Risk management strategies tend to comprise surveillance and the use of restrictive conditions (curfews, exclusion zones, etc.), with rather less attention to reintegrative techniques (Kemshall and Wood 2007b). Broader risk management using reintegrative techniques are the subject of the next sections.

Public health and community approaches to protection

Paralleling these statutory developments were initiatives and community partnerships rooted within the voluntary sector, faith-based communities or survivor groups (Kemshall and Wood 2007b; see also Chapter 5, this volume for a full discussion). These developments have taken a broader approach to community risk management utilizing the Public Health Approach (PHA). The characterization of sexual and violent offending as a public health problem is most easily attributable to the work of Richard Laws (1996, 2000). In brief, Laws argues that traditional, reactive responses to such offending located predominantly in the criminal justice system have not proved to be effective in reducing the incidence of sexual or violent offending, and that perversely such approaches inflate public fears and rejection, particularly of sex offenders (2000: 30). The public health approach is characterized as preventive and 'forward looking'. The PHA has gained ground as a novel and potentially more effective method of dealing with child sexual abuse and, to a lesser extent, violent offending.

The PHA is located at three levels: the primary, secondary and tertiary:

- *Primary level*: at which the goal is prevention of sexually deviant behaviour before it starts, for example the identification and prevention of sexually deviant behaviour in children, and the long-term prevention of adults in engaging in sexual abuse.
- *Secondary level*: at which the goal is the prevention of first time offenders from progressing, or the opportunistic and 'specific offence' offender from becoming a generalist.
- *Tertiary level*: at which the goal is effective work with persistent and more serious offenders. Specific goals are usually effective treatment programmes and relapse prevention.

(see Laws 2000: 31)

Laws argues that as an alternative to (largely ineffective) incarceration, increased efforts should be targeted at levels one and two. This requires increased attention to 'prevention goals' of which the following are seen as the most important:

- *Public awareness and responsibility*: This involves informing the public of 'the magnitude and characteristics of sexual offending', including how sex offenders groom their victims, but more importantly that sex offenders are part of the community. The emphasis is upon adult responsibility for responding to sex offending.
- *Public education*: This involves challenging the myth that all sex offenders are demons and incapable of change, and an emphasis upon treatment programmes that work. The message that something can be done and that treatment is worth investing in is a key one.

These prevention goals are supported by direct targeting of sex offenders and encourage both active and potential sex offenders/abusers to come forward for treatment. The emphasis is upon the prevention of those beginning to engage in abuse or to think about it, and relapse prevention for those with established behaviours. Harm reduction and risk minimization are seen as key components of such a strategy. Two examples of PHA approaches to sex offenders in the community will now be reviewed.

Partnerships with local communities: Circles of Support and Accountability (COSA)

Circles of Support and Accountability (COSA) grew out of negative public reaction to the release of a sex offender into the community, and perceptions that formal supervisory mechanisms could neither successfully reintegrate sex offenders nor guarantee public safety (Wilson 2003; Wilson and Picheca 2005; Wilson et al. 2005, 2007a).

As Wilson (2007: 36) puts it: 'One must ultimately ask: for every offender forced out of your community and into someone else's, how many offenders are forced out of that community and into yours? ... By forcing offenders underground, are we not inadvertently increasing secrecy and decreasing safety? There has to be a better way'. This 'better way' has its roots in faith-based communities agreeing to form circles of support and accountability around a sexual offender, offering on the one hand contact and support and, on the other, monitoring and vigilance. The approach takes a broadly restorative and reintegrative approach to sexual offending, and seeks to improve community safety through the successful reintegration of sex offenders into the community (Wilson et al. 2007a; for a detailed description of COSA see Correctional Service of Canada 2002; Wilson and Picheca 2005). This model has been adopted in the USA, UK, Netherlands,

South Africa and Bermuda. Volunteers are largely from faith-based communities with a proportion having had previous experience of corrections and being altruistically motivated (Wilson et al. 2007). As Wilson succinctly puts it: 'Volunteers act as concerned friends or surrogate family members for the core members but with support and accountability set prominently in their minds' (2007: 37).

COSA have been evaluated in Canada and the UK with positive results. The original pilot achieved a decrease in sexual offending of 70 per cent 'in comparison with either matched control subjects or actuarial projections' (Wilson 2007a: 37; Wilson et al. 2007b: 333), with the UK pilot achieving similar reconviction results in its early stages (Quaker Peace and Social Justice 2005). In the UK, a more subtle distinction has been drawn between reconviction rates and the identification and response to recidivist behaviours (Bates et al. 2007). With only 16 offenders participating in the Thames Valley COSA, drawing general conclusions is difficult. However, the following results are presented:

- no core member (CM) was reconvicted of a sexual offence;
- one CM was convicted for breach of a Sex Offence Prevention Order and thereafter made subject to a three-year Community Rehabilitation Order;
- four CMs were recalled to prison for breaching the conditions of their parole;
- five CMs were identified as exhibiting some kind of recidivist behaviour;
- six CMs had no further problematic behaviours identified in their management by COSA.

(from Bates et al. 2007: 23)

The early identification and response to recidivist behaviours is seen as a positive outcome of the Thames Valley COSA. The work of COSA also recognizes that many sex offenders are social isolates, and that re-integration following custody is particularly challenging. COSA provides a surrogate social network combined with practical assistance (Wilson 2007). Sex offenders are deemed as capable of rehabilitation, although barriers to successful rehabilitation are acknowledged and often the focus of the work of circles. The assumption of COSA is that without adequate help sex offenders will re-offend (Bates et al. 2007). The Canadian COSA has taken particularly high risk offenders, but has achieved notable success with sexual recidivism of COSA offenders – 70 per cent lower than offenders in a matched sample. In the three instances of sexual recidivism the re-offences were of less severity, thus achieving a harm reduction function (Wilson et al. 2007b: 333). Increasingly in the Canadian context, the community management of sex offenders is supported by relapse prevention programmes and treatment interventions as part of parole supervision

(Wilson et al. 2000). Data is beginning to indicate that COSA can achieve greater effectiveness for higher risk offenders (Wilson et al. 2007b).

In the Canadian context there are three types of circle:

- sentencing circles, which can be implemented at the sentencing stage – either as an alternative to custody or as well as custody;
- circles to support conditional release under parole licence;
- circles to support the reintegration of sex offenders at the end of custodial sentences and in the absence of statutory parole supervision.

Sentencing circles were initiated in Saskatchewan in 1992 (Church Council on Justice and Corrections 1996). The practice combines 'respect for due process, mediation and interest-based negotiation, and consensus-based decision making with aboriginal healing and peacekeeping concepts' (Wilson et al. 2002: 364). They are used for serious crime and while custodial sanctions can be given, the emphasis is upon 'accountability, rehabilitation and community integration' (Wilson et al. 2002: 366). The offender has to face the victim, family and significant others, and the focus is on correcting the criminal behaviour. Social control, censure and support is provided by the circle and wider community network. The circle also supports and helps the victim. The initiative has been particularly focused on youth, although not exclusively so (for a full review of key processes, issues and criticisms see Wilson et al. 2002). Wilson et al. argue that sentencing circles promote community engagement, dialogue, participatory democratic decision making, power sharing, and sharing responsibility for the offender and crime (2002: 368). However, the empirical evidence of community impact is more limited (as discussed below).

Circles to support parole supervision focus on two key factors in recidivism: 'anti-social attitudes and anti-social peer affiliations' (Wilson et al. 2002, drawing on the work of Andrews and Bonta 1998). Prosocial values, beliefs and behaviours are promoted and the emphasis is upon repairing harms done. It combines restoration with public safety (see Correctional Services of Canada 1999–2000; McWhinnie and Brown 1999). However, numbers of referrals and offenders using this option are still small and the scheme requires further, independent evaluations (Wilson et al. 2000, 2002).

The third type of circle is used for the reintegration of sex offenders released into the community without statutory supervision and support. Initially a response to public anxiety and potential vigilante action, such circles have grown in use (particularly in Canada, the UK and the USA). Increasingly they have formal links with local police, probation services and multi-agency panels (see Wilson 2003, 2007).

Professional criminal justice workers play a role on most COSA project steering groups, and the UK pilot (Thames Valley) has a formalized partnership between volunteers and professional workers with, 'Each circle

. . . maintained by means of consultancy and hands-on support by a practitioner team . . . The team members all have prior experience of working with sex offenders in both treatment and hospital settings' (Bates et al. 2007: 20). The COSA is linked to the local MAPPA, and provides 'soft data' taken from offender self-report and behavioural observation from volunteers and practitioners to assess the compliance and progress of sex offenders subject to MAPPA. In this sense, COSA is co-opted into the existing public protection arrangements. As Bates et al. (2007: 22) put it:

> . . . perhaps nowhere is this kind of detailed 'soft data' about sex offenders more available than within the file information and local knowledge held by professional and volunteer staff working with COSA. The level of detail in this information goes way beyond that held even by statutory agencies such as treatment providers (Prison, Probation) and Police and Social Services. COSA have detailed knowledge about the attitudes and behaviours of sex offenders which arise from regular contact with them in formal and informal group and individual settings within the context of COSA activity. The core member (i.e. the released prisoner) will often form closer relationships with those involved in COSA than with any others in society and the accountability aspect of the COSA role provides unique access to a questioning and understanding of the process of successful rehabilitation (or the lack of it) for the core member. It seems very likely that COSA is able to provide more information about sex offenders' attitudes and behaviour in the community than any other agency working in this field.

In the Thames Valley this has resulted in four recalls to prison for parole violations (out of 16 cases), with this seen as a positive indicator that COSA is working. Vigilance and reporting to professional staff is seen as crucial, with effective communication procedures with MAPPA seen as a key ingredient of COSA functioning (Bates et al. 2007). In essence, COSA volunteers are supporters to the sex offender but also exercise vigilance on behalf of MAPPA. This presents a potential role tension and ethical dilemma for volunteers, particularly around the rights of the offender and the risks presented by them to the community (see Chapter 6, this volume, for a full discussion of these challenges). In this UK pilot COSA is firmly embedded in the public protection arrangements, and COSA has become part of the 'community protection' approach to high risk offenders and is seen as contributing positively to the 'public protection challenge' (Bates et al. 2007: 38). This 'co-option' in itself sets the agenda and role boundary for COSA volunteers.

While COSA has the laudable aim of community engagement and enabling the community to take responsibility for a community issue (Bates et al. 2007: 39; Wilson 2007), the extent of this community engagement is questionable. Wilson et al. (2002) acknowledge that transferability to larger, more anonymized communities has been difficult, and that 'larger communities appear to be at a distinct disadvantage when it comes to hands-on, community based risk management' (2002: 379). This resonates with other evidence on the problems of transferability of restorative justice approaches from communitarian societies to those with weaker ties and looser networks (McAlinden 2005).

In a recent study of COSA in the Canadian context Wilson et al. (2007) found that 63 per cent of volunteers became aware of COSA through friends or family, and that 40 per cent had previous experience of corrections, with 28 per cent learning about COSA through their faith-based community. Volunteers are characterized by an interest in helping this client group and by a sense of altruism, and of course they self-select towards this type of activity. Most have employment or volunteering histories in work with marginal groups. In this sense, they may not be typical of the wider community's views of sex offenders, which is more usually characterized by negativity and hostility (Silverman and Wilson 2002). A body of concerned volunteers does not necessarily constitute community engagement. However, COSA has certainly been effective in reducing public–community anxiety, vigilantism and hostility to sex offenders (Wilson et al. 2000; Wilson 2003; Bates et al. 2007; Wilson et al. 2007).

Public engagement, awareness and public education are the aims of Stop It Now! UK and Ireland. Their work will be the subject of the next section.

Partnership with communities and public: building awareness and responsibility

Stop It Now! was initiated by Fran Henry in 1995 in Vermont, USA. Based upon her own survivor experiences of child sexual abuse she questioned the traditional approaches to the problem, and based upon the success of PHA in areas such as smoking, alcohol, and HIV and intravenous drug use she considered the potential transferability of PHA to sexual abuse. Central to her view was the inappropriate framing of children as the solution, in other words, placing the responsibility for reporting on children, teaching children to 'be safe', without recognizing their relative powerlessness and the reluctance of adults to act on the word of children. Stop It Now! USA has successfully established itself as a campaigning organization for the elimination of child sexual abuse, and has run an effective Helpline for abusers and families/partners of abusers since its inception (see www.stopitnow.org and Tabachnick and Dawson 1999). Stop It Now! UK and Ireland is run under the umbrella of the Lucy Faithfull Foundation and a working agreement with Stop It Now! in the USA. The Home Office and Department of Health have provided core funding to the Lucy Faithfull Foundation for the central operation, including the Helpline.

There are three strands to the work of Stop It Now! UK and Ireland:

- the Helpline;
- treatment and counselling for sexual offenders;
- public awareness, public education and media campaigning.

The Helpline has national coverage and seeks to provide information and advice for adults who are concerned about their own behaviour or the behaviour of someone they know. The targeted population for the Helpline is:

- adult abusers and those at risk of abusing;
- family and friends of abusers;
- parents of young people who are engaging in sexually inappropriate behaviours.

The goal of reaching those concerned about their own behaviour has been a core and novel feature of the Helpline, and a recent evaluation (Eldridge et al. 2006) found that the largest number of calls between June 2002 and May 2006 were from abusers or potential abusers, with 1804 calls from 674 different callers representing 45 per cent of calls. The Helpline aims to challenge and change attitudes, with an emphasis on raising awareness and supporting people to take appropriate action. With an overall focus on reducing the number of victims of abuse, the issue of child protection remains the foremost concern of the Helpline team. Thus confidentiality has limits, since Helpline operators will notify the relevant authorities if they feel an identifiable child is at risk. These limits of confidentiality are clearly communicated to callers when they contact the Helpline and form part of the Helpline protocols (Kemshall et al. 2004).

While the Helpline does not provide long-term counselling, a limited number of cases are selected for face-to-face treatment. Such treatment is severely limited by lack of resources and Stop It Now! campaigns for services for sexual abusers. Preventative work is hampered by a lack of treatment services and by the absence of treatment programmes outside of the criminal justice system. This makes direct work with offenders at Laws' primary and secondary levels of prevention difficult. However, Laws (2000) argued that the 'prevention goals' of public awareness and responsibility, and public education were also important. These goals are a key area of Stop It Now! work.

Building awareness and responsibility

In its public awareness and educative work Stop It Now! targets the following audiences:

- adults who are worried about their own behaviour and who can be encouraged to contact the Helpline and seek assistance;
- family and friends of abusers, with an emphasis upon how to encourage the abusers to seek advice and assistance, for example by contacting the Helpline;
- adults in the general public, with a view to raising both public awareness of the issue of child sexual abuse and conveying the message that combating such abuse is an adult responsibility.

Stop It Now! also aims to:

- influence the general debate and inform government policy;
- raise the awareness and influence the practice of professionals working within the broad child protection arena;
- target (through local projects) key community groups for Stop It Now! information.

Stop It Now! builds awareness and responsibility by disseminating information in a user-friendly way to key community groups and local opinion formers (Kemshall et al. 2004), and by attempting to influence media coverage of child sexual abuse and responses to it. Wood (see Kemshall et al. 2004), in a review of media coverage of Stop It Now!, found the campaign had an impact at both local and national levels, despite the known difficulties in influencing national print media in a climate of commercial interest and sensationalism (Critcher 2003). This was well supported by local initiatives on disseminating to professional groups such as teachers and local community groups (Kemshall et al. 2004). The subsequent evaluation recommended a formalized and systematic approach to communication and public awareness (see Fig. 4.2).

The review of the management of sex offenders in England and Wales 2006–07 initiated two public awareness pilots in West Midlands and Surrey by Stop It Now! currently the subject of evaluation (for further information contact: office@ stopitnow.org.uk).

However, public health campaigns are fraught with difficulty (Alaszewski 2006; Bennett and Calman 1999), not least in that messages are prone to distortion by the media and often result in panics rather than rational debate about the extent or otherwise of a risk (see Boseley 2002 on the MMR vaccine coverage; Burgess 2002 on telephone masts; Furedi 2002 on general coverage of hazards; Barnett and Breakwell 2003 on BSE). Messages are also prone to interpretation by the audience, and can be influenced by social context and the local networks within which the audience receives and reflects upon them (Pidgeon et al. 2002; Duff 2003; Hughes et al. 2006). Evaluations of extensive public health campaigns, such as those on sexual behaviour (Alder 1997) or smoking (Denscombe 2001), show that they have

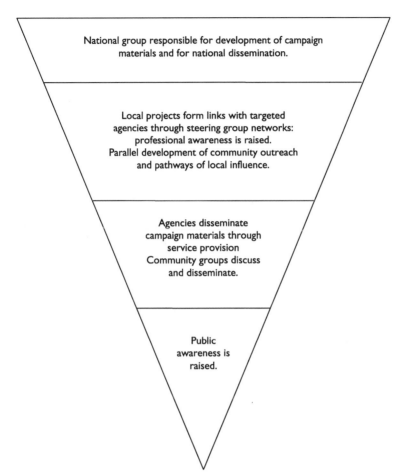

National group responsible for development of campaign materials and for national dissemination.

Local projects form links with targeted agencies through steering group networks: professional awareness is raised. Parallel development of community outreach and pathways of local influence.

Agencies disseminate campaign materials through service provision Community groups discuss and disseminate.

Public awareness is raised.

Figure 4.2 Communicating key messages to the public

Source: Kemshall et al. 2004.

little impact and that there can be considerable difference between expert and public perceptions of risk (Slovic 2000; see Miller and Kitzinger 1998 on AIDS). This has been particularly acute in public perceptions of child sexual abuse, and of high risk offenders generally (Soothill and Walby 1991; Kitzinger 2004). A key flaw in public health/awareness campaigns is to assume that the 'receiver' of information is a 'rational actor' and will respond to this information as the experts deem suitable. Denscombe (2001) found that young smokers are not ignorant of the risks but choose to diminish, justify and ignore them. Other studies of health risks indicate that knowledge of a risk does not necessarily change behaviours (Alaszewski 2006; see Ruston and Clayton 2002 on heart disease; Hobson-West 2003 on MMR; Thirlaway and Hegg 2005 on alcohol and cancer). Interestingly people tend to adopt strategies to manage their anxieties about risk, but they are less likely to change their behaviour (Thirlaway and Hegg 2005; Alaszewski 2006). Information can be used selectively to reinforce existing beliefs (for example, about violence and mental disorder, see Philo 1999), and local networks and associations are important in how risk information is sought, interpreted and used, which is particularly crucial in local vigilante responses to paedophiles (Kitzinger 2004). As Hughes et al. (2006: 262) put it: 'The circulation of everyday knowledge in routine conversation between friends and acquaintances is also key in supporting the focus on some sources of threat, and not others', a key ingredient in the Paulsgrove vigilante action (Nash 2006). This action took place on an English council estate when local residents protested against the location of sex offenders on the estate and the perceived lack of action by local statutory agencies. Rumour and misperception of the extent and nature of the risk played a significant role in inflating fears and responses (Nash 2006).

Media isn't there just to communicate risk. It also has a role in politicizing risks – in particular, debating their acceptability and whether risks have been/or are being adequately controlled. Media also has a role in blame allocation and holding government, corporations, public bodies and individuals to account for risk (see Hughes et al. 2006 for a full discussion of how this process operates in the print media). In this context, trust in the message source, but also in the risk managers, is crucial to audience perception of risk and to how acceptable it is (Kitzinger 2004; Hughes et al. 2006). In the case of sexual and violent offenders, coverage may highlight the shortcomings of the professionals charged with managing risk and bring the public protection system into disrepute. Raising awareness may raise expectations and erode trust in the risk management system itself. Campaigns have to be very careful to avoid such a backlash.

Building responsibility is also problematic. Communities and the public may resent 'being made responsible' for risks which they consider are the responsibility of paid professionals (e.g., police and probation); and involuntary risks are particularly resented (Slovic 2000). Increasing the awareness of professionals and parents about child sexual abuse is laudable, although the extent to which it is reducing child sexual abuse is more difficult to discern (Kemshall et al. 2004). The PHA displaces responsibility for risk management onto communities, treating them as a potential source of vigilance, monitoring, support and control – the community is seen as a resource for risk management (Kemshall and Wood 2007b). However, risks and the resources to manage them are inequitably distributed (Johnston 2000), and some communities literally struggle to manage the risks placed within them. As Kitzinger puts it, 'some communities already felt under siege', particularly on underresourced and underpoliced housing estates (2004: 151). These perceptions were heightened by housing inequalities, poor local services and the release of prisoners into strained communities, coupled with perceptions that professionals could not provide sufficient protection. In essence:

> Many protesters expressed anger and frustration at the fact that their fate was to be decided by faceless bureaucrats who rarely lived in such areas themselves. The question often asked at public meetings called to reassure people was 'How would you feel if he was living next door to you and your kids?' Council tenants who were expected to put up with living next to an incinerator, playgrounds built on polluted sites, damp housing or a failing local school, now were also expected to tolerate the country's most dangerous predators dumped on their doorsteps.
>
> (Kitzinger 2004: 152)

In this climate, the public may conclude that it is having risks foisted upon it, with a differential impact upon various communities.

Protection through partnership: a summary

The rhetoric of protection through partnerships is very strong (Kemshall 2003), although the nature of partnership can differ, ranging from exclusive, formal partnerships between State agencies to partnerships with communities and the wider public. Agency-based partnerships are almost exclusively rooted in the community protection discourse; adopt an 'arms length' attitude to the public; and frame the offender as a risk that requires managing, monitoring and controlling. Surveillance and restriction tend to outweigh rehabilitative concerns (with some notable exceptions), and protective partnerships of this type tend to fulfil a regulatory rather than reintegrative function. The public is characterized as being 'irrational' and difficult to manage, and on occasion as presenting a threat to risk management strategies through vigilante action (Kemshall and Wood 2007b). Such partnerships tend to operate almost exclusively at the tertiary level of crime prevention focused on the 'critical few' (Laws 1996).

By contrast, community-based partnerships tend to adopt a broader preventative and reintegrative approach, with particular attention to the primary and secondary levels of intervention. However, these community-based partnerships can differ, with COSA, for example, representing a limited partnership between criminal justice agencies and communities, utilizing the resource of volunteers to both reintegrate offenders and ameliorate local community anxiety. COSA, particularly in the UK, is embedded in the criminal justice management of offenders, and integrative work is heavily qualified by protection concerns. Inclusion and integration are seen as key ingredients for rehabilitation and hence for reducing recidivism. Accountability and prevention remain paramount. COSA is tending to operate at the tertiary level of sexual crime prevention, although it does have the capacity to operate at the secondary level (Laws 1996). With its roots in faith-based communities, it has had limited engagement with the public, although its ability to ameliorate public anxiety over released sex offenders has been important.

Stop It Now! works with offenders, relatives of offenders, community groups and with the wider public. It targets all levels of crime prevention, with greatest attention to the primary and secondary levels. Its public awareness and public educative aims are ambitious but have a clear primary level prevention goal. A significant contribution of Stop It Now! is the creation of a climate in which informed discussion of sex offending can take place, with an exploration of the most effective ways of responding to the range of harms presented by sexual offenders. The media rather than the public is seen as problematic, although the issues in influencing the media may be underestimated. Both public and offenders are seen as capable of cooperation and change.

Rather than being understood as alternative forms of sex offending risk management, it may be more productive to understand the various partnerships discussed above as complementary forms of risk management located along a State–public continuum of responsibility for delivery, and at differing levels of crime prevention (Kemshall and Wood 2007b). They are also beginning to elide: MAPPA, for example, are exploring other mechanisms for community engagement beyond lay advisors and annual reports; COSA and MAPPA have formed a strong link in the UK pilot, and COSA form a key part of parole supervision in Canada; Stop It Now! has developed links with MAPPA, police, probation and other State agencies involved in child protection and sexual offender management. Differences remain – most notably in the extent to which inclusion and reintegration are prioritized in the approach to sex offenders and in the extent to which responsibility for their management is shared and devolved. Despite some interesting initiatives, participatory and communicative mechanisms for engaging the public in approaches to high risk offenders remain limited, and the focus remains almost exclusively on sex offenders.

Further reading

Bates, A., Saunders, R. and Wilson, C. (2007) Doing something about it: a follow-up study of sex offenders participating in Thames Valley Circles of Support and Accountability, *British Journal of Community Justice*, 5(1): 19–42.

Kitzinger, J. (2004) *Framing Abuse: Media Influence and Public Understanding of Sexual Violence Against Children*. London: Pluto Press.

Laws, R. (2000) Sexual offending as a public health problem: a North American perspective, *Journal of Sexual Aggression*, 5(1): 30–44.

Stop it Now! Available at: www.stopitnow.org (accessed 24 September 2007).

Risk management

Introduction

Chapter 4 examined the types of partnership used in the community management of high risk offenders. The rhetoric of partnership is strong, and the boundaries between types of partnership, and the statutory and voluntary sectors is increasingly blurred. This chapter focuses on the strategies and interventions used by these partnerships to deliver protection. Risk management has become an essential ingredient of a penal policy driven by risk. In essence, public protection is about the correct identification and prevention of risks to the public, with zero risk an unstated but implicit aim. This chapter will review the main risk management strategies used in the 'community protection model' followed by a review of strategies rooted in the restorative and integrative approaches. As the community protection model has been extensively reviewed elsewhere (see Connelly and Williamson 2000; Kemshall 2001, 2003; Petrunik 2002; Nash 2006), greater weight will be given to the emerging alternative strategies. The potential and limits of each approach is reviewed, and the possibility that they can be effectively meshed to deliver a balanced 'blended protection' is examined.

Community protection risk management strategies

This approach to risk management has tended to emphasize controlling and restrictive measures on the offender, combined with intensive/intrusive supervision, various monitoring techniques (including electronic tagging) and corrective programmes based on cognitive behavioural therapy (CBT) techniques. Controlling and restrictive measures are those conditions attached to supervision orders or licences which restrict where an offender can go, where they can live, what they can or cannot do and who they must not approach or contact. For example, a sex offender may have a restriction against using certain leisure facilities (e.g., swimming pools), approaching local schools and may have a condition to reside in a certain place (e.g., a probation hostel). Offenders can also be made the subject of a curfew to restrict their activities at certain times of the day or night when they are known to be more risky. These conditions restrict the opportunity to commit offences and to 'groom' victims. Restrictive conditions are specific to individual offenders, and it is important that they are well matched to the assessed risk factors, that they are proportionate, justified and workable in practice. It is also important that the measures are monitored and enforced if breached. The lack of restrictive measures (or their lack of enforceability), have been indicted in recent SFOs (see the case of Damien Hanson, in HMIP 2006a).

However, restrictive conditions can sometimes have an adverse affect. The HMIP thematic on sex offenders noted sex offenders subject to restrictions prohibiting them from living in proximity to schools and parks resulted in social isolation, distance from their own families and support networks, and a lack of reintegration (HMIP and HMIC 2005; see also Levenson and Cotter 2005a). In addition, this type of policy can result in sex offenders being accommodated together in a small geographical area.

The community protection model also presumes that most community management will involve working with unmotivated offenders. In such cases, risk management is almost entirely about containment in the community, restriction of opportunities to re-offend, and protection of known or likely victims. Surveillance and police intelligence are usually the key components of such plans, along with rapid recall procedures (Kemshall 2001; Kemshall et al. 2006).

Reviews of best practice have summarised the following as key components of effective risk management:

- *Proactive planning* – before release from prison enables appropriate licence/parole conditions to be made, accommodation to be secured, victim protection and support work to take place, and surveillance and reporting requirements to be set up.
- *Police intelligence* – this helps to monitor grooming and targeting activities, and to identify offender networks.
- *Boundaries and swift enforcement* – written contracts with offenders can reinforce such conditions and hold offenders to account for programme attendance and compliance with conditions. (While not legally binding, such contracts may engender a stronger commitment by the offender and can be used in conjunction with a clear warning system and swift enforcement, including rapid parole recall.)
- *Targeted surveillance* – to establish key contacts and offender movements, to provide evidence of further offending, evidence to justify rapid recall.
- *Supervised accommodation* – can be crucial for effective risk management. It provides stability and can be combined with curfews, intensive treatment-based work, CCTV surveillance, electronic monitoring and high levels of staff contact.
- *Accredited programmes* – these can be used with positive effect with some offenders. However, programme selection and work must be done with care and as part of a wider risk management strategy. Offenders can present false compliance and on occasion a false reassurance to workers that risk is falling. In some cases offenders will have experienced similar programmes in prison or under earlier supervision and have 'learnt the responses'.
- *Victim protection* – this can include providing information, personal alarms, rapid response police numbers, restraining orders, conditions on licences or supervision orders.
- *Addressing criminogenic and welfare needs* – On release from custody, for example, a failure to meet the basic needs of the offender (e.g., benefit claims or accommodation) can undermine the risk management plan. However, these should not be the sole focus of the risk management plan.
(Adapted from Kemshall 2003; Kemshall et al. 2005;
Kemshall et al. 2006)

This can be translated into a typical risk management package for a paedophile on release from custody:

- electronic tagging;
- supervised accommodation;

- restriction of access to school locations;
- identification and intensive one-to-one work on key triggers, (e.g., mood change, attitudes to and the sexualization of children);
- use of local police intelligence about offending networks and surveillance on key movements;
- victim empathy work.

(Adapted from Kemshall et al. 2005; Kemshall et al. 2006)

Supervision and monitoring

Supervision and monitoring are key activities in the community protection model. Supervision can be described at the minimal level as oversight of the offender, but with high risk offenders is likely to comprise a focus on behaviours, enforcement of conditions, assessment and encouragement of motivation and change, interventions and treatment. Supervision can be stymied by at least two difficulties: lack of resources and an overemphasis on prohibitions/restrictions. The Chief Inspector of Probation in England and Wales has noted the significant impact of low resources and diminished capacity in the adequate supervision of offenders. He refers to the 'Long Squeeze' – a situation over a period of time where resources have not kept pace with rising workload, and increasing public and political expectations of what can be delivered (HMIP 2007a: 5–6). The Chief Inspector draws the conclusion that if the situation is not addressed then the capacity to supervise adult offenders satisfactorily will be compromised. While a simple causal relationship cannot necessarily be drawn between quantity and quality in the workload (HMIP 2007a), the Effective Supervision Inspections have found that less than 60 per cent of cases had a satisfactory risk of harm assessment carried out (similar to the findings of Kemshall et al. 2005 on MAPPA cases), although interventions were satisfactory in around 80 per cent of cases (HMIP 2007b).

An overemphasis on restrictive conditions has been noted as problematic, particularly on the grounds of reintegration, but also that such conditions can be counter to long-term change and self-risk management (Kemshall and Wood 2007a; Wood and Kemshall 2007). Practitioners report that offenders lack incentive to change when their needs remain unmet or when restrictions are overly intrusive. Increasingly, a motivational approach to offenders is advocated, emphasizing a 'meshing of motivational principles into the fabric of offender management' (Porporino and Fabiano 2007: 207). Supervision goals that are entirely couched in terms of prohibitions (e.g., avoid fighting; avoid sexual contact with children) can also be problematic and reframing goals into positive change language is more helpful (e.g., 'I will find three ways of controlling my temper'). This model reflects a more positive framing and approach to human agency, and utilizes more recent work on desistance (see Maruna 2001; Ward and Stewart 2003a; McMurran and Ward 2004; Ward and Maruna 2007). This 'Good Lives' model (GLM) has also been applied to work with sex offenders with some success (this is discussed in more detail below; see also Ward and Marshall 2004; and Ward and Maruna 2007). Greater attention to diversity and to more reflective practice has also been advocated. The latter is seen as essential to understanding the responsivity of offenders and in assisting workers to practice in a theoretically informed way from a solid knowledge base (Farrow et al. 2007).

Monitoring is also a key function of the community protection model, and comprises more than a 'watchful eye' over the offender. The Scottish Risk Management Authority states that monitoring may comprise differing combinations of surveillance, electronic tagging, drugs testing, contact with the offender's network and with other professionals, and home visits including unannounced visits (RMA 2007). Monitoring will assess compliance with supervision and conditions, assess the offender's functioning and monitor problematic behaviours for escalation and deterioration, assess the offender's social environment for cues (e.g., the presence of toys for children or pornographic literature), and whether the offender is grooming or obtaining access to victims (see RMA 2007).

Cognitive behavioural treatment and intervention programmes

Cognitive behavioural therapy (CBT) treatment is designed to assist offenders to change their criminal behaviour through control and/or management of thinking patterns, feelings, drives and attitudes (McGuire 1995, 2000, 2004; Home Office 2002; Hollin and Palmer 2006; see McGuire 2007 for a review of current programmes in the UK). CBT programmes targeted at *sex offenders* tend to focus on:

- changing patterns of deviant sexual arousal;
- correcting distorted thinking and educating offenders in the 'cycle of abuse';
- educating offenders about the effects and impact of abuse;
- increasing social competence;
- victim empathy;
- controlling sexual arousal;
- reducing denial;
- relapse prevention;
- problem recognition and problem solving;
- skills practice for improving interpersonal relationships.
  (see Marshall et al. 1999; Beech et al. 2001; Beech and Fisher 2002; Beech and Mann 2002; Loucks 2002; Carich and Calder 2003; Craissati 2004; Kemshall and McIvor 2004; Brown 2005).

A number of factors are significant to the effectiveness of sex offender programmes. In brief, these are amenability to treatment; timings of interventions; programme integrity; and relapse prevention. Amenability to treatment is important, as is motivation to change and whether the level of motivation has been established with integrity by the worker (McMurran 2002). In addition, some sexual offences are more difficult to treat than others. Serious, well established/entrenched behaviours involving penetrative sex and violence (e.g., rape) are less amenable to treatment (Beech and Fisher 2004; Fisher and Beech 2004).

Timings of interventions can be crucial. Beech et al. (1999) have argued that intensive challenge during 'denial' can be counterproductive as this reduces the likelihood of establishing victim empathy. In a hostile climate that challenges their activities, offenders can develop a strategy of blaming their victims in order to cope with confrontation. This may require intensive one-to-one work on denial prior to group work. Offenders with high deviancy and high denial have poorer success rates from programme interventions than low deviancy and low denial offenders (Beech et al. 1999; Beech and Fisher 2004). Longer programmes are more successful, and this reflects the intensive work often required to deal with entrenched behaviours (Beech et al 1999).

Programme integrity is also essential, with programmes (whether individual or group), delivered as specified (Grubin and Thornton 1994; Hollin 1995; Cooke and Philip 2000; Brown 2005).

Work on relapse prevention is also critical to long-term risk management and programme effectiveness (Brown 2005). Offenders need to be taught techniques for self-risk management and strategies for managing their own problematic behaviours once programmes have finished. Offenders need to recognize the signs of relapse and have a 'safety net' to deal with it. Workers also need to be alert to relapse and take appropriate action(s) (e.g., to act on non-attendance, non-compliance with conditions or treatment requirements; to increase the frequency of contact). However, relapse prevention programmes have attracted some criticism, with some commentators challenging the uncritical transference of these programmes from work with addictions to work with sex offenders (Ward and Hudson 1996), and pointing out that the evaluative evidence for the effectiveness of the relapse prevention programmes is limited. Mann (1996, 2000) has subsequently found limited evidence of effectiveness, although she has noted that the overemphasis upon 'avoidance goals' (e.g., avoid doing X) is more problematic as these are more difficult for offenders to achieve (Ward 2000).

Programmes for *violent offenders* usually focus on:

- interventions and programme content well matched to the nature, extent and type of violence;
- changing the violent thinking patterns of offenders;

- changing the violent behaviour patterns of offenders;
- changing the 'logic of violence' and the justifications used for offending;
- increasing victim empathy and reducing victim blaming;
- promoting alternative prosocial thinking and behaviour patterns;
- teaching prosocial problem-solving skills;
- teaching relapse prevention skills.

(see McGuire 2004; Quinsey et al. 2005; Kemshall et al. 2006;
DeLisi and Conis 2007; Maden 2007; Webster and Hucker 2007)

It is important that such work is placed within a broader risk management strategy emphasizing monitoring and where appropriate surveillance of violent behaviours/offending, alcohol and drug testing (key disinhibitors in violent offending), swift enforcement of conditions and action on non-compliance. Risk management strategies should also provide:

- strong incentives for individuals to manage their own behaviour;
- strong incentives to attend and comply with therapy/programmes;
- a thorough system of supervision with regular re-assessment;
- clear boundaries for acceptable behaviour and enforcement;
- integrated management of custody, therapy and community services.

(from MacLean 2000: 59)

These programmes can be delivered in groups or one-to-one (see Bush 1995; Connelly and Williamson 2000; Ireland 2000; McGuire 2000; Kemshall et al. 2006).

The factors for success are similar to those with sex offender programmes. Well matched programmes/interventions are crucial, delivered with integrity and the avoidance of 'false compliers'. Critical success factors include:

- appropriate targeting;
- programme integrity (deliver the content as intended);
- committed programme tutors;
- support to the programme by key workers;
- appropriate relapse prevention planning.

(see Kemshall et al. 2006)

Appropriate targeting was identified as a key issue in the Serious Further Offence committed by Damien Hanson (HMIP 2006a). In brief, Hanson had completed the CALM programme in prison and was deemed a low enough risk to be released. However, he had a lengthy record for violence, linked to drug use, and he went on to commit murder on release. The subsequent HMIP report was critical of the use of the CALM programme (designed to deal with aggression management and emotional anger) for an offender who had a long history of *instrumental violence*. Similarly, Loza and Loza-Fanous (1999) have noted the mistake in attempting to treat rape and violent recidivism through anger management programmes. Howells and Day (2003) have also noted poorer outcomes with prisoners, and argue that programme assessment must take account of motivation to change.

Evaluations of CBT

Brown (2005) outlines in some detail the difficulties in evaluating sex offender programmes, the current research evidence and the specifics of 'what works'.

In brief, the methodological issues are the difficulties in transferring North American evaluations uncritically to the UK (Grubin and Thornton 1994; Proctor 1994); lack of programme integrity – the 'same' programme is not necessarily the same in different contexts and locations; and the practical and ethical difficulties in constructing a randomized control trial – for example, allocating prisoners randomly to treatment and non-treatment groups.[1] Difficulties in evaluating outcomes can also be problematic, for example, is a sexual re-offence of lesser severity deemed a success or a failure? How long a period of follow-up time is required to demonstrate success? Measures of recidivism can also be difficult and they do not necessarily reflect re-offence rates (the latter may in fact be greater). Brown argues that a balance must be struck between researchers adopting 'the most rigorous methodology possible and draw conclusions that take account of the methodological weaknesses of each study' (2005: 192). In a review of the 'best' studies from North America, the UK and Ireland, Australia and New Zealand, and including meta-analyses (a statistical tool used to combine and evaluate the results of various effectiveness studies),[2] Brown concludes that the evidence is promising with treated sex offenders having lower rates of recidivism than non-treated sex offenders. However, Brown cites a note of caution from Marshall and Eccles (1991: 87): 'Not all forms are effective and not all applications of all forms are effective. We are not uniformly effective with all offender types, and find rapists the least responsive to our efforts to date. We need to modify our programs to deal with our current failures. But sex offenders can be treated'.

Research in the 1990s and the early part of the twenty-first century has focused on 'what works and with whom' (Brown 2005). The most notable points are that sex offenders who drop out of treatment have higher rates of recidivism, although it is not clear whether this is due to the profile of those who drop out or whether it is as a result of the programme content/experience. Violent sex offenders are more likely to be non-completers of programmes and motivation impacts on treatment compliance. Male abusers of children are among the most responsive (Beech and Fisher 2004); rapists do less well (McGrath 1995); and high risk offenders are the most resistant to treatment (Quinsey et al. 1998). There are some difficulties in making programmes culturally relevant and sensitive (Patel and Lord 2001), although this can be done. The English and Welsh Prison Service Sex Offender Treatment Programme (SOTP) has been adapted for ethnic minority sex offenders with some success (Webster et al. 2004). In New Zealand the original Kia Marama programme for Maori has been adapted to the Te Piriti programme and it is more effective (Hudson et al. 1995; Nathan et al. 2003). Treatment characteristics have been much discussed, with emphasis upon the 'risk responsivity' principle (Gendreau 1996); programme integrity; correct 'dosage'; a mixture of group and individual components; and group cohesion in the treatment of groups. Key therapeutic characteristics have also been identified, including staff capable of prosocial modelling, of being empathic and warm but non-collusive. Indeed, confrontational styles have been seen as producing negative outcomes (Marshall et al. 2003; Marshall and Eccles 1996). Limited feedback from sex offenders indicates that they value: the safe group experience; time to try and understand their behaviours; and learning techniques of relapse prevention (Scheela and Stern 1994; Drapeau et al. 2004; see also Clarke et al. 2004 on CBT programmes in prisons).

The evaluation of risk management strategies for violent offenders has also been restricted by difficulties in completing impact studies and by the severe ethical and methodological difficulties in constructing control groups (Kemshall 2001). Difficulties in measuring violence due to its 'multidimensional nature' and the differing range of acts and seriousness have added to the problem (Michie and Cooke 2006). Studies have mostly occurred within residential psychiatric settings with particular client groups (usually the severely mentally ill see Rice et al. 1992; Villeneuve and Quinsey 1995; Rice 1997; Wang et al. 2000); the case management of mentally disordered offenders in the community (Dvoskin and Steadman 1994); or the evaluation of domestic violence programmes (Dobash et al. 1999; Bowen and Gilchrist 2004) including the Duluth IDAP programme (Bilby and Hatcher 2004). Studies in the 1990s (including meta-analyses, see Dowden and Andrews 2000) indicated that CBT could achieve significant results with violent offenders (see Hollin 1993, 2005; Browne and Howells 1996; and Kemshall 2001 for a review) with the most notable programme of the period being the Cognitive Self-Change Programme for violent men piloted and evaluated in Vermont, USA (Bush 1995). Differences in recidivism rates were significant with only 45.5 per cent of those going through the Cognitive Self-Change Programme having a further conviction after three years compared to 76.6 per cent of a comparable sample who had not experienced the programme (Bush 1995: 152–3). However, as this was not a randomized control trial the figures need to be treated with some caution.

Although few studies have evaluated the effectiveness of programmes for serious violent offenders per se (Whitehead et al. 2007), Polaschek and Collie (2004) found that programme effectiveness was promising but that further robust research was required. More recent group work has emphasized the skills required to avoid violent situations and improving the thinking and decision-making skills of offenders (e.g., the IDEA group work used in Staffordshire Probation, see Courtney and Hodgkinson 1999); and intensive prison-based programmes in many of the Anglophone countries. Polaschek et al. (2005) have positively evaluated a prison-based programme in New Zealand and found that: 'in a comparison with untreated offenders, treated men were less likely to be reconvicted of a violent offence, and those who were took longer to fail. There was also a 12% difference in favour of the treated men on the two other indices, non-violent reconviction and re-imprisonment' (Polaschek et al. 2005: 1611).

An important feature of all programmes is their integration into broader risk management strategies that emphasize intensive supervision comprising: surveillance, alcohol and drug testing, warnings and reincarceration for any violations, and strong enforcement of rules and requirements (Kemshall 2001). Interestingly in the UK,

> violent crime has remained stable according to BCS interviews in 2006/07 compared with 2005/06. Recorded crime figures show a one per cent fall in violence against the person, a seven per cent fall in sexual offences and a three per cent increase in robbery for 2006/07 compared with 2005/06.
>
> (Nicholas et al. 2007)

However, this fall in crime rates has not necessarily been reflected in penal policy or sentencing trends.

Beyond the punishment paradigm – PHA, 'good lives' and risk management

McCulloch and Kelly (2007) have argued that probation work with sex offenders is dominated by the current societal stereotypes of 'stranger-danger' and a punishment paradigm. Importantly, they point out that work with sex offenders was never characterized by the welfarism of 'advise, assist and befriend' (2007: 11), but rather by 'challenge and change'. The rise of cognitive behavioural therapy (CBT) was perfectly suited to changing 'distorted thinking' and remoralizing the risky subject (Kemshall 2002b). CBT has been the mainstay of sexual offender treatment and interventions (Fisher and Beech 2004), with evidence that well targeted programmes can reduce reconviction rates (Beech and Fisher 2004; Marshall et al. 2004). CBT has had its critics, not least for its simplistic approach to sexual offending (Laws and Marshall 2003); lack of attention to the power dynamic in the commission of offences (Worrall 1997); and the overemphasis upon confrontational techniques (Sheath 1990; Vivian-Byrne 2004). CBT has been refined in more recent years with greater attention to social factors, prosocial modelling and the role of the therapist, and treatment integrity (Marshall et al. 2003; Dowden and Andrews 2004; Mann 2004). However, CBT is still largely characterized by control and a correctional agenda (Kemshall 2002b). To some extent the picture painted by Sheath in 1990 still prevails:

> Much of the work currently being undertaken by probation officers in this field appears to rely upon the use of structured confrontational interviews where sex offenders are required to give an account of their offending and to have that account challenged as to its veracity. Elements of victim blaming, distorted thinking, denial and the minimisation of responsibility are identified, confronted and, ultimately, changed.
>
> (Sheath 1990: 159)

Disillusionment with this approach has led to alternative approaches rooted in restorative justice and the 'Good Lives' model (Ward and Marshall 2004; McAlinden 2005, 2006). As McCulloch and Kelly put it, the 'Good Lives' model: 'proposes a more holistic and constructive way of conceptualising and engaging with offenders, focusing less on individual offender deficits and more on the personal, inter-personal and social contexts required to enable offenders to live and sustain a "good life" ' (2007: 15).

The GLM is essentially a strengths-based approach which 'focuses on promoting individuals' important personal goals, while reducing and managing their risk for future offending' (Whitehead et al. 2007: 579). In brief:

> It takes seriously offenders' personal preferences and values – that is, the things that matter most to them in the world. It draws upon these primary goods to motivate individuals to live better lives; and ... therapists seek to provide offenders with the competencies (internal conditions) and opportunities (external conditions) to implement treatment plans based on these primary goods.
>
> (Whitehead et al. 2007: 580)

For example, a sex offender may pursue relatedness and social/physical intimacy through inappropriate sexual relations with children (Ward and Stewart 2003b). GLM will focus on positive and prosocial approach goals to achieve legitimately these 'primary goods' of intimacy, and emphasize avoidance goals to prevent harm. The model has also been applied to violent offenders, although robust evaluative studies are still awaited (Whitehead et al. 2007). In brief, GLM works with the offender to reframe approach goals and the means to achieve them positively and legitimately, and assists the offender in reconstructing a new identity that can action personal goals legally (Whitehead et al. 2007). However, GLM has been criticized on a number of grounds, not least that it is culturally and context specific, developed from work with indigenous peoples and lacks transferability. It has to be combined with a risk management approach, but a therapeutic focus on needs may obscure attention to risks. The model also has limited efficacy with psychopaths who display limited empathy and remorse (Hemphill and Hart 2002; Whitehead et al. 2007). In addition, it is difficult to establish in a multimodal approach the impact achieved by GLM over and above more traditional risk management methods. Finally, comparison of GLM and more traditional risk management strategies are still lacking (see Bonta and Andrews 2003 for a full review).

However, in Scotland the Risk Management Authority has embedded the 'Good Lives' model within their approach to high risk offenders, and emphasizes the dual function of supervision, thus:

> Literature on risk management practice often defines the goal of super-vision as being the reduction of likelihood that an individual will re-offend through the restriction of liberty. In Scotland, a broader understanding of supervision is predominant. Therefore, for the pur-pose of this document, the supervision process has a dual focus of promoting rehabilitation and reducing harm, through restricting liberty as necessary, and engaging an offender in the process of change.
>
> (RMA 2007: 48)

In addition to emphasizing engagement and motivation as key processes of change, restorative approaches emphasize social inclusion and reintegration as key mechanisms for the prevention of offending, including sexual offend-ing. However, as McCulloch and Kelly (2007) argue, the taboo and fearful-ness surrounding sexual offending has legitimated an almost exclusively punitive paradigm, which under the umbrella of public protection has extended to violent offenders (Kemshall 2003). Within this climate it has been difficult for alternative approaches to take hold; however, Circles of Support, and Stop It Now! UK and Ireland are two prime examples (as discussed in Chapter 4).

This section will consider the following alternative approaches:

- prevention strategies and environmental/opportunity management strategies;

- social inclusion and integration techniques, including prosocial statutory supervision.

Prevention strategies and environmental/opportunity management strategies

As discussed in Chapter 4, prevention strategies are rooted in Richard Laws' public health approach to sexual offending (and, more latterly, violent offending). Laws (1995, 1999, 2000, 2003) argued that the prevalence and harm of sexual offending far outstripped the capacity of the criminal justice system to deal with it, indeed the latter wasted resources 'fire fighting' the consequences of such offending without effectively tackling the causes of sexual abuse. Laws argued that resources should be redistributed away from tertiary responses, such as dealing with offenders post-offending and those 'already known' to the system, to preventing the development of problematic behaviours (primary) and targeting those early in their criminal careers (secondary). Craven et al. (2006, 2007) apply this approach to sexual grooming, that is the targeting of children for sexual abuse by offenders. They argue that preventative work could be targeted at:

1 Identifying potential offenders at the onset of their sexual interest in children.
2 Intervening with these potential offenders as they begin grooming behaviours.
3 Intervening as they groom the environment and significant others (for example, gaining the confidence of parents).
4 Intervening once they are grooming the child.
5 Working with them long-term to prevent further offending.
(adapted from Craven et al. 2007: 69)

The Helpline work of Stop It Now! UK and Ireland described in Chapter 4 is a key example of work of this type (see www.stopitnow.org.uk and Kemshall et al. 2004). Stop It Now! also provide public awareness leaflets to enable the public to recognize grooming behaviours and to assist parents in identifying problematic sexual behaviours in their children.[3] However, such public awareness campaigns run the risk of raising anxiety and fear if they do not provide the knowledge and confidence about what actions to take if required, or if they do not inform the public of the types and effectiveness of interventions available (Kemshall et al. 2004). Leisurewatch provides a helpful example of a concrete response to grooming behaviours, and of how to actively engage the public in safely managing sex offenders within their own communities.

Leisurewatch is a branded project developed by the The Derwent Inititative

(TDI) (www.derwentinitiative.org.uk) to safeguard leisure sites (e.g., swimming pools) and, more recently, shopping centres and other public spaces. Initiated as a three-year pilot in 2002 under Home Office funding, the project has been extensively extended throughout the UK. The purpose of Leisurewatch is to:

- make staff of a leisure site more able to spot potentially dangerous behaviour and empower them to make safe challenges to customers;
- point out to managers any infrastructural aspects of a site which may make it easier for people to commit offending behaviour;
- promote an observant and vigilant image for the site which is off-putting to sex offenders and reassuring to the public;
- make strong and informed links with local police, who respect the fact that staff have been trained to observe behaviour;
- establish a formal referral procedure to inform police of suspect behaviour before an offence has been committed;
- provide more information to MAPPA units to ensure that offenders being managed in the community do not break the terms of their management arrangements.

(adapted from: www.derwentinitiative.org.uk/leisurewatch.htm
and TDI 2007)

Leisurewatch encourages CRB checks on staff, provides training in Leisurewatch techniques (e.g., how to spot and act on grooming behaviours) for at least 80 per cent of frontline staff, establishes protocols with local police and issues posters, information leaflets and a Leisurewatch manual. Continuity and stability of on-site Leisurewatch is facilitated by top-up visits, retraining if the 80 per cent rule is broken, a 'mystery visit' to ensure compliance and tracking of any referrals to the police to evaluate outcomes. The overall aim is to make those leisure facilities used regularly by children safer and to enable staff in those facilities to manage customers with protection in mind. It is of course possible that staff will also be offenders, and TDI accept this position on the basis that their training will make colleagues more vigilant (a position that has resulted in one successful prosecution). TDI are currently extending this work to parents' workshops aimed at helping parents to challenge inappropriate behaviour in their own families, but also extending the notion of community responsibility and vigilance.

The strategy is an interesting mix of public awareness campaigning, environmental and crime opportunity management (literally by managing crime away through increased vigilance) and targeting key staff for practical training (some 4000 staff had been trained at time of writing). Leisurewatch is being extended in 2007, and currently receives support from the Ministry of Justice and the Institute of Leisure and Amenities Management.

Leisurewatch operates primarily at Laws' primary and secondary levels of prevention, although it can operate with known and persistent sexual offenders. On Craven et al.'s (2007) model above, Leisurewatch targets points 1–4 in a very practical way.

Does giving the public information in this way work? TDI evaluate their training and have positive results indicating that the training gives confidence, enabling staff (and thereby members of the public) to challenge inappropriate behaviours not only in the Leisurewatch sites but also in other public places. Interestingly, TDI asks participants to complete an assessment form about their level of knowledge and awareness of sexual offending pre- and post-training. The post-training forms indicate that knowledge and awareness rises and 20 per cent of participants disclose that they or a close family member have been affected by sexual offending. Broader evaluation of impact is embryonic but developing, with TDI tracking the response of police, probation and MAPPA to any referrals made, and the subsequent outcomes (for example, parole recalls, prosecutions, successful convictions). This database also has the potential to track patterns of offending, identifying the *modus operandi* of individual offenders and the particular locations used by sex offenders.

In addition to Leisurewatch, TDI also contributes to public protection through training and consultancy (including to MAPPA), and developed the first multi-agency protocol for housing sex offenders. TDI also researches specific issues such as service provision for adolescent sex offenders and the service needs of elderly sex offenders. Through a holistic approach utilizing research, training and consultancy, TDI aims to find 'creative solutions' to sexual offending.

Prevention strategies have also extended to violent crime, particularly violent crime associated with alcohol abuse and the 'night time economy'. This comprises awareness campaigns on alcohol use, organizing public transport to ensure safe travel home, marshalling of taxi queues and crowds to avoid confrontation, and giving out lollipops at the end of club nights 'because no one feels angry when they've got a lollipop' (see Home Office 2005b). In some licensed premises, plastic glasses are used to reduce the number of woundings from 'glassing incidents'. Such approaches actively manage the environment to reduce opportunities for crime.

The 'World Health Organisation 2002 report on Violence and Health (Krug 2002) established violence as a global public health issue' (Shepherd 2007: 250). The death rate in the year 2000 from violence across the globe averages at 28.8 per 100,000 (Krug 2002), with Africa and the USA having extremely high rates. Varying levels of injury as well as death can also occur, although figures are less reliable (Krug 2002; Shepherd 2007). Both police and formal crime recording statistics are bedevilled by underreporting (Shepherd 2007), with the self-reports of the year 2000 British Crime Survey indicating that 75 per cent of 'moderately serious' violent offending does not appear in police records (Mirlees-Black et al. 2001; Shepherd 2007). For Shepherd this underreporting and subsequent lack of detection of perpetrators is problematic as the volume of victims presenting to hospital for treatment is increasing.

Night time alcohol related violence has been tackled by a pioneering programme in Cardiff – the Tackling Alcohol-related Street Crime (TASC) project. The project comprised effective liaison between police and licensees; improvements to the behaviour of door staff; training of bar staff; a cognitive behavioural therapy programme for repeat offenders; and targeted policing at 'hot-spots'. TASC was independently evaluated by Maguire and Nettleton (2003; Maguire and Hopkins 2003) for the Home Office, with researchers arguing that TASC resulted in an 8 per cent reduction in violent incidents and that TASC offered value for money in the reduction of health care services subsequently required. The researchers estimated savings of £3200 per offence; with £130,000 for 'serious wounding'; £2040 for other wounding; and £550 for 'common assault' (Maguire and Nettleton 2003).

TASC also illustrates how police intelligence and effective liaison with licensees can provide important information on the nature and context of violent incidents within the night time economy. These can be used to develop preventative strategies such as:

- opposition to entertainment and drinks licences;
- changes to late night transportation;
- changes to police patrols;
- marshalling of taxis;
- policing in pedestrian areas;
- using plastic glasses (to reduce facial injuries from 'glassing').
                    (see Goodwin and Shepherd 2000; Warburton and Shepherd
                                        2004, 2006; Shepherd 2007)

However, as Maguire and Nettleton (2003) importantly point out, TASC failed to influence local planning policy on the location of licensed premises and it failed to gain any agreement to change alcohol marketing strategies. Without these broader strategies, initiatives like TASC run the risk of making only a limited impact. In terms of the targeted nature of the initiative, TASC has made an important contribution to the management of violence in the night time economy, particularly in the volume of persons seeking emergency treatment, with a 35 per cent 'overall decrease' in Cardiff as compared to an '18% decrease in England and Wales over the same period' (Shepherd 2007). Writing from a medical perspective, Shepherd concludes that:

according to Home Office data, by 2005, with the exception of

Cambridge, Colchester, Southend, and York, Cardiff was experiencing lower levels of violence (including robbery) than any other of the 55 towns and cities in England and Wales with a population over 100,000 (Gibbs and Haldenbury 2006).

(Shepherd 2007: 255)

In some areas these measures have been combined with CCTV, enabling rapid deployment of police patrols, reducing both violent incidents and the harm levels arising from them (Sivarajasingam et al. 2003; Shepherd 2007). The TASC initiative has also paid attention to victims, providing a care pathway designed to:

target risk factors such as the locations in which injury was sustained, the weapons and alcohol misuse. It also takes account of the sequelae of violence for mental health (Shepherd 2005). In this care pathway, primary prevention is exemplified by the introduction of toughened and plastic beer glasses, secondary prevention is exemplified by trauma clinic and magistrates court brief alcohol misuse interventions (motivational interviews), and tertiary prevention is exemplified by cognitive-behavioural therapy to treat post-traumatic stress disorder when it occurs.

(Shepherd 2007: 257; see also Watt and Shepherd 2005)

Hall and Winlow (2005) have also examined alcohol related night time violence and place the hedonism of the night time economy (NTE) within a broader societal context of neo-liberalism which emphasizes instrumentalism, individual competitiveness and consumerism (see also Winlow and Hall 2005). Drawing on hospital records and police records they argue that there has been a rise of 100 assaults per year since 1997, and that the NTE are 'hot-spots' 'where over 75 per cent of these rising levels of street violence occur' (2005: 381). The fragmentation of traditional social bonds and collectivities has transformed Britain into a 'more atomized, competitive and aggressive place' (p. 384). The hedonism of the NTE is a prime example of this weakening of cultural and normative bonds: 'For young people whose lives seem to be characterised by personal ambition, anxiety and mounting debt, consumption in the shopping mall and the night time economy has replaced work, class politics and community as the principle locus of identity-construction' (Hall and Winlow 2005: 385). It is perhaps not surprising in these circumstances that the most effective risk management strategy currently on offer is environmental risk management: literally turning disorder into 'controlled disorder' (p. 381).

Social inclusion and integration techniques, including prosocial statutory supervision

Integrative approaches have their roots in restorative justice (Braithwaite 2002). While there is some debate about terminology and conceptual definitions (see McAlinden 2006), the 'general principles of providing restitution to victims and the communities, promoting offender reintegration and repairing relationships between victims, offenders and communities are well understood and increasingly accepted' (McAlinden 2006: 206). However reintegrative strategies with sexual and violent offenders have been seen as particularly challenging, and the reintegrative techniques of restorative justice have been most closely associated with low level crime (Johnstone 2003). Sexual and racial crime has been seen as particularly challenging to restorative approaches (see Hudson 1998).

However, increased criticism of the present legal and punitive approach to sex offenders (and latterly to violent offenders) has led to consideration of integrative approaches as a more effective way of ensuring community safety (see Morris and Gelsthorpe 2000; Hudson 2002; McAlinden 2005). Official statistics indicate that between 1999–2000 and 2001–02 sexual offences increased by 9.6 per cent and that over the last 25 years sexual offences have increased by 94.4 per cent (Recorded Crime Statistics 1898–2001/02). Research by Falshaw et al. (2003) found that actual recidivism rates for sexual offenders are 5.3 times the official reconviction rate.

In brief, commentators critical of retributive and punitive justice have argued that reintegrative approaches can apply to serious crimes, as they promote genuine engagement with offenders and assist the process of change; they hold offenders accountable for their actions; and victims and communities are empowered by becoming part of the solution(s) (see McAlinden 2005 for a review). Restorative approaches to sexual and violent offending have been largely restricted to the arena of intimate family violence, reflecting that around 80 per cent of sexual offending occurs within families or personal networks (Gelles 1997; Grubin 1998), and that most violence towards women by men occurs within family settings (Morris and Gelsthorpe 2000). In the arena of domestic violence, safety plans for women and children have gained from the reinforcement and monitoring of key family/network members as well as professionals (Morris and Gelsthorpe 2000), and from the censure that significant others can place on abusive behaviour. As Morris and Gelsthorpe put it, 'violence is no longer "private" or "personal" ' (2000: 416). The support and modelling of men who are 'anti-violence' is also critical (Braithwaite and Daly (1994), exemplified by probation programmes for violent and abusive men facilitated by male role models (see for example the CHANGE programme in Scotland, in Morran 1996). In addition, Daly (2006) examined 400 cases of youth sexual assault in South Australia and found that conferencing was less of a re-victimizing experience for victims, and that it could potentially produce more effective outcomes for youth sexual offence recidivism than court penalties. Newell (2007) has reviewed the use of restorative justice practice in work with prisoners. Interestingly, the project 'included randomised controlled trials on the medical model, testing the effects of restorative justice in cases where offenders have been remanded in custody awaiting sentence for serious burglary and robbery offences, and for offenders actually serving sentences for violent crime' (2007: 234).

The project is presented positively in terms of reducing prison violence and bullying (see Edgar and Newell 2006 for a full discussion) and has the potential to assist prisoners with handling conflict prosocially on release. Newell draws attention to recent research on work with violent offenders. In particular, the work of Sherman and Strang (2007) which draws on UK and international work to demonstrate the effectiveness of restorative justice with serious violent crime, including positive benefits for victims who suffer less post-traumatic stress. Recidivism for violent offenders in an earlier study dropped by 38 per cent (Sherman et al. 2000). Interestingly nearly 90 per cent of victims take up the restorative justice process and 'Over four-fifths of victims felt that they had received "restitution" as a result of a restorative conference, compared to less than a tenth in court, and, perhaps as a result, the proportion fearing re-victimisation fell from 25 per cent to less than 4 per cent (Strang, Barnes, Braithwaite, Sherman 1999)' (Newell 2007).

Recent work has identified a prosocial approach with offenders (including high risk offenders) as helpful in reducing re-offending (Rex 1999; Trotter 2000, 2007; McNeill and Batchelor 2002). This 'prosocial' approach is underpinned by an assumption that offenders, if given the opportunities to engage effectively, can and will change behaviours in most cases. Promoting change in offenders has been recognized as a key task for the Probation Service (HMIP 1998). Trotter has extensively examined how the supervisory relationship can promote and reinforce change (1993, 1999, 2000). His work emphasizes the key characteristics of both supervisors and supervision practices that promote change. This approach has been characterized as 'prosocial modelling' (Trotter 1999, 2007) and comprises:

- Being clear about the supervisory role, including purpose and expect-ations of supervision, the appropriate use of authority and the role of enforcement.
- Prosocial modelling and reinforcement, involving clear expectations about required values and behaviours, and their reinforcement through the use of rewards. Challenge and confrontation of undesirable behav-iours and the discouragement of procriminal attitudes and values.
- Negotiated problem solving, clear objective setting, monitoring and accountability of the offender's progress.

- Honest, empathic relationship with an emphasis upon persistence and belief in the offender's capacity to change.

(adapted from McNeill and Batchelor 2002: 38;
Trotter 1999, 2000, 2007)

Prosocial supervision has been strongly linked to subsequent falls in recidivism, and while most often associated with the supervision of 'young, high-risk, violent and drug-using offenders' (McNeill and Batchelor 2002: 38), there is growing evidence of its effectiveness with adult high risk offenders (Wood and Kemshall 2007).

Rex (1999) has also highlighted the significance of the worker–offender relationship, and that the 'style' and focus of supervision is significant. Negotiated engagement and partnership in problem solving is important, embedded in 'readiness to change'. This has to be supported by the worker's personal and professional commitment to the change process and to the recommended programme. The latter should be supported by one-to-one work and intensive, individualized relapse prevention work (Rex 1999). Offenders value and benefit from attention to their personal and social problems, and to their personal goals, needs and desires (Ward and Stewart 2003a, b). Feelings of loyalty, commitment and accountability that offenders have to the probation officer/worker can be important in ensuring compliance and commitment to the change process. Holding offenders to account is crucial (without rejection or stigmatization); reinforcing prosocial behaviour is a core activity of supervision (Rex and Matravers 1998); and staff should display a genuine interest in the well-being of offenders (Rex 1999; Ward and Stewart 2003a, b).

In a study of MAPPA, Wood and Kemshall (2007) found that the balance between external and internal controls was the key to effective risk management. Various external controls were employed, including legal requirements, parole conditions, curfews, exclusion zones, residence requirements and the use of unannounced home visiting. While some offenders saw external controls as intrusive, where they could perceive a link between such controls and the management of their behaviour they were more likely to accept and comply with them. In one MAPPA area this approach was supported by the use of contracts with offenders and, while not legal binding, these provided an important starting point for supervision and engaged offenders in planning their own risk management. Engaging the offender and emphasizing the 'Good Lives' model underpinned the best practice observed in the study, with one area achieving success in reintegrating sex offenders back into housing, employment and, for young sex offenders, back into education. Interestingly, this area separated out the delivery of broadly 'welfare' services from risk management services by using different members of staff. However, these services were complementary and offenders welcomed this more holistic approach to their supervision. Staff also noted that restrictive conditions (particularly their overuse) could have an adverse affect. The HMIP thematic on sex offenders noted that sex offenders subject to restrictive measures may struggle with social isolation and experience difficulties with community reintegration (HMIP and HMIC 2005; Levenson and Cotter 2005a). To some extent, reintegrative techniques such as COSA help to combat this. As Cesaroni puts it, circles help to reintegrate the 'worst of the worst' (2001).

In addition, sex offenders, and particularly high risk sexually violent offenders, lack social support and are social isolates. This can impact upon normal social learning and 'seems to have a decisive impact on normal and deviant behaviour' (Bandura 1977 in Gutierrez-Lobos et al. 2001).

Internal controls were defined as those used by the offender to manage their own behaviour and include how to recognize and avoid key offending triggers and risky situations, and how to employ relapse prevention techniques. Intensive treatment programmes supported by one-to-one work were perceived by staff to be the most effective method of promoting internal controls.

Relapse prevention

As stated above, relapse prevention was seen by staff as a key component of successful risk management strategies with high risk offenders (although the research evidence on the impact of relapse prevention is still emerging). The MAPPA area that focused more intensively on relapse prevention had emerging empirical evidence of higher success rates, although this would need to be the subject of further evaluation.

Relapse is a return to problematic behaviours and/or re-offending. Attention to preventing relapse and maintaining the impact of the programme intervention is required as well as to the delivery of the programme (Laws 1999, 2003; Ward and Hudson 2000; Ward, Purvis and Devilly 2004). Relapse prevention attempts to prevent the prisoner/offender returning to problematic behaviours and offending. It may target:

- negative attitudes and antisocial feelings – for example, victim blaming, justifying offending or behaviours as a legitimate way to get what is wanted;
- situations of high risk (such as contact with children);
- 'unconscious' or 'seemingly unimportant decisions' that result in grooming activities and offending – that is small, trivial decisions that appear individually reasonable but build up to offending (for example, choice of daily activities that create proximity to children or other potential victims);

- feelings of fatalism and lack of coping, failure to manage stressors and negative events in the offender/prisoner's life: 'I can't cope'; 'Why should I bother? I never succeed'; 'No one cares what I do', etc.

Relapse prevention programmes also promote self-regulation and self-risk management by offenders. This will include helping the offender to recognize the key factors of relapse for her/him and working out specific and detailed strategies to manage them. Programmes may target:

- the offender – for example, having helplines open at vulnerable times so that those tempted to re-offend can ring in and talk it through with their case manager;
- potential victims – for example, having a rapid response helpline for those who have been, or feel they are in danger of being, threatened.

(from Kemshall et al. 2006)

Integrative models, particularly those based on the GLM, tend to place greater emphasis upon relapse prevention rather than mere enforcement.

What is the potential for restorative approaches?

Despite recent positive research, particularly in Canada (e.g., on COSA), restorative approaches require more research, particularly longitudinal studies to establish their effectiveness on recidivism. However, these studies do indicate that they have enormous potential that requires further exploration (see for example Wilson et al. 2002). Lack of treatment programmes for offenders who do come forward has also been identified as problematic (for example, from the Stop It Now! Helpline, see Kemshall et al. 2004). It has also been contended that restorative approaches are more difficult to operate in communities and societies with looser networks and weaker social bonds (McAlinden 2005), and therefore transferability to all social contexts cannot be assumed. Daly (2006) has provided detailed empirical evidence of the effectiveness of restorative justice with 'gendered violence' although restorative approaches have also been criticized on the grounds that they cannot respond to serious crime and have a limited transferability from the realm of intimate family violence (e.g., domestic violence). Initiatives like COSA challenge this view, and, as McAlinden (2005) argues, restorative and retributive approaches are not necessarily mutually exclusive. They can be effectively combined as in COSA in Canada and in the UK, Thames Valley. The initiative is used post-custody and integrates with multi-agency, statutory supervision. This combined use of a penal sanction and a reintegrative strategy under statutory supervision ensures legitimacy, strengthens accountability and ensures safeguards (the usual criticisms of restorative approaches, see Paternoster et al. 1997; Ashworth 2002; Roche 2003).

As McAlinden argues:

> The restorative or re-integrative justice paradigm does not have all the answers. It is often met with controversy, particularly where 'gendered and sexualised violence' (Hudson 2002) is concerned. In the absence of workable alternatives, however, there is a need to extend the use of restorative justice to the most difficult of societal problems, like child sexual abusers and child sexual abuse. Its potential benefits for improving the safety of victims, for providing relief for communities and for rehabilitating offenders may mean that it is worth careful experiment.
>
> (2005: 388)

Restorative and reintegrative approaches may also make an important contribution to criminal justice and penal policy beyond their contribution in individual cases. Primarily they offer a different way of thinking and responding to crime and to offenders, particularly in a climate that is dominated by a 'tough on crime' paradigm. Violent and sexual offenders can be less demonized, and the contemporary caricature of the offender as the 'rational choice actor' who can be punished or corrected into more prudential choices can be challenged (Kemshall 2006a). Rather, the offender can be reconstituted more holistically as a person requiring social support and integration in order to change.

Summary

Community protection risk management strategies have been characterized by CBT programmes emphasizing corrective thinking often combined with restrictive conditions. While evaluations of 'what works' have increasingly identified 'what works for whom', the CBT approach has been recently refined by increased attention to the 'Good Lives' model, motivational goal setting, attention to relapse prevention and prosocial modelling/supervision. This has been paralleled by increased attention to integrative approaches rooted in the restorative justice paradigm – epitomized primarily by COSA and to a more limited extent by Stop It Now! and The Derwent Initiative. Integrative approaches have yet to be fully and independently evaluated, but early results are promising. In Canada and the UK in particular they are being effectively combined with more traditional community protection approaches such as MAPPA to good effect.

Notes

1 See Glossary for further definition and details of randomized control trials.
2 See Glossary for further details.
3 *Preventing Child Sexual Abuse; What We All Need to Know to Protect Our Children; Child's Play? Preventing Abuse Among Children and Young People; The Internet and Children: What's the Problem?* Available at: www.stopitnow.org.uk.

Further reading

Brown, S. (2005) *Treating Sex Offenders: An Introduction to Sex Offender Treatment.* Cullompton: Willan.

DeLisi, M. and Conis, P. (2007) *Violent Offenders: Theory, Research, Public Policy and Practice.* New York: Jones and Bartlett Publishers.

Ward, T. and Stewart, C. (2003a) Criminogenic needs and human needs: a theoretical model, *Psychology, Crime and Law*, 31(3): 282–305.

Ward, T. and Maruna, S. (2007) *Rehabilitation.* London: Routledge.

Wilson, R. J., Huculak, B. and McWhinnie, A. (2002) Restorative justice innovations in Canada, *Behavioural Sciences and the Law*, 20: 363–80.

chapter six

Key issues in managing high risk offenders

Introduction

This chapter reviews some of the key issues in the community management of high risk offenders, in particular: risks versus rights; ethical dilemmas in decision making; community notification and third party disclosure; and difficulties in evaluating the effectiveness of differing approaches to high risk offenders. These issues tax academics, practitioners and policy makers alike, and have been differently resolved in differing jurisdictions. While the Anglophone countries in particular have adopted the community protection model to varying degrees, the response to these issues is by no means uniform, either across them or within them. This chapter will draw on material from Canada, the USA, the UK and Australia/New Zealand to illustrate these differences.

Risks versus rights [1]

The tension between risks and rights was brought into sharp focus by the Serious Further Offence review on Anthony Rice (HMIP 2006b). Anthony Rice was a UK life sentence prisoner who murdered Naomi Bryant nine months after his release on licence. This report raised the key issue of the tension between public protection and human rights, expressed by the Chief Inspector of the English and Welsh Probation Service thus:

> The MAPPA faced comparable challenges to those faced by the Prison Service and the Parole Board – challenges from Rice and his solicitor that the restrictions he was under contravened his human rights. The MAPPA certainly did not roll over in response to these – the February 2006 meeting held to the 'lone woman', and to the boundary (as amended) licence conditions despite the threat of judicial review. But it is clear that in their deliberations they gave more attention to justifying the proportionality of the restrictions than to planning how to manage them effectively. This is where the available guidance on maintaining an investigative approach in this work might be especially useful.
>
> (HMIP 2006b: 63)

The subsequent recommendation made the Inspectorate's position clear:[2] 'When managing a High Risk of Harm offender in the community, although proper attention should be given to the human rights issues, the relevant authorities involved should maintain in practice a top priority focus on the public protection requirements of the case' (HMIP 2006b: 64). This report in effect presented public protection and human rights as pulling in opposite directions, and that practitioners are presented with difficult either/or choices.

However, the polarization of risks and rights has not been entirely helpful. The current government position in the UK is clear, with an unambiguous instruction that public bodies 'give proper priority to public protection when considering the individual rights of the offender' (Hansard 2006). Further guidance has since been issued, partially to make the position clear for staff in public bodies, but also to dispel the myths, media distortion and misunderstandings that have come to plague this area (see DCA 2006). The DCA review outlines the 'the overriding importance of the State's duty to take suitable measures to protect public safety' (2006: 35). In the case of Rice, the DCA notes that once a prisoner has passed his/her tariff date:

> the authorities have to justify keeping a prisoner in custody rather than having to justify why he should be released. In fact they should be balancing the prisoner's rights under the European Convention on

Human Rights with restrictions which are proportionate given the risk of harm to the public he presents. Secondly, there seems to be insufficient recognition that the prison, parole and probation services are themselves subject to a positive obligation under the Human Rights Act to take proper steps to protect the public from dangerous criminals such as Rice.

(DCA 2006: 27)

The DCA review notes that the Human Rights Act has been 'misunderstood by the public', has been misapplied, and 'too much attention has been paid to individual rights at the expense of the interests of the wider community' (2006: 29). The review notes a number of myths and misperceptions that have taken root in the imagination of both practitioners and public alike. The Lord Chancellor in February 2007 in the Harry Street lecture at Manchester University outlined the impact of a number of these myths and misperceptions on the work of criminal justice (see www.dca.gov.uk/speeches/2007/sp070209.htm accessed 23 November 2007). He argued that decisions were a 'matter of commonsense' and that: 'People's human rights have to work in a way in which they can resolve conflicts – day to day conflicts – where the rights of the individual have to be balanced against the rights of the community'. Commonsense is seen as the key to resolving conflicts that may arise, and in preserving public confidence in the Human Rights Act. In making this appeal to commonsense the Lord Chancellor also roots human rights within a particular value base. These values encompass protection for the individual from the State, flexibility when rights conflict, and a practical implementation of human rights which recognizes the need to protect the citizen: 'in the context that the rights of the community have in many cases to be balanced against the rights of the individual: freedom of expression versus privacy; liberty versus protection from crime' (www.dca.gov.uk/speeches/2007/sp070209.htm accessed 23 November 2007).

These values are firmly set within a community protection model that prioritizes victims and community safety. The emphasis is upon a practical, balanced and proportionate response to tensions between risks and rights. The current UK use of discretionary disclosure to third parties is one example of a proportionate, balanced and practical resolution of the right to privacy and the need for victim and community protection (this is discussed in more detail below). The public disclosure of information about sex offenders in the USA, or 'community notification' as it is known, is one area where the rights of the community have been significantly asserted over the rights of offenders. Within the UK a more pragmatic and balanced approach has been taken (this is discussed further below).

The recourse to 'commonsense' also serves to neutralize debate about risk, discrimination and potential injustice (see Whitty 2007 for a discussion of the complex interpretations of 'risk' and 'rights' in contemporary debates).

Commonsensically the 'Other' is seen as undeserving of justice. However, as Hudson (2003: 201) puts it:

> The great challenge postmodernism poses is: how are we to do justice to those who are incomprehensibly Other? How do we give a respectful, attentive hearing, accepting our responsibility to respond with justice, to the incomprehensibly outsider narrative, to the stories of those we react to as irrational, bizarre, hostile, perhaps monstrous, and of course risky?

Such individualization of risk and the creation of 'monsters' can obscure structurally-based risks and structural constraints on the opportunities for change afforded to offenders (Denney 2005); and the potential for such risks to become inflated and institutionalized (e.g., 'stranger-danger' as opposed to familial sexual abuse of children, see Kitzinger 2004). Denney (following Hudson 2000, 2001, 2003) has summarized this position well:

> The culture of rights is essentially inclusive, where no one is outside the constituency of justice, while an over-emphasis upon risk can serve to fracture society and stigmatise particular groups who are framed as a threat or danger (Hudson 2001). Justice and due process appear less important than 'risk' in that the politics of 'safety' have overwhelmed considerations of 'justice'. If someone, or some category of persons, is categorised as a risk to public safety, there seems to remain scarcely any sense that they are nevertheless owed justice. The vocabulary of justice is almost entirely absent from current debates about sexual offending, safety in public places and mass surveillance techniques (Hudson 2000).
> (Denney 2005: 130)

The commonsense presentation of rights may potentially exacerbate these issues, framed as it is within a 'culture of risks' rather than a 'culture of rights' – and it is essential to recognize this framing in order to interpret correctly the UK's current approach to risks and rights. This approach is repeated in most of the Anglophone countries, although Western Europe has largely resisted this approach. For example, sex offender registers are still uncommon across the European Union (Thomas 2004b). While the trend may be towards prioritizing risks above justice (Hudson 2000, 2001, 2003), there are significant 'firewalls' to the inexorable risk of risk (O'Malley 2001). For example, in the UK, the use of civil commitment as a mechanism for the social control and regulation of the 'dangerous' has been largely resisted (Royal College of Psychiatrists 1996, 2004), although its overuse in America has been well documented (Petrunik 2002). Extended supervision and compulsory treatment post-custody has also been criticized by mental health professionals, including criticism of the community protection benefits of the Serious Sex Offenders Monitoring Act (2005) in Australia. This act allows for up to 15 years extended post-custody supervision and compulsory treatment, including polygraph testing and chemical castration (Birgden 2007). Birgden argues that rather than being measures based on evidence and sound social policy, the current Australian measures to regulate sex offenders are rooted in a 'tough on crime' stance and 'populist punitiveness' – with little evaluative evidence that they will actually reduce sexual recidivism. Indeed Birgden argues that the Act may well have the opposite effect because of offender alienation and disengagement from therapeutic regimes.

There is, then, the potential for some resistance to an uncritical community protection paradigm, not least because practitioners do not always share or implement its objectives (Kemshall 1998a), and the erosion of rights and justice principles can be resisted and resented (Hudson 2000), for example by the legal profession continuing to promote 'due process', fairness and impartiality (Creighton 2007). It is important to recognize that policies are often mediated by the agencies and staff tasked with implementing them (Maynard-Moody et al. 1990). Workers bring their own values and ideologies to bear on policy interpretation and delivery. They may, for example, focus on reintegration and resettlement as well as risk, on rehabilitation as well as protection. The 'best practice' risk management in the English and Welsh Probation Service outlined in Chapter 5, this volume, is a key example of such practical daily balancing achieved by staff. The current best practice approaches to disclosure outlined below are another key example.

Ethical issues

The community management of high risk offenders presents a number of key ethical issues, not least risk prediction related to release from custody or mental health institutions. Prediction of risk, particularly where associated with restriction of liberty, has long challenged practitioners tasked with risk assessment. The mental health profession has resisted prediction on the grounds of both legal liability (see Monahan 1993 on 'Tarasoff liability') and the ethical dilemmas presented by fallible risk assessment tools (Royal College of Psychiatrists 1996, 2004). This is well expressed by Monahan:

> Imagine that one person in 1,000 will kill. Imagine also that an exceptionally accurate test has been devised which can predict with 95% accuracy those who will kill and those who will not. In a population of 100,000 out of the 100 who would have killed 95 will be correctly identified. Out of the 99,900 who will not kill, 4995 will be identified as potential murderers. The cost to the wrongly identified is enormous.
>
> (Monahan 1981: 90)

Moore (1996) has simply expressed the tension between True Positive Predictions and False Positive Predictions presented in Figure 6.1.

Box A and D are correct predictions: that a serious offence will occur (true positive) or that it will not (true negative). Box B identifies those cases in which a serious offence is not predicted but does occur, and Box C identifies those cases in which a serious offence is predicted but does not occur. In Box B the consequences can be severe, with victims and members of the public being harmed. Box C cases result in overintervention, misplaced resources and infringements on individuals' rights and liberties. Perversely, Box B and C errors can be reduced but usually only by transferring errors between them, and not by increasing true positive or true negative predictions. There is a potential for community protection models to produce more Box C errors due to the prioritization of community safety and the precautionary principle. The rate of Box B and C errors is often a matter of what society finds tolerable and acceptable – for example, Box C errors are readily accepted where paedophiles are concerned and the attitude to overprediction is 'better safe than sorry'. This 'precautionary principle' (Hood and Jones 1996) can be very powerful and leads to net widening, overintrusion and defensive (rather than defensible) practice (Kemshall 1998a).

Improvements in risk assessment tools, including the development of what Bonta and Wormith (2007) have called 'fourth generation' tools, have increased the certainty of risk prediction and, as importantly, the matching of offenders to interventions. Reducing methodological, organizational and human error can improve the quality and reliability of decision making, therefore reducing the ethical dilemmas for practitioners by raising the certainty of risk assessments (see Kemshall et al. 2006).

In managing high risk offenders, practitioners will also be required to balance the rights and safety of victims and public against the rights and

		Prediction	
		Yes	No
O u t c o m e	Yes	A True positive prediction	B False negative prediction
	No	C False positive prediction	D True negative prediction

Figure 6.1 Prediction outcomes

Source: Moore 1996: 10.

safety of offenders. This most often arises where offenders reside near to, or begin to 'groom', children or other potential victims. Within the UK, decisions regarding such third party disclosure have been addressed in law, and latterly within the MAPPA Guidance (Home Office 2004a; Ministry of Justice 2007); and in the USA and Canada they are largely covered by community notification. Within the UK the disclosure of information between agencies is supported and enshrined in legislation (Crime and Disorder Act 1998; see Power 2003). A much discussed landmark case is *R v Chief Constable of North Wales ex p Thorpe and another* (1998) in which the court allowed disclosure not just to a known past victim of their immediate family, but to selected members of the wider public. In this case, North Wales police wished to disclose that a couple with previous convictions for child sexual abuse were living on a caravan park, and revealed their identities and offence history to the owners/managers of the park (Power 2003: 85). The decision was supported although 'blanket disclosure' was not approved. An earlier case, *R v Devon County Council ex parte L* (1991) had also upheld the right of a social services department to disclose to a woman with children that her new co-habitee was suspected of abusing children (Nash 2006). In essence, the offender's right to privacy can be overridden to prevent further crime and to protect victims (particularly vulnerable victims).

Community notification

Sex offender registration requires sexual offenders to register their addresses, personal information, offence history and employment (Petrunik 2002; Cohen and Jeglic 2007), and can be used without community notification – that is without notifying the public. Registers are administered by the police. In the UK, the Sex Offender Register was introduced in 1997 and currently does not extend to public disclosure. Limited or 'discretionary disclosure' occurs in the UK with professionals disclosing to targeted individuals where the risk justifies it (see below for full discussion). In the USA, community notification applies to sex offenders once released into the community, and allows for both registration and public/community disclosure about sex offenders. In practice it can take many forms and in the USA community notification is known colloquially as 'Megan's Law', named after Megan Kanka, a young girl sexually assaulted and murdered by a known sex offender.[3] Within the USA following this initial state law, community notification is now a federal law (see the Jacob Wetterling Act, Cohen and Jeglic 2007; Levenson 2003), and applies in all states, requiring states to 'make relevant information on released offenders available to the general public' (Cohen and Jeglic 2007: 374). However, the law does not mandate how states should do this, and in practice community notification is variable. Cohen and Jeglic identify four different models:

1   The first model is active notification based upon a three-tier model of dangerousness. Tier 1 are low risk, have not committed predatory sexual acts and have successfully completed treatment. Tier 2 present a moderate risk and are seen as more likely to re-offend. Tier 3 offenders are seen as high risk, with an inclination to re-offend if they have the opportunity to do so. Notification is driven by these tiers, with tier 1 not required to notify; tier 2 required to notify specific groups deemed to be at risk (e.g., boy scouts); and tier 3 required to notify all relevant persons the offender may come into contact with, and the process can include the use of posters, placards, press releases and so on (see Russell 2005).

2   The second model uses notification by a designated agency, according to state determined categories of risk and methods of notification. The agencies merely carry out the process but have no input into determining the process of notification (Finn 1997).

3   The third model requires sex offenders to carry out notification under the supervision of state agencies. This can include personally telling neighbours, giving out letters, posters and putting up placards.

4   The fourth model is a passive system and requires members of the community to make a request for information. This can be done through state sponsored websites, e.g., www.klaaskids.org (accessed 22 November 2007).

(Cohen and Jeglic 2007: 374)

Evaluation of the effectiveness of community notification in protecting children and communities is difficult given these radically different models operating across the USA. From the few studies available there are some important emerging issues to consider. Community notification laws do little to protect children from sexual assaults carried out by adults they know, which is still the source of most sexual offending against children (Catalano 2005). Community notification may also have a minimal effect on recidivism (Berliner et al. Milloy 1995; Lieb 1996; Adkins et al. 2000; Pawson 2002). In a study comparing registered and unregistered sex offenders (the latter were released prior to the implementation of the law), no statistical difference was found in a comparison of tier 3 offenders (the most risky). Indeed, 'sex offenders who were registered recidivated more quickly than those who were not' (Schram and Milloy 1995 in Cohen and Jeglic 2007: 375) – although an explanation for this is not clear. Further difficulties have been encountered, not least the resource difficulty in implementing community notification by criminal justice agencies; difficulties in enforcing registration and notification; sex offenders 'going underground'; and the negative impact on sex offenders themselves from vigilante action and social isolation (see Scholle 2000; Zevitz and Farkas 2000a, b; Petrunik 2002). Zevitz and Farkas (2000a, b) found that community notification drained police resources, especially in those areas where public notification meetings are routinely held.

In addition, information on registers has been found to be inaccurate, and there are difficulties in maintaining the integrity of the system (Tewksbury 2002; Levenson and Cotter 2005b). Fitch, in a review for the NSPCC on the viability of a Megan's Law for the UK, came to similar conclusions (Fitch 2006; see also Lovell 2001). In September 2006, Gerry Sutcliffe, the Home Office Minister of the time, announced after an extensive review and visit to USA schemes, that the UK would not be adopting a Megan's Law.

In a study comprising 30 interviews with sex offenders, Zevitz and Farkas (2000b) found that offenders' fear of community retribution made them less likely to register and that notification laws would not necessarily make them less likely to offend. Indeed they contend that stress, fear and anxiety may be the precursors of relapse and lead to higher rates of recidivism. Levenson (2003) has argued that community notification can erode treatment compliance and effectiveness by removing responsibility for rehabilitation and risk management from the offender. However, Elbogen et al. (2003) found that perceptions of 'fairness' or 'unfairness' were related to offender perceptions of their likely compliance with community notification, take-up of treatment and incentives to avoid re-offending. However, Elbogen et al. did not assess the impact of community notification on treatment and recidivism, and the study is small scale and restricted to the Nebraska notification system.

Offender perceptions of community notification are therefore complex, and how these perceptions relate to issues of treatment compliance and recidivism requires further research. Tewksbury and Lees (2007), for example, found that sex offenders could accept the rationale for a register, but wished to distinguish themselves from 'dangerous' or 'predatory' sex offenders, and many believed that they themselves did not warrant registration. This is supported by the research of Sample and Bray (2006) who found that sex offenders are not the homogeneous group presumed by sex offender policy and legislation, and that differing categories of sex offender have differing re-arrest patterns and differing levels of risk. Sex offenders also saw the length of registration as overly punitive and not helpful in seeking treatment or in achieving rehabilitation. The majority of offenders expressed 'the cynical view that registries are highly inefficient and ineffective for reducing recidivism' (Tewksbury and Lees 2007: 402). The 'collateral consequences' of registration for sex offenders are social stigmatization, loss of employment and relationships, loss of housing and increased homelessness, and physical assaults/harassment (Tewksbury 2005).

More recently, community notification has been combined with supervision on the grounds that merely knowing where an offender is has little actual impact on risky behaviours and, in particular, community notification has been more effectively combined with initiatives like Circles of Support and Accountability (see Chapter 5, this volume). COSA has also lowered community anxiety and retribution, as merely telling communities leaves them feeling anxious, fearful and resentful (Beck and Travis 2004). As Cohen and Jeglic put it: '. . . in a community that receives multiple sex offender warnings, community members may feel overwhelmed or even fatigued by the notifications because they cannot maintain their everyday lives while simultaneously trying to protect themselves and their families . . . notification induces fear' (2007: 377).

The situation in the UK

The Sex Offenders Act 1997 created the UK's Sex Offender Register which came into effect on 1 September 1997 (see Thomas 2004b for a full review). As with the USA, the origins of the UK Register lay in increased anxiety about sex offenders and a desire to improve interagency working and child protection processes (Thomas 2004b). By 2000, the Home Office had published an evaluation of the Register (Plotnikoff and Woolfson 2000), revealing that while multi-agency work had improved, there were difficulties in adequately maintaining the Register and in ensuring offender compliance with registration procedures. Notwithstanding such issues, compliance was put at 94.7 per cent (Plotnikoff and Woolfson 2000) although, as Thomas states, whether this effectively reduced recidivism was unclear (2004b; Hebenton and Thomas 1997). The Register requirements were subsequently strengthened by Schedule Five of the Criminal Justice and Court Services Act 2000. Despite pressure from the public and media campaigns for public access to the Register, this was resisted, although lay representation on MAPPA was put in place to allay public clamours for access.

More recently, a Violent and Sexual Offender Register (VISOR) has been piloted in the UK (PC 2006d). VISOR is in essence, a 'dangerous offenders' data-base, containing personal details, offence histories, risk assessments, risk management plans and photographs. It is intended to assist MAPPA with the identification, risk assessment and management of violent and sexual offenders. Originating in police forces, 2006–07 saw VISOR fully extended to the Probation Service and to criminal justice social work departments in Scotland. The joint use of VISOR should enable 'the sharing of risk assessment and risk management information on individual offenders in a timely way . . . and increases the ability to share intelligence and enable the safe transfer of key information when these offenders move, in turn enhancing public protection' (PC 2006d: 2). The VISOR pilots are currently the subject of evaluation.

Despite calls for a UK Megan's Law following the abduction and murder of Sarah Payne by Roy Whiting in 2000 (see the *News of the World* campaign for Sarah's Law, *News of the World* 2000a, b, 2001), the UK has not adopted public disclosure or community notification as per the USA models. Within the UK 'discretionary' or 'limited' disclosure is adopted (although there are currently five pilots allowing parents to gain further information about adults their children have contact with).

Current UK arrangements for discretionary disclosure allow MAPPA to disclose to third parties with the criteria for disclosure set out by the MAPPA Guidance (Home Office 2004a: paras. 93–5; and Ministry of Justice 2007):

- the offender presents a serious risk of harm to the person;
- there is no other practicable, less intrusive means of protecting the individual(s), and failure to disclose would put them in danger;
- the risk to the offender should be considered although it should not outweigh the potential risk to others were disclosure not to be made;
- the disclosure is to the right person;
- consider consulting the offender;
- ensure that whoever has been given the information knows what to do with it;
- before disclosing, ask them what they know about the offender.

Hence disclosures are heavily controlled, carried out by professionals to a limited number of persons and justified on the grounds of individual and public safety.

In a study of three MAPPA areas, Wood and Kemshall (2007) found that all areas were using their discretionary powers to disclose. This was confirmed by Cann's research of 40 police areas on the use of discretionary disclosure (Cann 2007). In Cann's study the primary reason for disclosure was child protection, either of a known or potential victim or to protect children in specific places such as swimming pools. While Cann found some variation in disclosure practice and makes recommendations for improving consistency of use, third party limited disclosure had been used on the whole positively. Wood and Kemshall's study focused in-depth on practice in three MAPPA areas and presents detailed examples of 'best practice'.

In Wood and Kemshall's study MAPPA areas reported that most disclosures were made with the consent of the offender, and areas encouraged offenders to self-disclose and then followed this up for accuracy, this might include staff accompanying offenders when disclosures were made. Where offenders do not consent or undertake the disclosure themselves, a consistent process is operated. The multi-agency public protection panel considers disclosure and makes a recommendation to the Assistant Chief Constable and, if approved, a disclosure takes place (nationally this is also the usual process, see Cann 2007). Such disclosures are usually checked with legal services. Figure 6.2 outlines this best practice process.

Confirming the national findings of Cann (2007), discretionary disclosure

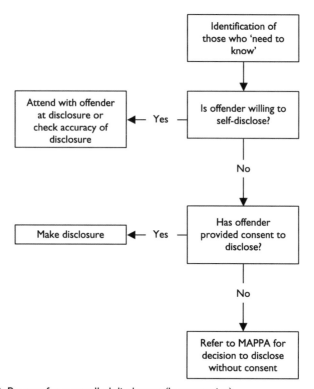

Figure 6.2 Process for controlled disclosure (best practice)

Source: Wood and Kemshall 2007: 17; reproduced with the kind permission of the Crown.

is made to a range of personnel and agencies, including employers, land-lords, educational institutions (e.g., colleges), voluntary groups, church groups and individuals deemed to be 'at risk' (see Cann 2007: 7 for a full breakdown). Residence and employment are the main reasons precipitating disclosure. Supervising officers and public protection panels consider dis-closure carefully, and the following factors are significant in their decisions:

- there is evidence that grooming behaviours are occurring (e.g., through churches, scout groups, volunteering, employment);
- where others (including service users) might be at risk (for example, in accommodation) – it is extremely rare for service users to be told, but staff and managers are routinely told in order to facilitate monitoring and for greater vigilance to be exerted;
- to protect past and potential victims – sex offenders may enter new relationships where children and grandchildren are at risk; in these cases, partners and family members will be told, and in a very few cases, neighbours with children have been told;

- in the case of young sex offenders, disclosures may be made to college staff to ensure protection of other students.

(from Wood and Kemshall 2007: 18)

MAPPA staff were aware that disclosures had to be handled with care to avoid potential vigilante action, retribution against offenders, and disrupting or undermining risk management plans. To achieve this, staff prepared third parties for the information and thoroughly discussed it with them. Differing levels of disclosure were also used, for example the MAPPA may decide to disclose key triggers and risk factors but to withhold a full offence history. The trigger factors enable third parties to know what to look out for and what to do if they see them. Full offence histories may only heighten fear and anxiety. Consistent and robust procedures for supporting third parties are essential, for example rapid telephone contact with key personnel or supervising officers. MAPPA personnel and supervising officers were consistent in their view that this discretionary approach was effective. In particular, it was seen to reduce anxiety for third party recipients who were clear as to what to do and why, and who else they could or could not disclose to. Disclosure had also engaged other agencies and professionals (particularly the voluntary sector) in the effective management of sex offenders. In a few instances, third parties had disclosed to others, presenting some problems of public disorder and increasing the drain on police resources. Staff recognized the importance of trying to assess carefully the integrity of third parties to whom they disclosed, although it was recognized that there would always be some limited cases in which inadvertent further disclosure might take place.

Consequences of disclosure are not always negative for the offender. As Cann (2007) notes, disclosure did not always lead to the termination of intimate relationships or employment. As Cann states: 'In some cases an offender's partner engaged with the MAPPA in managing risk, while remaining in the relationship' (2007: 9) and 'many offenders continued with work and other activities (e.g., church attendance), but disclosure allowed this to take place under supervision or when children were not present' (2007: 9). The alleviation of potentially negative consequences was greatly assisted by the use of 'behavioural contracts' in one MAPPA area (Wood and Kemshall 2007). These contracts enabled offenders to return to college, employment, or to attend church or work with voluntary groups. Contracts typically comprise:

- I will attend church only at the 8.30 am and 6.30 pm services;
- I will ensure that I sit apart from children and young people in the church;
- I will ensure that I am never alone with children and young people at church or at church groups/activities;

- I will not involve myself in any way with children and young people;
- I accept that certain people within the church will need to be aware of this contract and that this will be on a 'need to know basis'; I understand that I will be aware of the people who are given this information and the reason why they need to have this information;
- I understand that if these conditions are broken the church will have no alternative but to prohibit me from attending and will have a responsibility to report this to my probation officer.

(from Wood and Kemshall 2007: 19; reproduced in the MAPPA Guidance, Ministry of Justice 2007b: Section 15).

Interestingly offenders appreciate such behavioural contracts and understand the rationale for disclosure. Those disclosure strategies that actively involved the offender were most accepted, and offenders who had experienced disclosure in this way saw it as justified and reasonable (Wood and Kemshall 2007). Offenders feared public disclosure and felt this would make registration and supervision compliance more difficult, and their resettlement into communities and into employment would be compromised (a position supported by the research of Hudson 2005). Tewksbury and Lees in an American study found that registered sex offenders fear public access, and saw it as leading to stigmatization and harassment. However, the need for a register was generally accepted by sex offenders (Wood and Kemshall 2007).

MAPPA staff saw community notification as counterproductive, not least because of the potential for public disorder (already experienced on a limited scale); offenders 'disappearing'; the potential for risk management plans to be severely undermined by local residents (some instances had already occurred and the risk had escalated); the costs of administering a public disclosure system (a position adopted nationally, see Cann 2007). In a climate where MAPPA resources were seen as overstretched, adding to the burden was seen as problematic, particularly as the positive outcomes of public disclosure were doubted. In interview and focus groups, MAPPA staff expressed the view that while a reasonable political measure and while it may initially reassure the public, a Megan's Law had limited (if any) positive outcomes to offer, and the current system of discretionary limited disclosure was seen as working effectively (Wood and Kemshall 2007: 20). More recently, a limited use of public disclosure has been utilized to find high risk sex offenders who have 'gone missing'. This has been through the Child Exploitation and Online Protection Centre (CEOP) 'Most Wanted' list with some announcements on TV and radio (www.crimestoppers-uk.org/ceop/ accessed 20 November 2006). This has been restricted to a few cases per year and has had some success in locating missing offenders. Following the 2006–07 sex offender review the Ministry of Justice has proposed a pilot scheme to allow parents to 'register a child-protection interest in a named individual with whom they have a personal relationship and who has regular unsupervised access to their child' (Ministry of Justice 2007a: 1). This pilot is currently running in five areas in England and Wales.

Supervision and monitoring

Supervision and monitoring have recently been seen as important complementary processes to community notification in the USA (Cohen and Jeglic 2007), and in the UK they are seen as essential to the effective community management of high risk offenders (HMIP 2006a, b). Global Positioning System (GPS) electronic monitoring has been used in the USA to counter registration non-compliance and to track offenders who 'go underground', and similar initiatives have been considered in the UK (see Mair 2005; Nellis 2005, 2006, 2007; NAO 2006). Studies indicate success in locating and monitoring the whereabouts of sex offenders, notwithstanding some technical problems, and that tracking can be used to monitor compliance with exclusion zones (Beck and Klein-Staffan 1990; Vollum and Hale 2002; Cohen and Jeglic 2007). However, the overuse of exclusion zones has been seen as problematic, preventing employment/education and destroying access to supportive or family networks (Levenson and Cotter 2005a; Worth 2005). Levenson and Cotter identify 14 states that have exclusion zones prohibiting sex offenders from living within close proximity to a school, park, daycare centre or school bus stop (p. 168). They note that the zones range from 500 feet to up to 2000 feet and in California to a quarter of a mile from a school, and prohibits sex offenders residing within 35 miles of a victim or witness. Interestingly, they cite studies in which the evidence for proximity to children resulting in recidivism is mixed (see Walker et al. 2001; Minnesota Department of Corrections 2003; Colorado Department of Public Safety 2004). They contend that the overuse of exclusion zones may result in homelessness and transience thus making risk management harder. It also produces illogical responses to risk, potentially displacing risk onto more vulnerable people, summed up by one offender thus: 'I couldn't live in an adult mobile home park because a church was 880ft away and had a children's class that met once a week. I was forced to move to a motel where right next door to my room was a family with three children – but it qualified under the rule' (Levenson and Cotter 2005a : 175).

Supervision has been seen as an important component of monitoring, including electronic monitoring, to ensure offender compliance with behaviour change as well as merely being in certain places (Cohen and Jeglic 2007). Supervision has also been seen as central to enhancing offender accountability and responsibility for their actions, and in facilitating regular review of progress (Cohen and Jeglic 2007). However, questions remain as to whether merely extending supervision periods impacts on recidivism

(Cohen and Jeglic 2007), and whether intensive supervision is targeted at the riskiest offenders (Petrunik 2002; see also Hanson et al. 2007).

In a large study of 917 sex offenders on probation across 17 states in the USA, Melloy (2005) found that informal social controls, in particular a committed partner and stable accommodation with social support networks were important factors in ensuring success on probation. In addition, sex offenders were not a homogeneous group and had differing failure rates on probation depending on formal and informal social control factors and the types of risk triggers associated with specific offence types. Melloy argues that further research informing practice in selecting offenders for probation would be welcome.

Craissati, a consultant forensic psychologist at the Bracton Centre in the UK, has argued that overly restrictive risk management may have paradoxical results by reducing compliance and precipitating failure and that there is 'a fine line between control and persecution' (2007: 227). She concludes by saying:

> social exclusion – in the current climate – seems to be an unavoidable consequence of rigorous risk management. It seems to be counter-intuitive, and yet some of these higher-risk offenders appear to do better when left alone and given freedom, although judging just when that should happen seems impossibly difficult. However, such offenders are hypersensitive to perceived injustice and are unusually astute in recognising when stringent risk management has lost its focus and become a defensive institutional measure. The possibility that stringent risk management approaches embodied within the MAPPA re-creates – for some offenders – the disturbing experiences of their early lives seems absolutely clear. That it may paradoxically result in triggering greater levels of offending is an uncomfortable idea, as is the suggestion that in order to reduce risk, sometimes professionals and agencies may need to take risks.
>
> (Craissati 2007: 227)

Evidence of effectiveness

The difficulties in evaluating community notification, or intensive and extended supervision processes are indicative of the broader difficulties in evaluating the community protection model. There are severe methodological and ethical issues in using control groups, comparing 'like with like' and in correctly attributing causal factors to particular outcomes. Hebenton and Thomas (1997) completed a review of USA community notification and consider the potential transferability to the UK setting. They concluded:

> In reviewing the available public literature on evaluation of registration

as an investigative and preventive tool, one is struck by the dearth of good research studies . . . This lack of research, in our view, has to be seen in the light of the general political and legislative background against which State registration schemes emerged.

(Hebenton and Thomas 1997: 34)

In essence, politicians and policy makers were not concerned with effectiveness, but with votes, gaining public confidence in the criminal justice system, and in responding to populist punitiveness (Birgden 2007).

However, emerging studies indicate areas for caution, notably the negative impact of community notification, restrictive conditions and exclusion zones on offenders; and the mismatch of resources to risk, particularly in the use of costly intensive supervision. The expected impact of community protection legislation on recidivism is not always met, and in some instances there is potential for legislation to have a perverse outcome in terms of increased recidivism. However, studies are few and small scale, and this is an area that would benefit from further research. In particular, further comparisons of offenders subject to community notification without supervision and support with those who do receive supervision and resettlement support. Additional work is required on the impact, both negative and positive, of restrictive measures and exclusion zones; and further work to refine the 'risk tiers' so that resources and measures are better targeted at the most risky. The impact of such measures should then be re-evaluated. Commentators have also criticized the evidence base upon which legislation and justice policy in respect of high risk offenders (and particularly sex offenders) has developed, noting that 'moral panic' (Jenkins 1998, 2001) and public/victim advocacy have played a significant role in policy development (Petrunik 2002). There is also growing concern that the legislation may not be cost effective, with increased bureaucracy to administer systems and processes, greater demands on criminal justice staff, and growing prison populations (Petrunik 2002).

Restorative and reintegrative approaches have similar methodological and ethical issues. Again studies have been few and small scale although the evidence base is building (Newell 2007; Edgar 2008). Studies have also been targeted at particular types of offending (notably domestic violence), although both the approach and its evaluation is being transferred to other high risk offenders, and across both community and custodial settings (Newell 2007; Edgar 2008). Initiatives like COSA are promising, although it is interesting to note that the biggest impact on recidivism rates appears to be when combined with community protection approaches such as MAPPA (Bates et al. 2007) and parole supervision (Wilson et al. 2000). This raises the important question of whether community protection and restorative/reintegration approaches are mutually exclusive or complementary.

Community protection or reintegration: competing or complementary approaches to the community management of high risk offenders?

Community protection has been classified as a panoptical system of regulation and control (Petrunik 2002), with the few observing and regulating the many (see Foucault 1977; Mathiesen 1997). The panopticon has its origins in Bentham's prison design that facilitated 360 degree surveillance of prison cells and prisoners. The concept was applied to systems of discipline, social regulation and punishment by Foucault (1977), who identified systems of social control rooted in the routine surveillance of most aspects of social life and daily living by professional experts (usually agents of the welfare state). This panoptical system uses the expertise and knowledge of professionals to risk assess, categorize, manage and monitor the risky (Garland 2001), through which both individuals and populations are regulated (Foucault 1977). In essence, the few watch the many.

Drawing on the work of Mathiesen (1997), Petrunik (2002) contrasts this with the synoptic form of social control, in which the many (in this case, members of the community) survey the few (sex offenders). Panoptic forms of social control, particularly of offenders, are almost exclusively located in State agencies, often heavily influenced by media coverage and populist demand for more retributive and punitive measures as well as safety (Garland 2001). Petrunik (2002) has argued that these demands can elide panoptic controls into increasingly synoptic ones, with the community demanding a greater role (a greater 'say') in the risk management of offenders (particularly sex offenders) 'in their midst' (Simon 1998). In effect, the 'eyes of the many' are on the 'predatory sex offender'. Vigilante action is, of course, the most extreme expression of synoptic control.

COSA, Leisurewatch and other reintegrative approaches can also be placed in the synoptic control category, albeit a professionally mediated and restrained version of community synoptic control. It is also important to note that synoptic approaches have also been initiated and promoted by criminal justice workers, dissatisfied with the overreliance on panoptic techniques and seeking a 'better way' (Wilson et al. 2000). As such, their meshing should come as no surprise, with Mathiesen noting that: 'Panopticism and synopticism have developed in intimate interaction even fusion with each other' (1997: 223).

However, Petrunik (2002) sounds a note of caution. Synoptic approaches can be based on differing conceptions of justice – for example, exclusionary, retributive and punitive – or inclusionary and reintegrative. COSA in its original inception in Canada was based on principles of community reintegration. In its subsequent development it will be important to see whether these principles can be preserved or whether COSA is co-opted to the broader community protection panoptical agenda. Similar tensions can be discerned in the work of The Derwent Initiative and Leisurewatch. Are protection and reintegration mutually exclusive or can they be 'blended' into effective packages? Emerging evaluations of new initiatives such as the Thames Valley COSA suggest that both practically and pragmatically they are being blended – with promising effect. Indeed the review by Connelly and Williamson (2000) found many instances in varying jurisdictions of a 'hybrid approach' to high risk offenders.

Wood and Kemshall (2007), in an evaluation of supervision strategies with high risk MAPPA offenders, identified practice which effectively blended community protection with rehabilitative and reintegrative concerns (see Chapter 5, this volume). These strategies could be described as *'protective reintegration'* and seek to offer a balanced approach to the community management of high risk offenders. Strategies seek to achieve rehabilitation, change behaviour, meet needs and manage risks; and have the desired outcome of reducing serious further offences from the critical few, resisting overmanaging those whose risk does not justify it, and targeting scarce resources at those who present the greatest risk. These risk management strategies sustain offenders in treatment longer, enable relapse prevention work, teach self-risk management techniques and re-link offenders to their communities. Further evaluation of 'protective integration' techniques and their impact on recidivism is required, including their transferability to other high risk offenders such as violent offenders.

Importantly, Petrunik reminds us that community protection and community reintegration approaches value and prioritize differing voices and differing solutions to the problem of high risk offenders in the community (2002; see also Lafond 1992). Protection increasingly prioritizes the voices of victims and communities, with less attention to either offenders or workers. Particular 'voice' is given to vulnerable groups (children and women) and the 'major voices heard are those of victims rights and public safety advocates and those of politicians and law enforcement officials who recognise the necessity of responding to the community's demands if they wish to be considered successful in their jobs' (Petrunik 2002: 492).

In contrast, reintegration emphasizes the voices of community and offender, and focuses on 'healing the harm' rather than 'punishing the harm'. Reintegrative voices attempt to avoid the scape-goating and alienation of sex offenders. Risk remains a primary concern, and sex offenders are made responsible for their actions and held accountable. However, as Petrunik puts it: 'the sex offender is given the chance to redeem himself [sic] under the caring and ever so watchful eyes of a concerned community' (2002: 506).

Summary

In the Anglophone countries that have prioritized community protection, community safety tends to be asserted over the rights of the individual, although tensions in individual cases can still be discerned (usually risk management failures). The framing of rights in the community protection model is presented as a matter of 'commonsense', although this value-neutral language can obfuscate issues of discrimination, exclusion and injustice. Community notification is one of the clearest examples of community safety being prioritized over human rights, and the various examples of community notification were examined. The emerging evidence on the effectiveness of community notification was reviewed and the potential for perverse outcomes (such as lack of compliance and increased recidivism) were discussed. The UK position on community notification was examined in some detail, with a best practice presentation of discretionary disclosure. Difficulties in evaluating the effectiveness of community protection and reintegrative models were briefly examined, followed by a discussion on whether these models are mutually exclusive, or whether they can be 'blended' into strategies of 'protective reintegration' to offer a more balanced and effective approach to the community management of high risk offenders.

Notes

1 My thanks to Gill Mackenzie for providing some of the material referred to in this section, see 'Public protection and human rights' in Kemshall et al. (2006). The views expressed in this section are entirely the author's.
2 The position of the Chief Inspector caused consternation with the local MAPPA, Parole Board and legal profession, most notably expressed in a conference on 'Who to release? Parole, fairness and criminal justice' Cambridge, 15–16 September 2006. See Padfield (2007) for relevant conference papers. Subsequently the Chief Inspector of Probation in evidence to the All-Party Penal Affairs Committee accepted that extended imprisonment of high risk offenders would have a limited impact on public protection.
3 For further information on Megan's Law see: www.apbnews.com/safetycenter/family/kanka/sooo/03/28/kanka0328 ol.htm (accessed November 2007).

Further reading

DCA (Department of Constitutional Affairs) (2006) *Making Sense of Human Rights: A Short Introduction*. Available at: www.dca.gov.uk (accessed 23 November 2007).
DCA (Department of Constitutional Affairs) (2006) *Human Rights: Human Lives –*

A Handbook for Public Authorities. Available at: www.dca.gov.uk (accessed 23 November 2007).

Hudson, B. (2003) *Justice in the Risk Society*. London: Sage.

Petrunik, M. (2002) Managing unacceptable risk: sex offenders, community response and social policy in the United States and Canada, *International Journal of Offender Therapy and Comparative Criminology*, 46(4): 483–511.

chapter seven

Concluding comments

Pulling the threads together
Blending protection

Pulling the threads together

This book has explored the rise of risk-focused community protection as the dominant model for dealing with high risk offenders across a number of jurisdictions in Anglophone countries and Western Europe. While legislation and policy in many of these countries has consolidated the community protection model, in practice the approach rarely operates in a pure form. Connelly and Williamson in their review (2000) argued for a 'hybridization' of protection and treatment, although the recent legislative and policy evidence for this is mixed (see Petrunik 2002). Retributive and deterrent approaches to high risk offenders have increased, literally 'piggy-backing' on community protection concerns. Protection has become political, attracting media and public debate, and extensive blame and censure when risk management fails.

In this climate, the accurate identification of the 'dangerous', or 'critical few' for special measures has become both imperative and fraught. Chapter 1 reviewed the significant tensions between policy and legislation in defining and identifying the 'dangerous', and difficulties in establishing both criteria and evidence of a 'significant risk of serious harm'. The differing contexts within which risk is defined and 'played out' are important to how risk is interpreted and responded to. This framing of risk and dangerousness was explored in some detail in Chapter 2, and the 'long view' reminds us that both the problem and its solutions are perennial. Contemporary problems in risk work were examined in Chapter 3, with an important emphasis upon systemic and organizational sources of error and failure.

These organizational sources of error are increasingly important in partnership work, where the multi-agency dimension has the potential to exacerbate and magnify such failings (Kemshall et al. 2005).

Partnership has been seen as the route to greater protection, and within the community protection model this has tended to mean statutory partnerships of criminal justice agencies such as MAPPA. While there is evidence for the improved performance of MAPPA (and similar multi-agency working in other jurisdictions), there is increased recognition that criminal justice agencies cannot deliver all the risk management required, and that failure in even one case undermines public confidence in the community protection model. Chapter 4 examined statutory partnerships, but also reviewed new initiatives that promote partnerships with local communities, partnerships between faith-based groups and criminal justice agencies, and partnerships utilizing public health and reintegrative approaches to high risk offenders. These initiatives are also the result of a growing disillusionment with community protection, particularly unintended outcomes of driving offenders underground, alienating communities when offenders are resettled, and undermining rehabilitative and reintegrative aims. In essence, these initiatives argue for a 'better way'. Located broadly within Public Health Approaches and restorative justice models of dealing with offenders, these initiatives stress prevention, rehabilitation and reintegration. Community engagement is also central to these initiatives, including public awareness and educative campaigns about the likely risks presented by high risk offenders and how communities can effectively respond to them. A key objective is to turn 'community protection' into 'protective communities' (TDI 2007: 13).

Chapter 5 explored the differing risk management strategies offered by community protection and more reintegrative approaches. Importantly the chapter noted increased attention to rehabilitation and reintegrative aims in those MAPPA seeking to promote prosocial supervision; and increased liaison and cooperative working between COSA, Leisurewatch/TDI and statutory agencies such as police and probation. While important differences remain, particularly the extent to which resettlement and reintegration are prioritized, it is potentially more helpful to conceive of them as complementary strategies of risk management rather than as alternative forms of risk control.

Chapter 6 reviewed some of the key issues in the community management of high risk offenders, particularly the tension between risks and rights, the usefulness (or otherwise) of community notification and ethical dilemmas in decision making. Within the community protection model, risks have tended to outweigh rights (at least in terms of political rhetoric), although this tension is handled differently across various jurisdictions. The current UK response to calls for a Megan's Law expressed in the use of 'discretionary disclosure' is a good example of the largely pragmatic and commonsense approach to rights adopted by the UK. This example again illustrates that both the political and social contexts are significant in framing risk policy. The chapter also commented upon the need for further evaluations of the effectiveness of both community protection and those initiatives rooted within restorative justice, and potentially on how they could best be combined.

Blending protection

This book has highlighted how community protection and reintegrative approaches are already being blended into a 'protective integration', although the extent to which this is a genuine partnership of complementary approaches or a co-option of alternative useful strategies by a dominant community protection discourse is a moot point. Petrunik (2002, drawing on the work of Mathiesen 1997) has argued that the divide between panoptical and synoptical strategies is already closing (see Chapter 6, this volume), the question is, to what extent they can be blended appropriately to provide effective community risk management? As Petrunik reminds us, these strategies have their roots in differing discourses of risk, differing conceptions of the offender and differing conceptions of justice. Potentially these discourses could present challenges to combining community protection and reintegrative approaches. However, the COSA examples in Canada and the UK indicate that such issues are not necessarily insurmountable, although further research is required to establish the nature of the partnership between COSA and criminal justice agencies, how this is perceived by staff, offenders and community, and the extent to which panoptical and synoptical strategies are effectively combined in practice to produce protective reintegration.

Leisurewatch/TDI has also forged strong links with police and probation, and close working relationships with local MAPPA. Again the extent to which this is a genuinely collaborative partnership requires further investigation. Currently Leisurewatch/TDI makes referrals to MAPPA, for example Leisurewatch-trained staff at swimming pools, concerned about the potentially grooming behaviours of adult users, can make referrals to local police public protection units. These are fed into the local MAPPA, and risk management plans made according to the risk level determined. Where offenders are already known to MAPPA this can provide important information on treatment compliance, daily risk activities and *modus operandi*. Thus vigilance in public places is combined with statutory risk management plans.

'Blended' protective integration, in order to work, will need at least the following key ingredients:

- environmental, public space and opportunity management to reduce grooming behaviours, targeting (e.g., Leisurewatch), and to reduce potential conflict (e.g., management of the night time economy and alcohol related violence);
- public awareness and public education on likely risks and how to effectively manage them (including direct work with potential victims, see Shepherd 2007 on work with victims of violence);
- supportive and integrative strategies such as COSA;
- prosocial supervision and an emphasis upon the 'Good Lives' model;
- appropriate and balanced restrictive measures;
- community vigilance combined with statutory vigilance (e.g., tracking, tagging);
- effective partnership work, including closer working relationships between MAPPA and other agencies offering alternative strategies.

On a broader front the discourse of reintegrative approaches has the potential to engage communities 'as active participants in – rather than passive recipients of – public protection' (TDI 2007: 7). As such, it may ameliorate the retributive and populist punitiveness that currently fuels the community protection model and that ultimately makes protection ever more difficult to achieve.

Glossary

Bifurcated/bifurcation: This is a sentencing policy in which longer sentences should be reserved for harmful offences against the person and high risk offenders, and shorter sentences are used for less harmful offences and less risky offenders. In practice this is difficult to operate, not least due to public and sentencer views on offences and their particular risk, for example burglary where the divide between property crime and personal harm is difficult to draw. Bifurcation is also affected by media and public disquiet over particular crimes, reactions to crime trends and differing perceptions of harm.

Meta-analysis: This is a statistical tool used to combine the results of a range of effectiveness studies in order to establish 'what works'. This aggregation of data has been used not only to provide broad overviews of outcome studies, but also statistically to generate the most significant risk factors for (re)offending and more latterly for the commission of sexual and violent offences. Meta-analysis may be limited by the quality and methodologies of the original studies, although proponents such as Lipsey (1995) have developed more sophisticated techniques. See McGuire and Priestley (1995: 7–9) for a helpful introduction to meta-analysis.

Panopticon/panoptical control: The panopticon has its origins in Bentham's prison design that facilitated 360-degree surveillance of prison cells and prisoners. The concept was applied to systems of discipline, social regulation and punishment by Foucault (1977), who identified systems of social control rooted in the routine surveillance of most aspects of social life and daily living by professional experts (usually agents of the welfare state). In essence, a few experts, usually working through State agencies such as social, health, education and criminal justice services collect information on individuals and categorize them accordingly. By such mechanisms populations are effectively regularized and managed.

Preventative strategies: A technique in social and penal policy that emphasizes prevention, for example early interventions to prevent crime. In contemporary policy such strategies are justified by the rationale of risk, that is, to prevent future risks.

Randomized control trial (RCT): This is usually regarded as a high standard in research, with two comparable samples – one allocated, for example, to treatment and one not (the latter is usually known as the 'control group'). Comparison then enables a conclusion to be reliably drawn that an intervention or treatment has had the required impact, i.e., where the treatment group has lower levels of recidivism than the control group. Findings from studies not able to use RCT are usually regarded with more caution. There can be severe ethical issues against using RCT – for example, it is not ethically permissible to randomly allocate some prisoners or probationers to treatment and exclude others.

Responsibilization: A term describing a form of governance dependent upon what Rose (2000) has described as 'responsiblization', that is, individuals are made responsible for their own actions, including their own risks, and for their own effective risk management.

Restorative justice: A justice system and penal policy based upon notions of restoration, i.e., that the offender should 'make good the harm', and often associated with acts of restitution. In broader terms, the approach emphasizes 'healing the harm' rather than 'punishing the harm', and attempts to reintegrate offenders and heal the rift between offender and society.

Retributive justice/retribution: A justice system and penal policy based upon notions of retribution, i.e., that the 'punishment should fit the crime'. Retributive justice is often associated with public expressions of punitiveness, that is, public demands for retribution particularly against paedophiles.

Surveillance: This is defined as being more than mere observation. It refers to the routine and systematic collection of personal data and the control of populations through monitoring (see Lyon 2003).

Synopticon/synoptical control: Synoptic systems of regulation, in contrast to panoptical ones, use the 'eyes of the many' to provide constant monitoring and vigilance of individuals in the community. In the context of sex offenders, synoptic approaches have mobilized communities into Circles of Support and Accountability, or community groups (e.g., resident groups and neighbourhood watch) to 'watch' over offenders and to monitor local crime levels. Synoptic control has the potential to positively engage local communities in the community management of offenders in their midst (to elicit their help and support for offenders), but also it has the potential to develop into vigilante action, as communities 'out' and 'harass' unwanted offenders (e.g., paedophiles) in their midst.

References

Aas, K. (2005) *Sentencing in the Age of Information: from Faust to Macintosh*. London: Glasshouse Press.

Adams, J. (1995) *Risk*. London: UCL.

Adkins, D., Huff, D. and Stageberg, P. (2000) *The Iowa Sex Offender Registry and Recidivism*. Des Moines: Iowa Department of Human Rights.

Alaszewski, A. (2006) Health and risk, in P. Taylor-Gooby and J. Zinn (eds), *Risk in Social Science*. Oxford: Oxford University Press, pp: 160–79.

Albrecht, H-J. (1997) Dangerous criminal offenders in the German criminal justice system, *Federal Sentencing Reporter*, 10(2): 69–73.

Alder, M. W. (1997) Sexual health: a health of the nation failure, *British Medical Journal*, 314: 1743–6.

Ansbro, M. (2006) What can we learn from serious incident reports? *Probation Journal*, 53(1): 57–60.

Armstrong, D. (2004) A risky business? Research, policy and governmentality and youth offending, *Youth Justice*, 4(2): 100–16.

Ashenden, S. (1996) Reflexive governance and child sexual abuse: liberal welfare rationality and the Cleveland Inquiry, *Economy and Society*, 25(1): 64–88.

Ashenden, S. (2002) Policy perversion: the contemporary governance of paedophilia, *Cultural Values*, 6(1–2): 197–222.

Ashworth, A. (2002) Responsibilities, rights and restorative justice, *British Journal of Criminology*, 42: 578–95.

Attrill, G. and Liell, G. (2007) Offenders' views on risk assessment, in N. Padfield (ed.), *Who to Release? Parole, Fairness and Criminal Justice*. Cullompton: Willan, pp: 191–201.

Bandura, A. (1977) *Social Learning Theory*. Englewood Cliffs, NJ: Prentice Hall.

Barnett, J. and Breakwell, G. M. (2003) The Social amplification of risk and the hazard sequence: the October 1995 oral contraceptive pill scare, *Health, Risk and Society*, 5: 301–13.

Bartrip, P. W. J. (1981) Public opinion and law enforcement: the ticket of leave scares in mid-Victorian Britain, in V. Bailey (ed.), *Policing and Punishment in Nineteenth Century Britain*. London: Croom Helm.

Bates, A. (2005) Evaluation, *Circles of Support and Accountability in the Thames*

Valley: The First Three Years April 2002–March 2005. London: Quaker Communications.

Bates, A., Saunders, R. and Wilson, C. (2007) Doing something about it: a follow-up study of sex offenders participating in Thames Valley Circles of Support and Accountability, *British Journal of Community Justice*, 5(1): 19–42.

Bazerman, M. H. (1994) *Judgement in Managerial Decision Making*. Chichester: Wiley.

Beck, U. (1992) *Risk Society: Towards a New Modernity*. London: Sage.

Beck, U. (2005) *Power in the Global Age*. Cambridge: Polity Press.

Beck, J. L. and Klein-Staffan, J. (1990) Home confinement and the use of electronic monitoring with federal parolees, *Federal Probation*, 54: 23–4.

Beck, V. S. and Travis, L. F. (2004) Sex offender notification and fear of victimisation, *Journal of Criminal Justice*, 32(5): 455–63.

Beckett, R., Beech, A., Fisher, D. and Fordham, A. (1994) *Community-based Treatment for Sex Offenders: An Evaluation of Seven Treatment Programmes*. London: HMSO.

Beech, A. R. and Fisher, D. (2002) The rehabilitation of child sex offenders, *Australian Psychologist*, 37(3): 206–14.

Beech, A. and Fisher, D. (2004) Treatment of sex offenders in the UK prison and probation settings, in H. Kemshall and G. McIvor (eds), *Managing Sex Offender Risk*, Research Highlights 46. London: Jessica Kingsley Publishers.

Beech, A. R. and Mann, R. E. (2002) Recent developments in the treatment of sex offenders, in J. McGuire (ed.), *Offender Rehabilitation: Effective Programmes and Policies to Reduce Offending*. Chichester: Wiley.

Beech, A. R., Fisher, D. and Beckett, R. (1999) *STEP 3: An Evaluation of the Prison Sex Offender Treatment Programme*. London: HMSO.

Beech, A., Erikson, M., Friendship, C. and Ditchfield, J. (2001) *A Six Year Follow-up of Men Going Through Probation-based Sex Offender Treatment Programmes*, Findings 144. London: Home Office, Research, Development and Statistics Directorate.

Bennett, P. and Calman, K. (eds) (1999) *Risk Communication and Public Health*. Oxford: Oxford University Press.

Berliner, L., Schram, D., Miller, L. and Milloy, D. (1995) A sentencing alternative for sex offenders: a study of decision making and recidivism, *Journal of Interpersonal Violence*, 10: 487–502.

Bilby, C. and Hatcher, R. (2004) *Early Stages in the Development of the Integrated Domestic Abuse Programme (IDAP): Implementing the Duluth Domestic Violence Pathfinder*, Online Report 29/04. London: Home Office.

Birgden, A. (2007) Serious Sex Offenders Monitoring Act 2005 (Vic): a therapeutic jurisprudence analysis, *Psychiatry, Psychology and Law*, 14(1): 78–94.

Blom-Cooper, L., Hally, H. and Murphy, E. (1995) *The Falling Shadow: One Patient's Mental Health Care*. London: Duckworth.

Bonta, J. (1996) Risk-needs assessment and treatment, in A. T. Harland (ed.), *Choosing Correctional Options that Work*. Thousand Oaks, CA: Sage.

Bonta, J. and Andrews, D. A. (2003) A commentary on Ward and Stewart's model of human needs, *Psychology, Crime and Law*, 9: 215–18.

Bonta, J. and Wormith, S. J. (2007) Risk and need assessment, in G. McIvor and

P. Raynor (eds), *Developments in Social Work with Offenders*. London: Jessica Kingsley Publishers, pp: 131–52.

Boseley, S. (2002) Multi-jabs pose no risk to babies, say US researchers, *Guardian*, 8 January, p. 9.

Bottoms, A. (1977) Reflections on the renaissance of dangerousness, *Howard Journal of Criminal Justice*, 16: 70–96.

Bottoms, A. (1995) The politics and philosophy of punishment and sentencing, in C. Clarkson and R. Morgan (eds), *The Politics of Sentencing Reform*. Oxford: Oxford University Press.

Boutellier, H. (2000) *Crime and Morality: The Significance of Criminal Justice in the Post-modern Culture*. Dordrecht: Kluwer Academic.

Bowen, E. and Gilchrist, E. (2000) Comprehensive evaluations: a holistic approach to evaluating domestic violence offender programmes, *International Journal of Offender Therapy and Comparative Criminology*, 48(2): 215–34.

Braithwaite, J. (2002) *Restorative Justice and Response to Regulation*. Oxford: Oxford University Press.

Braithwaite, J. and Daly, K. (1994) Masculinities and communitarian control, in T. Newburn and E. Stanko (eds), *Just Boys Doing Business*. London: Routledge.

Brown, M. (2000) Calculations of risk in contemporary penal practice, in M. Brown and J. Pratt (eds), *Dangerous Offenders: Punishment and Social Order*. London: Routledge, pp. 93–108.

Brown, M. and Pratt, J. (eds) (2000) *Dangerous Offenders: Punishment and Social Order*. London: Routledge.

Brown, S. (2005) *Treating Sex Offenders: An Introduction to Sex Offender Treatment Programmes*. Cullompton: Willan.

Browne, K. and Howells, K. (1996) Violent offenders, in C. R. Hollin (ed.), *Working With Offenders: Psychological Practice in Offender Rehabilitation*. Chichester: John Wiley and Sons.

Budd, T., Sharp, C. and Mayhew, P. (2005) *Offending in England and Wales: First Results from the 2003 Crime and Justice Survey*, Research Study 275. London: Home Office.

Bumby, K. M. and Maddox, M. C. (1999) Judges' knowledge about sexual offenders, difficulties presiding over sexual offense cases, and opinions on sentencing, treatment and legislation, *Sexual Abuse: A Journal of Research and Treatment*, 11(4): 305–15.

Burgess, A. (2002) Comparing national responses to perceived health risks from mobile phone masts, *Health, Risk and Society*, 4: 175–88.

Bush, J. (1995) Teaching self-risk management to violent offenders, in J. McGuire (ed.), *What Works: Reducing Reoffending. Guidelines from Research and Practice*. Chichester: John Wiley and Sons, pp. 139–54.

Butler-Schloss, RH (1988) *Report of the Inquiry into Child Abuse in Cleveland 1987*, presented to the Secretary of State for Social Services by the Right Honorable Lord Butler-Schloss. DBE, Cm 412. London: HMSO.

Cann, J. (2007) *Assessing the Extent of Discretionary Disclosure Under the Multi-Agency Public Protection Arrangements (MAPPA)*, Online Report 13/07. London: Home Office.

Canton, R. (2005) Risk assessment and compliance in probation and mental health practice, in B. Littlechild and D. Fearns (eds), *Mental Disorder and Criminal Justice Policy, Provision and Practice.* Lyme Regis: Russell House.

Carich, M. S. and Calder, M. C. (2003) *Contemporary Treatment of Adult Male Sex Offenders.* Lyme Regis: Russell House Publishing.

Carpenter, A. (1998) Belgium, Germany, England, Denmark and the US: the implementation of registration and castration laws, *Dickenson Journal of International Law*, 16(2): 435–57.

Catalano, S. (2005) *Criminal Victimisation, 2004* (NCJ 210674). Washington, DC: US Department of Justice.

Carter Review of Prisons (Lord Carter) (2007) *Securing the Future: Proposals for the Efficient and Sustainable Use of Custody in England and Wales.* London: Ministry of Justice.

Cavadino, M., Crow, I. and Dignan, J. (2000) *Criminal Justice 2000.* Winchester: Waterside Press.

Cesaroni, C. (2001) Releasing sex offenders into the community through 'Circles of Support': a means of reintegrating the 'worst of the worst', *Journal of Rehabilitation*, 34(2): 85–98.

Church Council on Justice and Corrections (1996) *Satisfying Justice: Safe Community Options that Attempt to Repair Harm from Crime and Reduce the Use or Length of Custody.* Ottawa, ON: Church Council.

Clark, D. (2002) OASys – an explanation. Paper presented to Home Office Criminal Justice Conference: Using Risk Assessment in Effective Sentence Management, Pendley Manor Hotel, Tring, 14–15 March.

Clarke, A., Simmonds, R. and Wydall, S. (2004) *Delivering Cognitive Skills Programmes in Prison: A Qualitative Study*, Online Report 27/04. London: Home Office.

Clarkson, C. M. V. (1997) Beyond just desserts: sentencing violent and sexual offenders, *Howard Journal of Criminal Justice*, 36(3): 284–92.

Cleveland Inquiry (1988) *Report of the Inquiry into Child Sexual Abuse in Cleveland 1987.* Presented to the Secretary of State for Social Services by the Right Honourable Lord Butler-Schloss DBE, Cm 412. London: HMSO.

Cohen, M. and Jeglic, E. (2007) Sex offender legislation in the United States: what do we know? *International Journal of Offender Therapy and Comparative Criminology*, 51(4): 369–83.

Colorado Department of Public Safety (2004) *Report on Safety Issues Raised by Living Arrangements for and Location of Sex Offenders in the Community.* Denver, CO: Sex Offender Management Board.

Columbo, A., Bendelow, G., Fulford, K. W. M., and Williams, S. (2003) Evaluating the influence of implicit models of mental disorder on processes of shared decision making within community mental health teams, *International Journal of Social Science and Medicine*, 56: 1557–70.

Connelly, C. and Williamson, S. (2000) *A Review of the Research Literature on Serious Violent and Sexual Offenders.* Edinburgh: Scottish Executive Central Research Unit.

Cooke, D. J. and Philip, L. (2000) To treat or not to treat? An empirical perspective, in C. R. Hollin (ed.), *Handbook of Offender Assessment and Treatment.* Chichester: John Wiley and Sons, pp. 17–34.

Copas, J. (1995) *Some Comments on Meta-analysis*. Warwick: Department of Statistics, Warwick University.

Copas, J. and Marshall, P. (1998) The Offender Group Reconviction Scale: the statistical reconviction score for use by probation officers, *Journal of the Royal Statistical Society, Series C*, 47: 159–71.

Correctional Service of Canada (1999–2000) *Alternatives to Revocation: Safely Sustaining the Offender in the Community*. Ottawa, ON: Strategic Planning and Policy Branch, Correctional Services of Canada.

Correctional Service of Canada (2002) *Circles of Support and Accountability: A Guide to Training Potential Volunteers. Training Manual 2002*. Ottawa, ON: Correctional Services of Canada.

Courtney, J. and Hodgkinson, I. (1999) The 'IDEA' approach to groupwork with violent offenders, *Probation Journal*, 46: 192–4.

Cowie, I. (2007) Risk it wisely, 29 June, pp. 24–5. Available at: www.policereview.com (accessed 8 August 2007).

Craissati, J. (2004) *Managing High Risk Sex Offenders in the Community: A Psychological Approach*. Hove: Brunner-Routledge.

Craissati, J. (2007) The paradoxical effects of stringent risk management, in N. Padfield (ed.), *Who to Release? Parole, Fairness and Criminal Justice*. Cullompton: Willan, pp. 215–27.

Craven, S., Brown, S. and Gilchrist, E. (2006) Sexual grooming of children: review of literature and theoretical considerations, *Journal of Sexual Aggression*, 12(3): 287–99.

Craven, S., Brown, S. and Gilchrist, E. (2007) Current responses to sexual grooming: implication for prevention, *The Howard Journal*, 46(1): 60–71.

Creighton, S. (2007) The Parole Board as a court, in N. Padfield (ed.), *Who to Release? Parole, Fairness and Criminal Justice*. Cullompton: Willan, pp: 109–26.

Critcher, C. (2003) *Moral Panics and the Media*. Buckingham: Open University Press.

Cross, S. (2005) Paedophiles in the community: Inter-agency conflict, news leak and the local press, *Crime, Media and Culture*, 1(3): 284–300.

Cullen, Lord (1990) *The Public Enquiry into the Piper Alpha Disaster*. London: HMSO.

Daly, K. (2006) Restorative justice and sexual assault: an archival study of court and conference cases, *British Journal of Criminology*, 46: 334–56.

DCA (Department of Constitutional Affairs) (2006) *Review of the Implementation of the Human Rights Act*. Available at: www.dca.gov.uk (accessed 23 November 2007).

D'Cruze, S., Walklate, S. and Pegg, S. (2006) *Murder*. Cullumtpon: Willan.

Dean, M. (1997) Sociology after society, in D. Owen (ed.) *Sociology after Postmodernism*. London: Sage.

Dean, M. (1999a) Risk, calculable and incalculable, in D. Lupton (ed.), *Risk and Sociocultural Theory: New Directions and Perspectives*. Cambridge: Cambridge University Press.

Dean, M. (1999b) *Governmentality: Power and Rule in Modern Society*. London: Sage.

DeLisi, M. and Conis, P. (2007) *Violent Offenders: Theory, Research, Public Policy and Practice*. New York: Jones and Bartlett Publishers.

Denney, D. (2005) *Risk and Society*. London: Routledge.

Denscombe, M. (2001) Uncertain identities: the value of smoking for young adults in late modernity, *British Journal of Sociology*, 52: 157–77.

Dingwall, R. (1998) Selective incapacitation after the Criminal Justice Act 1991: a proportional response to protecting the public? *Howard Journal of Criminal Justice*, 37(2): 177–87.

Dobash, R. P., Dobash, R. E., Cavanagh, K. and Lewis, R. (1999) A research evaluation of British programmes for violent men, *Journal of Social Policy*, 28(2): 205–33.

Dodd, T., Nicholas, S., Povey, D. and Walker, A. (2004) *Crime in England and Wales 2003/2004*, Home Office Statistical Bulletin. London: Home Office.

DoH (Department of Health) (2002) *Safeguarding Children*. London: Department of Health.

Donzelot, J. (1980) *The Policing of Families*. London: Hutchinson.

Douglas, M. (1986) *Risk Acceptability According to the Social Sciences*. London: Routledge.

Douglas, M. (1992) *Risk and Blame*. London: Routledge.

Douglas, M. and Wildavsky, A. (1982) How can we know the risks we face? Why risk selection is a social process, *Risk Analysis*, 2(2): 49–51.

Dowden, C. and Andrews, D. A. (2000) Effective correctional treatment and violent re-offending: a meta-analysis, *Canadian Journal of Criminology*, 42: 449–67.

Dowden, C. and Andrews, D. A. (2004) The importance of staff practice in delivering effective correctional practice, *International Journal of Offender Therapy and Comparative Criminology*, 48(2): 203–14.

Drapeau, M., Korner, A., Brunet, L. and Granger, L. (2000) Treatment at La Macaza Clinic: a qualitative study of the sexual offenders' perspective, *Canadian Journal of Criminology and Criminal Justice*, 46(1): 27–44.

Draper, A. and Green, J. (2002) Food safety and consumers: constructions of choice and risk, *Social Policy and Administration*, 36(6): 610–25.

Duff, C. (2003) The importance of culture and context: rethinking risk and risk management in young drug using populations, *Health, Risk and Society*, 5: 285–99.

Dunbar, I. and Langdon, A. (1998) *Tough Justice Sentencing and Penal Policies in the 1990s*. London: Blackstone Press.

Dvoskin, J. A. and Steadman, H. J. (1994) Using intensive case management to reduce violence by mentally ill persons in the community, *Hospital and Community Psychiatry*, 45(7): 679–84.

ECHR (European Convention on Human Rights) (1998) London: Stationery Office. Available at: www.opsi.gov.uk/acts/acts1998/80042--d.htm (accessed 16 March 2007).

Edgar, K. (2008) Justice restored, *Prison Report*, Winter, pp. 20–1.

Edgar, K. and Newell, T. (2006) *Restorative Justice in Prisons – A Guide to Making It Happen*. Winchester: Waterside Press.

Einhorn, H. J. (1986) Accepting error, to make less error, *Journal of Personality Assessment*, 50(3): 387–95.

Elbogen, E. Patry, M. and Scalora, M. (2003) The impact of community notification laws on sex offender attitudes, *International Journal of Law and Psychiatry*, 26(2): 201–19.

Eldridge, H. Fuller, S. Findlater, D. and Palmer, T. (2006) *Stop It Now! Helpline Report.* Available at: www.stopitnow.org (accessed 30 September 2007).

Falshaw, L., Friendship, C. and Bates, A. (2003) *Sexual Offenders: Measuring Reconviction, Reoffending and Recidivism,* Home Office Research Findings No. 183. London: RDS Directorate, Home Office.

Farnham, F. R. and James, D. V. (2001) Dangerousness and dangerous law, *Lancet,* 8 December 358: 1256.

Farrall, S. (2002) *Rethinking What Works with Offenders: Probation, Social Context, and Desistance from Crime.* Cullompton: Willan.

Farrington, D. P. (2000). Explaining and preventing crime: the globalization of knowledge (The American Society of Criminology 1999 Presidential Address), *Criminology,* 38: 1–24.

Farrow, K., Kelly, G. and Wilkinson, B. (2007) *Offenders in Focus: Risk, Responsivity and Diversity.* Cullompton: Willan.

Feeney, A. (2003) Dangerous severe personality disorder, *Advances in Psychiatric Treatment,* 9: 349–58.

Fennell, S. (1988) *Investigation into the Kings Cross Underground Fire.* London: Department of Transport.

Finn, P. (1997) *Sex Offender Community Notification,* NCJ 162364. Washington, DC: US Department of Justice.

Fischoff, B. (1975) Hindsight=foresight: the effect of outcome knowledge on judgement under conditions of uncertainty, *Journal of Experimental Psychology, Human Perception and Performance,* 1: 288–99.

Fisher, D. and Beech, A. (2004) Adult male sex offenders, in H. Kemshall and G. McIvor (eds), *Managing Sex Offender Risk*, Research Highlights 46. London: Jessica Kingsley.

Fitch, K. (2006) *Megan's Law: Does it Protect Children? (2).* London: NSPCC.

Fitzgibbon, D. W. (2007) Institutional racism, pre-emptive criminalisation and risk analysis, *Howard Journal,* 46(2): 128–44.

Floud, J. and Young, W. (1981) *Dangerousness and Criminal Justice.* London: Heinemann.

Flynn, E. E. (1978) Classification for risk and supervision: a preliminary conceptualisation, in J. C. Freeman (ed.), *Prisons Past and Future.* London: Heinemann.

Folkard, M. S., Smith, D. E. and Smith, D. D. (1976) *IMPACT Vol.II: The Results of the Experiment.* London: HMSO.

Foucault, M. (1965) *Madness and Civilisation: The History of Insanity in the Age of Reason.* New York: Pantheon.

Foucault, M. (1973) *The Birth of the Clinic: An Archaeology of Medical Perception.* London: Tavistock.

Foucault, M. (1977) *Discipline and Punish: The Birth of the Prison.* London: Allen and Unwin.

Foucault, M. (1978) About the concept of the 'dangerous individual' in 19th century legal psychiatry, *International Journal of Law and Psychiatry,* 1: 1–18.

Foucault, M. (ed.) (1988) The dangerous individual, *Politics, Philosophy and Culture.* London: Routledge, pp. 125–51.

Freiberg, A. (2000) Guerillas in our midst? Judicial responses to governing the dangerous, in M. Brown and J. Pratt (eds), *Dangerous Offenders: Punishment and Social Order.* London: Routledge.

Frenken, J. (1999) Sexual offender research and treatment in the Netherlands, *Journal of Interpersonal Violence*, 14(4): 347–71.

Furedi, F. (2002) *Culture of Fear: Risk-taking and the Morality of Low Expectations*, 2nd edn. London: Cassell.

Furedi, F. (2005) Terrorism and the politics of fear, in C. Hale, K. Hayward, A. Wahidin and E. Wincup (eds), *Criminology*. Oxford: Oxford University Press.

Furlong, A. and Cartmel, F. (2006) *Young People and Social Change: Individualization and Risk in Late Modernity*, 2nd edn. Buckingham: Open University Press.

Gallagher, B. (2007) Stranger-danger, *Police Review*, 5 October, pp. 24–5.

Gandy, O. (1993) *The Panoptic Sort: A Political Economy of Personal Information*. Boulder, CO: Westview Press.

Garland, D. (1985) *Punishment and Welfare: A History of Penal Strategies*. Aldershot: Gower.

Garland, D. (1990) *Punishment and Modern Society: A Study in Social Theory*. Oxford: Clarendon Press.

Garland, D. (1997) Governmentality and the problem of crime: Foucault, criminology and sociology, *Theoretical Criminology*, 1(2): 173–214.

Garland, D. (2001) *The Culture of Crime Control: Crime and Social Order in Contemporary Society*. Oxford: Oxford University Press.

Gelles, R. J. (1997) *Intimate Violence in Families*. London: Sage.

Gendreau, P. (1996) The principles of effective intervention with offenders, in A. T. Harland (ed.), *Choosing Correctional Interventions that Work: Defining the Demand and Evaluating the Supply*. Newbury Park, CA: Sage, pp. 117–30.

Gibbs, B. and Haldenbury, A. (2006) *Urban Crime Rankings*. London: Reform.

Giddens, A. (1984) *The Constitution of Society*. Cambridge: Polity Press.

Goldson, G. (2005) Taking liberties: policy and the punitive turn, in H. Hemdrick (ed.), *Children and Social Policy: An Essential Reader*. Bristol: Policy Press.

Goodwin, V. and Shepherd, J. (2006) The development of an assault patient questionnaire to allow accident and emergency departments to contribute to Crime and Disorder Act local crime audits, *Journal of Accident and Emergency Medicine*, 17: 196–8.

Greenwood, P. and Abrahamse, A. (1982) *Selective Incapacitation*. Santa Monica, CA: RAND Corporation.

Grover, C. and Soothill, K. (1995) Miscarriages of justice: sex crime appeals in the news, *Police Journal*, April, pp. 120–8.

Grubin, D. (1998) *Sex Offending Against Children: Understanding the Risk*. Police Research Series Paper 99. London: Home Office.

Grubin, D. and Thornton, D. (1994) A national program for the assessment and treatment of sex offenders in the English prison system, *Criminal Justice and Behaviour*, 21(1): 55–71.

Guardian (2007) In chatrooms and message boards, Madeleine hysteria grips the world, Emma Brockes, 19 May.

Gutierrez-Lobos, K., Eher, R., Grunhut, C. et al. (2001) Violent sex offenders lack male social support, *International Journal of Offender Therapy and Comparative Criminology*, 45(1): 70–82.

Hacking, I. (1990) *The Taming of Chance*. Cambridge: Cambridge University Press.

Hall, S. and Winlow, S. (2005) Night-time leisure and violence in the breakdown of the pseudo-pacification process, *Probation Journal*, 52(4): 376–89.

Hall, C. et al. (2007) Implementing the common assessment framework: surveillance, social sorting and categorisation, Paper presented at ESRC E-Society Seminar, Grange Hotel, York, 14–15 May.

Hansard (2006) House of Commons debate, July, Col. 473.

Hanson, R. K., Harris, A. J. R., Scott, T. and Helmus, L. (2007) *Assessing the Risk of Sexual Offenders on Community Supervision: The Dynamic Supervision Project*, User Report Number 2007–05. Ottawa: Public Safely Canada.

Health and Safety Executive (1988) *Blackspot Construction*. London: HMSO.

Hebenton, B. and Thomas, T. (1996) Tracking sex offenders, *Howard Journal of Criminal Justice*, 35(2): 97–112.

Hebenton, B. and Thomas, T. (1997) *Keeping Track? Observations on Sex Offender Registers in the US*, Crime Detection and Prevention Series Paper 83. London: Police Research Group and Home Office.

Hemphill, J. F. and Hart, S. D. (2002) Motivating the unmotivated: psychopathy, treatment, and change, in M. McMurran (ed.), *Motivating the Offender to Change: A Guide to Enhancing Engagement in Therapy*. Chichester: John Wiley and Sons, pp: 193–200.

Hidden, A. (1989) *Investigation into the Clapham Junction Railway Accident*. London: HMSO.

HMIP (Her Majesty's Inspectorate of Probation) (1998) *A Guide to Effective Practice*. London: HMIP

HMIP (Her Majesty's Inspectorate of Probation) (2006a) *An Independent Review of a Serious Further Offence Case: Damien Hanson and Elliot White*. London: HMIP.

HMIP (Her Majesty's Inspectorate of Probation) (2006b) *An Independent Review of a Serious Further Offence Case: Anthony Rice*. London: HMIP.

HMIP (Her Majesty's Inspectorate of Probation) (2007a) *Independent Inspection of Probation and Youth Work: Annual Report 2006–7*. London: HMIP.

HMIP (Her Majesty's Inspectorate of Probation) (2007b) *Effective Supervision Inspection of the National Probation Service for England and Wales*. London: HMIP.

HMIP (Her Majesty's Inspectorate of Probation) and HMIC (Her Majesty's Inspectorate of Constabulary) (2005) *Managing Sex Offenders in the Community: A Joint Inspection on Sex Offenders*. London: HMIP and HMIC.

HM Prison Service (2004) *Violence Reduction: Prison Service Order 2750*. London: HM Prison Service.

Hobson-West, P. (2003) Understanding vaccination resistance: moving beyond risk, *Health, Risk and Society*, 5: 273–83.

Hollin, C. R. (1993) Contemporary psychological research into violence: an overview, in P. J. Taylor (ed.), *Violence in Society*. London: Royal College of Physicians, pp. 55–67.

Hollin, C. R. (1995) The meaning and implications of 'programme integrity', in J. McGuire (ed.), *What Works: Reducing Reoffending. Guidelines from Research and Practice*. Chichester: John Wiley and Sons, pp. 195–208.

Hollin, C. R. (2005) Working with aggression and violence: assessment, treatment and prevention, *Psychology, Crime and Law*, 11: 344–5.

Hollin, C.R. and Palmer, E. J. (eds) (2006) *Offending Behaviour Programmes: Development, Application and Controversies*. Chichester: John Wiley and Sons.

Holmes, R. M. and Holmes, S. T. (1998) *Serial Murder*, 2nd edn. London: Sage.

Home Office (2002) *Working with Offenders: Offending Behaviour Programmes*. Available at: www.crimereduction.gov.uk/workingoffenders3.htm (accessed 9 November 2007).

Home Office (2004a) *MAPPA Guidance (Version 2)*. London: Home Office.

Home Office (2004b) *Safety and Justice: Sharing Personal Information in the Context of Domestic Violence – An Overview*, Home Office Development and Practice Report 30. London: Home Office.

Home Office (2005a) *Restructuring Probation to Reduce Reoffending*. London: Home Office.

Home Office (2005b) *Tackling Violent Crime Programme Strategic Communications Toolkit*. Available from: Chris.Kirby@homeoffice.gsi.gov.uk

Home Office (2006a) *Rebalancing the Criminal Justice System in Favour of the Law Abiding Majority: Cutting Crime, Reducing Reoffending and Protecting the Public*. London: Home Office.

Home Office (2006b) *The Home Secretary's Five Year Strategy for Protecting the Public and Reducing Reoffending*. London: Home Office (announced 9 February).

Home Office (2006c) Home Secretary announces new public protection measures, Press release, 20 April. London: Home Office. Available at: www.press.homeoffice.gov.uk (accessed 8 August 2006).

Home Office (2006d) Home Secretary pledges 8,000 new prison places – putting public protection first, Press release, 21 July. London: Home Office. Available at: www.press.homeoffice.gov.uk (accessed 8 August 2006).

Home Office (2007a) *OASys Handbook*. London: Home Office.

Home Office (2007b) *MAPPA – The First Five Years: A National Overview of the Multi-Agency Public Protection Arrangements*. London: Home Office.

Home Secretary (2006) Annual Speech to the Parole Board, May. London: Home Office. Available at: www.press.homeoffice.gov.uk (accessed 8 August 2006).

Hood, C. and Jones, D. K. C. (1996) *Accident and Design: Contemporary Debates in Risk Management*. London: UDL Press.

Hood, R. and Shute, S. (2000) *The Parole System at Work: A Study of Risk Based Decision Making*, Home Office Research Study 202. London: Research, Development and Statistics Directorate, Home Office.

Hope, T. (2001) Crime victimisation and inequality in the risk society, in R. Matthews and J. Pitts (eds), *Crime Disorder and Community Safety*. London: Routledge.

Hope, T. and Sparks, R. (eds) (2000) *Crime, Risk and Insecurity*. London: Routledge.

Horlick-Jones, T. (1998) Meaning and contextualisation in risk assessment, *Reliability Engineering and System Safety*, 59: 79–89.

Howard, P. (2006) *The Offender Assessment System: An Evaluation of the Second Pilot*, Research Findings 278. London: Home Office. Available at: www.homeoffice.gov.uk/red/pdfs06/r278.pdf.

Howard, P., Clark, D. and Garnham, N. (2006) An evaluation of the Offender Assessment System (OASys) in three pilots 1991–2001. Available at: www.noms.homeoffice.gov.uk/news-publications/policy-consultation/.

Howells, K. and Day, A. (2003) Readiness for anger management, *Clinical Psychology Review*, 23: 319–37.

Hudson, B. (1998) Restorative justice: the challenge of sexual and racial violence, *Journal of Law and Society*, 25(2): 237–56.

Hudson, B. (2000) *Human Rights, Public Safety and the Probation Service: Defending Justice in the Risk Society*, Bill McWilliams Memorial Lecture, 28 June. Cambridge: Cambridge University Press.

Hudson, B. (2001) Punishment, rights and difference: defending justice in the risk society, in K. Stenson and R. Sullivan (eds), *Crime, Risk and Justice*. Cullompton: Willan.

Hudson, B. (2002) Restorative justice and gendered violence: diversion or effective justice? *British Journal of Criminology*, 42: 616–34.

Hudson, B. (2003) *Justice in the Risk Society*. London: Sage.

Hudson, K. (2005) *Offending Identities: Sex Offenders' Perspectives on their Treatment and Management*. Cullompton: Willan.

Hudson, B. and Bramhall, G. (2005) Assessing the 'Other', *British Journal of Criminology*, 45(5): 721–40.

Hudson, S. M., Marshall, W. L., Ward, T., Johnston, P. W. and Jones, R. L. (1995) Kia Marama: a cognitive-behavioural program for incarcerated child molesters, *Behaviour Change*, 12(2): 69–80.

Hughes, E., Kitzinger, J. and Murdoch, G. (2006) The media and risk, in P. Taylor-Gooby and J. Zinn (eds), *Risk in Social Science*. Oxford: Oxford University Press.

Inter-Departmental Liaison Group (ILGRA) (2002) *The Precautionary Principle: Policy and Application*. London: Health and Safety Executive.

Ireland, J. (2000) Bullying among prisoners: a review of research, *Aggression and Violent Behaviour*, 5: 201–15.

James, A. and Raine, J. (1998) *The New Politics of Criminal Justice*. London: Longman.

Janus, E. (2000) Civil commitment as social control: managing the risk of sexual violence, in M. Brown and J. Pratt (eds), *Dangerous Offenders: Punishment and Social Order*. London: Routledge, pp. 71–90.

Jenkins, P. (1998) *Moral Panic: Changing Concepts of the Child Molester in Modern America*. New York, CT: Yale University Press.

Jenkins, P. (2001) How Europe discovered its sex offender crisis, in J. Best (ed.), *How Claims Spread: Cross-national Diffusion of Social Problems*. Hawthorne Creek, NY: Aldine, pp. 147–67.

Johnston, L. (2000) *Policing Britain: Risk, Security and Governance*. London: Longman.

Johnstone, G. (ed.) (2003) *A Restorative Justice Reader: Texts, Sources and Context*. Devon: Willan Publishing.

Kemshall, H. (1996) *Reviewing Risk: A Review of the Research on the Assessment and Management of Risk and Dangerousness. Implications for Policy and Practice in the Probation Service*, Report for the Home Office Research and Statistics Directorate. London: Home Office.

Kemshall, H. (1997) The dangerous are always with us: dangerousness and the role of the Probation Service, *VISTA*, 2(3): 136–53.

Kemshall, H. (1998a) *Risk in Probation Practice*. Aldershot: Ashgate.

Kemshall, H. (1998b) Defensible decisions for risk: or it's the doers wot get the blame, *Probation Journal*, 45(2): 67–72.

Kemshall, H. (2000) Conflicting knowledges on risk: the case of risk knowledge in the Probation Service, *Health, Risk and Society*, 2(2): 143–58.

Kemshall, H. (2001) *Risk Assessment and Management of Known Sexual and Violent Offenders: A Review of Current Issues*, Police Research Series 140. London: Home Office.

Kemshall, H. (2002a) Risk assessment and management, in M. Davies (ed.), *The Blackwell Companion to Social Work*. Oxford: Blackwell Publishing.

Kemshall, H. (2002b) Effective practice in probation: an example of 'advanced liberal responsibilisation'? *The Howard Journal*, 41(1): 41–58.

Kemshall, H. (2003) *Understanding Risk in Criminal Justice*. Maidenhead: Open University Press.

Kemshall, H. (2004) Female sex offenders, in H. Kemshall and G. McIvor (eds), *Managing Sex Offender Risk*, Research Highlights 46. London: Jessica Kingsley.

Kemshall, H. (2006a) Crime and risk, in P. Taylor-Gooby and J. Zinn (eds), *Risk in Social Science*. Oxford: Oxford University Press.

Kemshall, H. (2006b) Social policy and risk, in G. Mythen and S. Walklate (eds), *Beyond the Risk Society: Critical Reflections on Risk and Human Security*. Maidenhead: Open University Press.

Kemshall, H. (2007) MAPPA, parole and the management of high-risk offenders in the community, in N. Padfield (ed.), *Who to Release? Parole, Fairness and Criminal Justice*. Cullompton: Willan, pp. 202–14

Kemshall, H. and Maguire, M. (2001) Public protection, partnership and risk penality: the Multi-Agency Risk Management of sexual and violent offenders, *Punishment and Society*, 3(2): 237–64.

Kemshall, H. and McIvor, G. (eds) (2004) *Managing Sex Offender Risk*. London: Jessica Kingsley.

Kemshall, H. and Wood, J. (2007a) High-risk offenders and public protection, in L. Gelsthorpe and R. Morgan (eds), *Handbook of Probation*. Cullompton: Willan, pp. 381–97.

Kemshall, H. and Wood, J. (2007b) Beyond public protection: an examination of community protection and public health approaches to high-risk offenders, *Criminology and Criminal Justice*, 7(3): 203–22.

Kemshall, H. and Wood, J. (2008) Risk management, accountability and partnerships in criminal justice, in B. Stout, J. Yates and B. Williams (eds), *Applied Criminology*. London: Sage Publications.

Kemshall, H., Mackenzie, G. and Wood, J. (2004) *Stop It Now! UK and Ireland: An Evaluation*. Leicester: De Montfort University Press.

Kemshall, H., Wood, J., Mackenzie, G., Bailey, R. and Yates, J. (2005) *Strengthening Multi-Agency Public Protection Arrangements (MAPPA)*. London: Home Office.

Kemshall, H., Mackenzie, G., Miller, J. and Wilkinson, B. (2006) *Risk of Harm Guidance and Training Resource*, CD-rom. Leicester and London: De Montfort University and NOMS.

Kemshall, H., Mackenzie, G., Miller, J., and Wilkinson, B. (2007) *Assessing and Managing Risk*. Leicester and Paisley, Scotland: De Montfort University and the Risk Management Authority.

Kim, K. and Lee, B. (2001) *An Analysis of Policy Response to Protect Youths from Sexual Crimes*. Seoul: Korean Commission on Youth Protection.

Kinzig, J. (1997) Preventative measures for dangerous recidivists, *European Journal of Crime, Criminal Law and Criminal Justice*, 5(1): 27–57.

Kitzinger, J. (1999) The ultimate neighbour from hell? Stranger danger and the media representation of paedophilia, in B. Franklin (ed.), *Social Policy, the Media and Misrepresentation*. London: Routledge, pp. 207–21.

Kitzinger, J. (2004) *Framing Abuse: Media Influence and Public Understanding of Sexual Violence Against Children*. London: Pluto Press.

Kropp, P. (2004) Some questions regarding spousal assault in risk assessment, *Violence Against Women*, 10(6): 676–97.

Kropp, P., Hart, S. D., Webster, C. D. and Eaves, D. (2004) *Spousal Assault Risk Assessment Guide*. Ontario: Multi-Health Systems.

Krug, E. G. (2002) *World Report on Violence and Health*. Geneva: World Health Organisation.

La Fond, J. (1992) Washington's sexually violent predator statute: law or lottery? A response to professor brooks, *University of Puget Sound Law Review*, 15(3): 755–99.

Laming, Lord (2003) *The Victoria Climbié Inquiry*. London: Crown Copyright. Available at: www.victoria-climbie-inquiry.org.uk/finreport/finreport.htm (accessed 16 March 2007).

Lawrie, C. (1997) The role and responsibility of middle managers, in H. Kemshall and J. Pritchard (eds), *Good Practice in Risk Assessment and Risk Management, Vol 2*. London: Jessica Kingsley Publishers, pp. 301–11.

Laws, D. R. (1995) Central elements in relapse prevention procedures with sex offenders, *Psychology, Crime and Law*, 21(1): 41–53.

Laws, D. R. (1996) Relapse prevention or harm reduction? *Sexual Abuse: A Journal of Research and Treatment*, 8(3): 243–8.

Laws, D. R. (1999) Relapse prevention: the state of the art, *Journal of Interpersonal Violence*, 8: 285–302.

Laws, D. R. (2000) Sexual offending as a public health problem: a North American Perspective, *Journal of Sexual Aggression*, 5(1): 30–44.

Laws, D. R. (2003) The rise and fall of relapse prevention, *Australian Psychologist*, 38(1): 22–30.

Laws, D. R. and Marshall, W. (2003) A brief history of behavioural and cognitive behavioural approaches to sexual offenders, Part 1: early developments, *Sexual Abuse: A Journal of Research and Treatment*, 15(2): 93–120.

Levenson, J. (2003) Policy interventions designed to combat sexual violence: community notification and civil commitment, *Journal of Child Sexual Abuse*, 12: 17–52.

Levenson, J. and Cotter, L. (2005a) The impact of sex offender residence restrictions: 1,000 feet from danger or one step from absurd? *International Journal of Offender Therapy and Comparative Criminology*, 49(2): 168–78.

Levenson, J. and Cotter, L. (2005b) The effects of Megan's Law on sex offender reintegration, *Journal of Contemporary Criminal Justice*, 21(1): 49–66.

Lianos, M. and Douglas, M. (2000) Dangerization and the end of deviance: the institutional environment, *British Journal of Criminology*, 40: 261–78.

Lieb, R. (1996) Community notification laws: 'a step towards more effective solutions', *Journal of Interpersonal Violence*, 11: 298–300.

Lieb, R. (2003) Joined-up worrying: the Multi-Agency Public Protection Panels, in:

A. Matravers (ed.), *Sex Offenders in the Community: Managing and Reducing Risk*. Cullompton: Willan.

Lips, M., Organ, J. and Taylor, J. (2007) The service state and the surveillance society: e-benefits and e-assessments in information age public service provision, Paper presented to the ESRC e-Society Information Sharing, Assessment in e-Technology and Social Care, The Grange, York, 14–15 May.

Lipsky, M. (1980) *Street-Level Bureaucracy: Dilemmas of the Individual in Public Services*. New York: Russell Sage.

Loader, I. and Sparks, R. (2002) Contemporary landscapes of crime, order and control: governance, risk and globalisation, in M. Maguire, R. Morgan and R. Reiner (eds), *The Oxford Handbook of Criminology*. Oxford: Oxford University Press.

Lord Chancellor (2007) The Harry Street Lecture, Manchester University. Available at: www.dca.gov.uk/speeches/2007/sp070209.htm (accessed 23 November 2007).

Loucks, N. (2002) *Recidivism Amongst Serious Violent and Sexual Offenders*. Edinburgh: Scottish Executive, Crime and Criminal Justice Social Research Series.

Lovell, E. (2001) *Megan's Law: Does it Protect Children? (1)*. London: NSPCC.

Loza, W. and Loza-Fanous, A. (1999) The fallacy of reducing rape and violent recidivism by treating anger, *International Journal of Offender Therapy and Comparative Criminology*, 4(4): 492–502.

Lupton, D. (1999) *Risk*. London: Routledge.

Lynch, M. (2000) Rehabilitation and rhetoric: the ideal of reformation in contemporary parole discourse and practice; *Punishment and Society*, 2(1): 40–65.

Lyon, D. (2003) *Surveillance as Social Sorting: Privacy, Risk and Automated Discrimination*. London: Routledge.

Macgill, S. (1989) Risk perception and the public: insights from research around Sellafield, in J. Brown (ed.), *Environmental Threats: Perception, Analysis and Management*. London: Belhaven Press, pp. 48–66.

MacLean Report (2002) *A Report on the Committee on Serious Violent and Sexual Offenders*. Edinburgh: Scottish Executive Social Research.

Maden, T. (2007) *Treating Violence: A Guide to Risk Management in Mental Health*. Oxford: Oxford University Press.

Maguire, M. (2004) The crime reduction programme: reflections on the vision and the reality, *Criminal Justice*, 4(3): 213–38.

Maguire, M. and Hopkins, M. (2003) Data analysis for problem-solving: alcohol and city centre violence, in K. Bullock and N. Tilley (eds), *Crime Reduction and Problem-Oriented Policing*. Devon: Willan, pp. 126–53.

Maguire, M. and Nettleton, H. (2003) *Reducing Alcohol-Related Violence and Disorder: An Evaluation of the TASC Project*, Home Office Research Study No. 265. London: Home Office.

Maguire, M., Kemshall, H., Noaks, L. and Wincup, E. (2001) *Risk Management of Sexual and Violent Offenders: The Work of Public Protection Panels*, Police Research Series 139. London: Home Office.

Mair, G. (ed.) (1997) *Evaluating the Effectiveness of Community Penalties*. Aldershot: Avebury.

Mair, G. (2005) Electronic monitoring in England and Wales: evidence-based or not? *Criminal Justice*, 5: 257–78.

Mann, R. E. (1996) Measuring the effectiveness of relapse prevention intervention with sex offenders, paper presented at the 15th Annual Research and Treatment Conference of the Association for the Treatment of Sexual Abusers, Chicago IL. November.

Mann, R. E. (2000) Managing resistance and rebellion in relapse prevention intervention, in D. R. Laws, S. M. Hudson and T. Ward (eds), *Remaking Relapse Prevention with Sex Offenders*. Thousand Oaks, CA: Sage.

Mann, R. E. (2004) Innovations in sex offender treatment, *Journal of Sexual Aggression*, 10(2): 141–52.

Marshall, W. and Eccles, A. (1991) Issues in clinical practice with sex offenders, *Journal of Interpersonal Violence*, 6(1): 68–93.

Marshall, W. and Eccles, A. (1996) Cognitive behavioural treatment of sex offenders, in V. B. Van Hasselt and M. Hersen (eds), *Sourcebook of Psychological Treatment Manuals for Adult Disorders*. London: B. T. Batsford.

Marshall, W. L., Anderson, D. and Fernandez, Y. (1999) *Cognitive Behavioural Treatment of Sexual Offenders*. Chichester: John Wiley and Sons.

Marshall, W., Serran, G., Fernandez, Y., Mann, R. and Thornton, D. (2003) Therapist characteristics in the treatment of sexual offenders: tentative data on their relationship with indices of behaviour change, *Journal of Sexual Aggression*, 9(1): 25–30.

Marshall, W., Serran, G. and Moulden, H. (2004) Effective interventions with sexual offenders, in H. Kemshall and G. McIvor (eds), *Managing Sex Offender Risk: Research Highlights 46*. London: Jessica Kingsley, pp. 111–36.

Martinson, R. (1974) What works? Questions and answers about prison reform. *The Public Interest*, 10: 22–54.

Maruna, S. (2001) *Making Good: How Ex-Convicts Reform and Rebuild their Lives*. Washington, DC: American Psychological Association.

Mathiesen, T. (1997) The viewer society: Michel Foucault's 'Panopticon' revisited. *Theoretical Criminology*, May, 1: 215–34.

Matravers, A. (2005) *Managing Modernity: Politics and the Culture of Control*. Abingdon: Routledge.

Maynard-Moody, S., Musheno, M. and Palumbo, D. (1990) Street-wise social policy: resolving the dilemma of street-level influence and successful implementation, *Western Political Quarterly*, 43: 831–48.

McAlinden, A. (2005) The use of 'shame' with sexual offenders, *British Journal of Criminology*, 45(3): 373–94.

McAlinden, A. (2006) Managing risk: from regulation to reintegration of sexual offenders, *Criminology and Criminal Justice*, 6(2): 197–218.

McCulloch, T. and Kelly, L. (2007) Working with sex offenders in context: Which way forward? *Probation Journal*, 54(1): 7–21.

McGrath, R. J. (1995) Sex offender treatment: does it work? *Perspectives*, 19: 24–6.

McGuigan, J. (2006) Culture and risk, in G. Mythen and S. Walklate (eds), *Beyond the Risk Society: Critical Reflections on Risk and Human Security*. Berkshire: Open University Press.

McGuire, J. (ed.) (1995) *Offender Rehabilitation and Treatment: Effective Practice and Policy*. Chichester: John Wiley and Sons.

McGuire, J. (1997) A short introduction to meta-analysis, *VISTA*, 3(3): 163–76.

McGuire, J. (ed.) (2000) *Offender Rehabilitation: Effective Programmes and Policies to Reduce Offending.* Chichester: Wiley.

McGuire, J. (2004) *Understanding Psychology and Crime: Perspectives on Theory and Action.* Maidenhead: Open University Press/McGraw-Hill Education.

McGuire, J. (2007) Programmes for probationers, in G. McIvor and P. Raynor (eds), *Developments in Social Work with Offenders*, Research Highlights 48. London: Jessica Kingsley Publishers, pp. 153–83.

McMurran, M. (2002) *Motivating Offenders to Change: A Guide to Enhancing Engagement in Therapy.* Chichester: John Wiley and Sons.

McMurran, M. and Ward, T. (2004) Motivating offenders to change: an organizing framework, *Legal and Criminal Psychology*, 9: 295–311.

McNeill, F. and Batchelor, S. (2002) Chaos, containment and change: responding to persistent offending by young people, *Youth Justice*, 2(1): 27–43.

McNeill, F. and Maruna, S. (2007) Giving up and giving back: desistance, generativity and social work with offenders, in G. McIvor and P. Raynor (eds), *Developments in Social Work with Offenders*, Research Highlights 48. London: Jessica Kingsley Publishers, pp. 224–39.

McWilliams, W. (1986) The English probation system and the diagnostic ideal, *Howard Journal*, 25: 241–60.

McWilliams, W. (1987) Probation, pragmatism and policy, *Howard Journal of Criminal Justice*, 25: 97–121.

Melloy, M. (2005) The sex offender next door: an analysis of recidivism, risk factors, and deterrence of sex offenders on probation, *Criminal Justice Policy Review*, 16(2): 211–36.

Melossi, D. (2000) Changing representations of the criminal, *British Journal of Criminology*, 40(2): 296–320.

Michie, C. and Cooke, D. (2006) The structure of violent behaviour: a hierarchical model, *Criminal Justice and Behaviour*, 33(6): 506–738.

Miller, D. and Kitzinger, J. (1998) *The Circuit of Mass Communications: Media Strategies, Representation and Audience Reception in the AIDS Crisis.* London: Sage.

Ministry of Justice (2007a) Ministerial foreword, *MAPPA Annual Reports.* London: Ministry of Justice.

Ministry of Justice (2007b) *MAPPA Guidance* 2007 (*Version 2.0*), produced by the National MAPPA Team, National Offender Management Service Public Protection Unit. London: Ministry of Justice.

Minnesota Department of Corrections (2003) *Level Three Sex Offenders Residential Placement Issues.* St Paul, MN: Minnesota Department of Corrections.

Mirlees-Black, C., Budd, T. and Partridge, S. (2001) *The 2000 British Crime Survey.* London: HMSO.

Monahan, J. (1981) *The Clinical Prediction of Violence.* Beverley Hills, CA: Sage.

Monahan, J. (1993) Limiting therapist exposure to Tarasoff liability: guidelines for risk containment, *American Psychologist*, 48: 242–50.

Moon, G. (2000) Risk and protection: the discourse of confinement in contemporary mental health policy, *Health and Place*, 6(3): 239–50.

Moore, B. (1996) *Risk Assessment – A Practitioners Guide to Predicting Harmful Behaviours.* London: Whiting and Birch.

Moore, R., Howard, P. and Burns, M. (2007) The further development of OASys: realising the potential of the Offender Assessment System, *Prison Service Journal*, 167: 36–42.

Morran, D. (1996) Working in the 'Change' Programme, probation-based group-work with male domestic violence offenders, in T. Newburn and G. Mair (eds), *Working with Men*. Lyme Regis: Russell House Publishing, pp. 108–22.

Morgan, S. (2004) Positive risk-taking: an idea whose time has come, *Health Care Risk Report*, 10(10): 18–19.

Morris, A. and Gelsthorpe, L. (2000) Re-visioning men's violence against female partners, *Howard Journal*, 39(4): 412–28.

Mossman, D. (1994) Assessing predictions of violence: being accurate about accuracy, *Journal of Consulting and Clinical Psychology*, 62(4): 783–92.

Munro, E. (1996) Avoidable and unavoidable mistakes in child protection work, *British Journal of Social Work*, 26: 795–810.

Munro, E. (1999) Common errors of reasoning in child protection work, *Child Abuse and Neglect*, 23(8): 745–58.

Munro, E. (2002) *Effective Child Protection*. London: Sage.

Murray, C. (1990) *The Emerging British Underclass*. London: Health and Welfare Unit, Institute for Economic Affairs.

Mythen, G. and Walklate, S. (2006) Criminology and terrorism: which thesis? Risk society or governmentality? *British Journal of Criminology*, 46: 379–98.

NAO (National Audit Office) (2006) *The Electronic Monitoring of Adult Offenders*. London: National Audit Office. Available at: www.nao.org.uk/publiciations/nao_reports/05-06/0506800.pdf.

Nash, M. (1999a) *Police, Probation and Protecting the Public*. London: Blackwell Press.

Nash, M. (1999b) Enter the polibation officer, *International Journal of Police, Science and Management*, 1(4): 360–8.

Nash, M. (2006) *Public Protection and the Criminal Justice Process*. Oxford: Oxford University Press.

Nathan, L., Wilson, N. and Hillman, D. (2003) *Te Whakakotahitanga: An Evaluation of the Te Piriti Special Treatment Programme for Child Sex Offenders in New Zealand*. Wellington: New Zealand Department of Corrections.

Nelken, D. (ed.) (1994) *The Futures of Criminology*. London: Sage.

Nellis, M. (2005) Electronic monitoring, satellite tracking and the new punitiveness in England and Wales, in J. Pratt (ed.), *The New Punitiveness*. Cullompton: Willan.

Nellis, M. (2006) NOMS, contestability and the process of technocractic innovation, in M. Hough and U. Padel (eds), *Reshaping Probation and Prisons: The New Offender Management Framework*. Bristol: Policy Press.

Nellis, M. (2007) Electronic monitoring, in R. Canton and D. Hancock (eds), *Dictionary of Probation and Offender Management*. Cullompton: Willan.

Newell, T. (2007) Face to face with violence and its effects, *Probation Journal*, 54(3): 227–38.

Newman, J. (2001) *Modernising Governance*. London: Sage

News BBC (2006a) Killer psychiatric care panned. Available at: www.news.bbc.co.uk (accessed 9 March 2007).

News BBC (2006b) Call for stiffer sentence for attacker of girl, 3. Available at: www.news.bbc.co.uk (accessed 8 March 2007).

News BBC (2007a) Limit jail sentences. Available at: www.news.bbc.co.uk (accessed 8 March 2007).
News BBC (2007b) Child porn sentence is condemned. Available at: www.news.bbc.co.uk (accessed 8 March 2007).
News BBC (2007c) Full jails change child porn term. Available at: www.news.bbc.co.uk (accessed 8 March 2007).
News BBC (2007d) World prison populations. Available at: www.news.bbc.co.uk (accessed 8 March 2007).
News BBC (2007e) Some murderers in jail 'too long'. Available at: www.news.bbc.co.uk (accessed 9 March 2006).
News BBC (2007f) Reid loses Afghan hijack ruling. Available at: www.news.bbc.co.uk (accessed 9 March 2007).
News of the World (2000a) Named, Shamed, 23 July, p. 1.
News of the World (2000b) Sign here for Sarah, 30 July, p. 1.
News of the World (2001) Named, Shamed. 16 December, p. 1.
NHS London (2006) *Report of the Independent Inquiry into the Care and Treatment of John Barrett*. London: NHS London.
Nicholas, S., Kershaw, C. and Walker, A. (eds) (2007) *Crime in England and Wales 2006/07*, Home Office Statistical Bulletin. London: Home Office.
Norris, C. (2006) CCTV: beyond penal modernism? *British Journal of Criminology*, 46(1): 97–118.
Norris, C. (2007) The intensification and bifurcation of surveillance in British criminal justice policy, *European Journal on Criminal Policy and Research*, 13(1–2): 139–58.
NPS (National Probation Service) Briefing (2003) *Issue 16 2003 – Criminal Justice Act 2003*. London: Home Office.
NPS (National Probation Service) (2004) *Sex Offender Strategy*. London: NPS.
NPS (National Probation Service) (2005) *Learning Points from Serious Further Offence Full Reviews*. London: NOMS/NPS.
NSPCC (1992) *The NSPCC Fort Park*. London: NSPCC.
O'Malley, P. (1999) Volatile and contradictory punishment, *Theoretical Criminology*, 3(2): 175–96.
O'Malley, P. (2001) Discontinuity, government and risk, *Theoretical Criminology*, 5(1): 85–92.
O'Malley, P. (2004a) The uncertain promise of risk, *The Australian and New Zealand Journal of Criminology*, 37(3): 323–43.
O'Malley, P. (2004b) *Risk, Uncertainty and Government*. London: The Glass House Press.
O'Malley, P. (2006) Criminology and risk, in G. Mythen and S. Walklate (eds), *Beyond the Risk Society: Critical Reflections on Risk and Human Security*. Maidenhead: Open University Press.
O'Malley, P, Weir, L. and Shearing, C. (1997) Governmentality, criticism and politics, *Economy and Society*, 26(4): 501–17.
Padfield, N. (2007) *Who to Release? Parole, Fairness and Criminal Justice*. Cullompton: Willan.
Parton, N. (1986) The Beckford Inquiry: a critical appraisal, *British Journal of Social Work*, 16(5): 531–56.

Patel, K. and Lord, A. (2001) Ethnic minority sex offenders' experiences of treatment, *Journal of Sexual Aggression*, 7: 40–51.

Paternoster, R., Backman, R., Brame, R., and Sherman, L. (1997) Do fair procedures matter? The effect of procedural justice on spousal assault, *Law and Society Review*, 31: 163–204.

Pawson, R. (2002) *Does Megan's Law Work? A Theory-driven Systematic Review*, Working paper 8. London: ESRC UK Centre for Evidence Based Policy and Practice, University of London. Available at: www. evidencenetwork.org/cgi win/enet.exe/biblioview?780 (accessed 23 November 2007).

Payne, L. (2004) Information sharing and assessment (ISA): can data management reduce risk? *Children and Society*, 18(5): 383–6.

PC (Probation Circular) (2004a) *PC 53/2004 Pre-sentence Reports and OASys*. London: National Probation Directorate.

PC (Probation Circular) (2004b) *54/2004 The MAPPA Guidance*. London: National Probation Service.

PC (Probation Circular) (2005a) *PC/49 2005 Assessment and Management of Risk of Harm Action Plan*. London: National Probation Directorate.

PC (Probation Circular) (2005b) *PC 82/2005 Monitoring Risk of Harm*. London: National Probation Directorate.

PC (Probation Circular) (2006a) *PC 15/2006 Guidance on the Implementation of Practice Recommendations Arising from HMIP Independent Review of Serious Offence Case*. London: National Probation Directorate.

PC (Probation Circular) (2006b) *PC22/2006 Implementation of the Risk of Harm Guidance and Training Resource Pack*. London: National Probation Directorate.

PC (Probation Circular) (2006c) *PC 36/2006 OASys Manual Revised Chapter on Risk of Serious Harm*. London: National Probation Directorate.

PC (Probation Circular) (2006d) *PC 40/2006 VISOR*. London: National Probation Directorate.

Peay, J. (2003) *Decisions and Dilemmas Working with Mental Health Law*. London: Hart Publishing.

Perrow, C. (1984) *Normal Accidents: Living with High-Risk Technologies*. New York: Basic Books.

Petersen, A. (1997) Risk, governance and the new public health, in A. Petersen and R. Bunton (eds), *Foucault, Health and Medicine*. London: Routledge.

Petersen, A. and Lupton, D. (1996) *The New Public Health: Health and Self in the Age of Risk*. London: Sage.

Petrunik, M. (1993) The hare and the tortoise: dangerous and sex offender policy in the United States and Canada, *Canadian Journal of Criminology and Criminal Justice*, 45: 1.

Petrunik, M. (1994) *Models of Dangerousness: A Cross Jurisdictional Review of Dangerous Offender Legislation and Practice*. Ottawa: Solicitor General Canada.

Petrunik, M. (2002) Managing unacceptable risk: sex offenders, community response and social policy in the United States and Canada, *International Journal of Offender Therapy and Comparative Criminology*, 46(4): 483–511.

Philo, G. (1999) Media and mental illness, in G. Philo (ed.), *Message Received*. Harloco, UK: Addison Wesley Longman, pp. 54–61.

Pidgeon, N., Kasperson, R., and Slovic, P. (eds) (2002) *Social Amplification of Risk and Risk Communication*. Cambridge: Cambridge University Press.

Plotnikoff, J. and Woolfson, R. (2000) *Where Are They Now? An Evaluation of Sex Offender Registration in England and Wales*. London: Home Office.

Polaschek, D. L. L. and Collie, R. M. (2004) Rehabilitating serious violent adult offenders: an empirical and theoretical stoke-take, *Psychology, Crime and Law*, 10: 321–34.

Polaschek, D. L. L., Wilson, N. J., Townsend, M. R. and Daly, L. R. (2005) Cognitive-behavioural rehabilitation for high risk violent offenders: an outcome evaluation for the Violence Prediction Unit, *Journal of Interpersonal Violence*, 20(12): 1611–27.

Porporino, F. and Fabiano, E. (2007) Case managing offenders within a motivational framework, in G. McIvor and P. Raynor (eds), *Developments in Social Work with Offenders*, Research Highlights 48. London: Jessica Kingsley Publishers, pp. 184–213.

Power, H. (2003) Disclosing information on sex offenders: the human rights implications, in A. Matravers (ed.), *Sex Offenders in the Community: Managing and Reducing the Risk*. Cullumpton: Willan.

Pratt, J. (1997) *Governing the Dangerous*. Sydney: Federation Press.

Pratt, J. (2000a) The return of the wheelbarrow men or the arrival of postmodern penality? *British Journal of Criminology*, 40: 127–45.

Pratt, J. (2000b) Emotive and ostentatious punishment: its decline and resurgence in modern society, *Punishment and Society*, 2(4): 127–45.

Pratt, J. (2006) The dark side of paradise: explaining New Zealand's history of high imprisonment, *British Journal of Criminology*, 46: 541–60.

Presidential Commission (1986) *Report of the Presidential Commission on the Space Shuttle Challenger Accident*. Washington, DC: Government Printing Agency.

Priestley, P. and Vanstone, M. (2006) Abolishing probation – a political crime? *Probation Journal*, 53(4): 408–16.

Prins, H. (1999) *Will They Do It Again? Risk Assessment and Management in Criminal Justice and Psychiatry*. London: Routledge.

Prins, H. (2002) *Will They Do It Again? Risk Assessment and Management in Criminal Justice and Psychiatry*. London: Routledge.

Proctor, E. (1994) Sex offender programmes: do they work? *Probation Journal*, 41(1): 31–42.

Quaker Peace and Social Justice (2005) *Circles of Support and Accountability in the Thames Valley: The First Three Years April 2002 to March 2005*. Available at: www.quaker.org.uk.

Quinsey, V., Khanna, A. and Malcolm, P. B. (1998) A retrospective evaluation of the Regional Treatment Centre sex offender treatment program, *Journal of Interpersonal Violence*, 13(5): 621–44.

Quinsey, V. L., Harris, G. T., Rice, M. E., and Cormier, C. A. (2005) *Violent Offenders: Appraising and Managing Risk*, 2nd edn. New York: American Psychological Association.

Radzinowicz, L. (1948) *A History of English Criminal Law, Vol. 2*. London: Stevens and Sons.

Ray, M. and Craze, L. (1991) *Provisions for Violent Offenders: Perpetuating Myths* or *Confronting Challenges. Serious Violent Offenders: Sentencing, Psychiatry, and Law Reform.* Australia: Australian Institute of Criminology.

Rayner, S. (1992) Cultural theory and risk analysis, in S. Krimsky and D. Golding (eds), *Social Theories of Risk.* Westport, CT: Praeger.

Raynor, P. (1999) Risk, needs and effective practice: the impact and potential of new assessment methods in probation, paper presented to the British Criminology Conference, July.

Recorded Crime Statistics (1898–2001/02) Available at: www.homeoffice.gov.uk/rds/pdfs/100yers.xls.

Reder, P. and Duncan, S. (1999) *Lost Innocents: A Follow-up Study of Fatal Child Abuse.* London: Routledge.

Rex, S. (1999) Desistance from offending: experiences of probation, *Howard Journal of Criminal Justice,* 38(4): 366–83.

Rex, S. and Matravers, A. (1998) *Pro-social Modelling and Legitimacy.* Cambridge: Cambridge Institute of Criminology.

Rice, M. E. (1997) Violent offender research and the implications for the criminal justice system, *American Psychologist,* 52(4): 414–23.

Rice, M. E. and Harris, G. T. (1995) Violent recidivism: assessing predictive validity, *Journal of Consulting and Clinical Psychology,* 63: 737–48.

Rice, M. E., Harris, G. T. and Cormier, C. A. (1992) An evaluation of a maximum security therapeutic community for psychopaths and other mentally disordered offenders, *Law and Human Behaviour,* 16: 399–412.

Rigakos, G. and Hadden, R. W. (2001) Crime, capitalism and the 'risk society': towards the same old modernity? *Theoretical Criminology,* 5(1): 61–84.

Rio Declaration (1992) On environment and development, made at UNCED, ISBN 9 21 1000509 4. Available at: www.unep.org/Documents/Default.asp?DocumentsID=78&ArticleID=1163 (accessed 8 August 2007).

RMA (Risk Management Authority) (2006) *Standards and Guidelines for Risk Assessment (Version 1 April).* RMA: Paisley. Available at: www.RMAScotland.gov.uk.

RMA (Risk Management Authority) (2007) *Standards and Guidelines for Risk Management (version 1).* RMA: Paisley. Available at: www.RMAScotland.gov.uk.

Roberts, Y. (2007) Where John Reid could do some good, *First Post,* online magazine, 1 February. Available at: www.The First Post 'paedopals'cutreoffendingrates.htm (accessed 13 March 2007).

Robinson, A. (2005) *Domestic Violence MARACS (Multi-Agency Risk Assessment Conferences) for Very High Risk Victims in Cardiff, Wales: A Process and Outcome Evaluation.* Cardiff: School of Social Sciences, Cardiff University.

Robinson, A. and Tregidga, Y. (2005) *Domestic Violence MARACS (Multi-Agency Risk Assessment Conferences) for Very High Risk Victims in Cardiff, Wales: Views from the Victims.* Cardiff: School of Social Sciences, Cardiff University.

Robinson, G. (1999) Risk management and rehabilitation in the Probation Service: collision and collusion, *Howard Journal of Criminal Justice,* 38(4): 421–33.

Robinson, G. (2001) Power, knowledge and 'what works' in Probation, *Howard Journal of Criminal Justice,* 40(3): 235–54.

Robinson, G. (2002) A rationality of risk in the Probation Service: its evolution and contemporary profile, *Punishment and Society,* 4(1): 5–25.

Robinson, G. (2003) Risk and risk assessment, in W. C. Chui and M. Nellis (eds), *Moving Probation Forward: Evidence, Arguments and Practice*. Harlow: Pearson Education.

Robinson, G. and Raynor, P. (2006) The future of rehabilitation: what role for the Probation Service? *Probation Journal*, 53(4): 334–46

Roche, D. (2003) *Accountability in Restorative Justice*, Clarendon Studies. Oxford: Oxford University Press.

Rose, N. (1996a) Governing 'advanced' liberal democracies, in A. Barry, T. Osborne and N. Rose (eds), *Foucault and Political Reason: Liberalism, Neo-liberalism and Rationalities of Government*. London: UCL Press.

Rose, N. (1996b) The death of the social? Re-figuring the territory of government, *Economy and Society*, 25(3): 327–56.

Rose, N. (1998) Living dangerously: risky thinking and risk management in mental health care, *Mental Health Care*, April, 1(8): 249.

Rose, N. (1999) *Powers of Freedom: Reforming Political Thought*. Cambridge: Cambridge University Press.

Rose, N. (2000) Government and control, *British Journal of Criminology*, 40: 321–39.

Rose, N. (2001) Society, madness and control, in A. Buchanan (ed.), *The Care of the Mentally Disordered Offender in the Community*. Oxford: Oxford University Press.

Rose, N. (2004) Governing the social, in N. Gane (ed.), *The Future of Social Theory*. London: Continuum.

Royal College of Psychiatrists (1996) *Response to the Home Office Consultation Document on Dangerous Severe Personality Disorder*. London: Royal College of Psychiatrists.

Royal College of Psychiatrists (2004) *Psychiatrists and Multi-Agency Public Protection Arrangements*. Available at: www.rcpsych.ac.uk (accessed 14 March 2007).

Royal Society Study Group (1992) *Risk: Analysis, Perception and Management*. London: Royal Society.

Runciman, W. B. (1993) System failure: an analysis of 2000 incident reports, *Anaesthesia and Intensive Care*, October, 21(5): 684–95.

Russell, B. Z. (2005) Idaho leaves most violent and sexual predators unsupervised, *Spokesman Review*, 24 July, p.1.

Ruston, A. and Clayton, J. (2002) Coronary heart disease: women's assessment of risk – a qualitative study, *Health, Risk and Society*, 4: 125–37.

Ruszczyski, A. P. and Greengard, C. (2002) *Decision Making Under Conditions of Uncertainty*. London: Springer.

Sample, L. and Bray, T. (2006) Are sex offenders different? An examination of re-arrest patterns, *Criminal Justice Policy Review*, 17(1): 83–102.

Sanders, C. R. and Lyon, E. (1995) Repetitive retribution: media images and the cultural construction of criminal justice, in J. Ferrell and C. Sanders (eds), *Cultural Criminology*. Boston, MA: Northeastern University Press.

Satayamurti, C. (1981) *Occupational Survival*. Oxford: Blackwell Publishers.

Scheela, R. and Stern, P. (1994) Falling apart: a process integral to the remodelling of male incest offenders, *Archives of Psychiatric Nursing*, 22: 749–67.

Scholle, A. D. (2000) Sex offender registration, *FBI Law Enforcement Bulletin*, 69(7): 18–24.

Schon, D. A. (1983) *The Reflective Practitioner*. New York: Basic Books.

Schram, D. and Milloy, C. D. (1995) *Community Notification: A Study of Offender Characteristics and Recidivism*. Olympia: Washington State Institute for Public Policy.

Scott, P. (1977) Assessing dangerousness in criminals, *British Journal of Psychiatry*, 131: 127–42.

Seidel, G. and Vidal, L. (1997) The implications of 'medical' gender in 'development' and 'culturalist' discourses for HIV/AIDS policy in Africa, in C. Shore and S. Wright (eds), *Anthropology of Policy*. London: Routledge.

Senior, P., Crowther-Dowey, C. and Long, M. (2007) *Understanding the Modernisation of Criminal Justice*. Maidenhead: Open University Press/McGraw-Hill.

Sheath, M. (1990) Confrontative work with sex offenders: legitimised nonce bashing? *Probation Journal*, 37(4): 159–62.

Shepherd, J. (2005) Victims in the National Health Service: combining treatment with violence prevention, *Criminal Behaviour and Mental Health*, 15: 75–82.

Shepherd, J. (2007) Preventing alcohol-related violence: a public health approach, *Criminal Behaviour and Mental Health*, 17: 250–64.

Sheppard, D. (1996) *Learning the Lessons: Mental Health Inquiry Reports published in England and Wales Between 1969–1996 and their Recommendations for Improving Practice*, 2nd edn. London: Zito Trust.

Sherman, L. and Strang, H. (2007) *Restorative Justice: The Evidence*. London: The Smith Institute.

Sherman, L., Strang, H. and Woods, D. (2000) *Recidivism Patterns in the Canberra Reintegrative and Shaming Experiments*. Canberra: Australian National University.

Shute, S. (2004) The Sexual Offences Act 2003 (4) New civil prevention orders; sexual offences prevention orders; foreign travel orders; risk of sexual harm orders, *Criminal Law Review*, pp. 417–40.

Shute, S. (2007) Parole and risk assessment, in N. Padfield (ed.), *Who to Release? Parole, Fairness and Criminal Justice*. Cullompton: Willan, pp. 21–42.

Silverman, J. (2006) *Vocal Judiciary Nothing New*. Available at: www.news.bbc.co.uk (accessed 8 March 2007).

Silverman, J. and Wilson, D. (2002) *Innocence Betrayed: Paedophilia, the Media and Society*. Cambridge: Polity Press.

Simon, J. (1998) Managing the monstrous: sex offenders and the new penology, *Psychology, Public Policy and Law*, 4(1–2): 452–67.

Sivarajasingham, V., Shepherd, J. and Matthew, K. (2003) Effect of urban closed circuit television on assault injury and violence detection, *Injury Prevention*, 9: 312–16.

Slovic, P. (1987) Perceptions of risk, *Science*, 236: 280–5.

Slovic, P. (1992) Perceptions of risk: reflections on the psychometric paradigm, in S. Krimsky and D. Golding (eds), *Social Theories of Risk*. Westport, CT: Praeger.

Slovic, P. (2000) *The Perception of Risk*. London: Earthscan.

Smart, C. (1989) *Feminism and the Power of Law*. London: Routledge.

Social Exclusion Unit (2002) *Reducing Re-offending by Ex-prisoners*. London: Office of the Deputy Prime Minister (OPDM).

Soothill, K. (2003) Serious sexual assault: using history and statistics, in A. Matravers (ed.), *Sex Offenders in the Community: Managing and Reducing the Risk.* Cullompton: Willan.

Soothill, K. and Walby, C. (1991) *Sex Crime in the News.* London: Routledge.

Sparks, R. (2000) Risk and blame in criminal justice controversies: British press coverage and official discourse on prison security (1993–1996), in M. Brown and J. Pratt (eds), *Dangerous Offenders: Punishment and Social Order.* London: Routledge.

Sparks, R. (2001a) 'Bringin' it all back home': populism, media coverage and the dynamics of locality and globality in the politics of crime control, in K. Stenson and R. R. Sullivan (eds), *Crime, Risk and Justice: The Politics of Crime Control in Liberal Democracies.* Cullumpton: Willan.

Sparks, R. (2001b) Degrees of enstrangement: the cultural theory of risk and comparative penology, *Theoretical Criminology,* 5(2): 159–76.

Stalans, L. J., Yarnold, P. R., Seng, M., Olson, D. E. and Repp, M. (2004) Identifying three types of violent offenders and predicting violent recidivism while on probation: a classification tree analysis, *Law and Human Behaviour,* 28(3): 252–71.

Stanko, E. M. (1990) *Everyday Violence.* London: Pandora.

Starbuck, W. H. and Milliken, J. (1988) Challenger: Fine tuning the odds until something breaks, *Journal of Management Studies,* 25(4): 319–40.

Stenson, K. (2001) The new politics of crime control, in K. Stenson and R. R. Sullivan (eds), *Crime, Risk and Justice: The Politics of Crime Control in Liberal Democracies.* Cullompton: Willan.

Stenson, K. and Edwards, A. (2001) Crime control and liberal government: the 'third way' and the return of the local, in K. Stenson and R. R. Sullivan (eds), *Crime, Risk and Justice: The Politics of Crime Control in Liberal Democracies.* Cullompton: Willan.

Stenson, K and Sullivan, R. R. (eds) (2001) *Crime, Risk and Justice: The Politics of Crime Control in Liberal Democracies.* Cullompton: Willan.

Stone, M. (2005) Psychiatrists devise depravity rating to help courts decide in death sentences, *Daily Telegraph,* 20 February.

Stone, N. (2004a) 'Dangerous' offenders: early guidance on the CJA 2003, *Probation Journal,* 53(2): 193–8.

Stone, N. (2004b) 'Dangerous' Offenders: No basis for concluding a risk of 'serious harm', *Probation Journal,* 53(3): 299–303.

Stone, N. (2004c) 'Dangerous' offenders, *Probation Journal,* 53(4): 439–44.

Stop it Now! (2007) Available at: www.stopitnow.org (accessed 24 September 2007).

Strachan, R. and Tallant, C. (1997) Improving judgement and appreciating biases in the risk assessment process, in H. Kemshall and J. Pritchard (eds), *Good Practice in Risk Assessment and Risk Management, Vol. 2.* London: Jessica Kingsley, pp. 15–26.

Strang, H., Barnes, G. C., Braithwaite, J. and Sherman, L. (1999) *Experiments in Restorative Policing: A Progress Report on the Canberra Reintegrative Shaming Experiments (RISE).* Canberra: Australian National University.

Sunday Times, The (2006) A crisis in our jails, 18 June, p. 16.

Tabachnick, J. and Dawson, E. (1999) *Stop It Now! Vermont: Four Year Program Evaluation, 1995–1999.* Available at: www.stopitnow.org (accessed 24 September 2007).

Taylor, P. J. and Gunn, J. (1999) Homicides by people with mental illness: myth and reality, *British Journal of Psychiatry*, 174: 9–14.

Taylor, R., Wasik, M. and Leng, R. (2004) *Blackstone's Guide to The Criminal Justice Act 2003*. Oxford: Oxford University Press.

TDI (The Derwent Initiative) (2007) *Tackling Sex Offending Together*. Newcastle upon Tyne: TDI.

Tewksbury, R. (2002) Validity and utility of the Kentucky sex offender registry, *Federal Probation*, 66(1): 21–6.

Tewksbury, R. (2005) Collateral consequences of sex offender registration, *Journal of Contemporary Criminal Justice*, 21(1): 67–81.

Tewksbury, R. and Lees, M. (2007) Perceptions of punishment: how registered sex offenders view registeries, *Crime and Delinquency*, 53(3): 380–407.

Thames Valley Circles of Support and Accountability (2005) *Circles of Support and Accountability in the Thames Valley: The First Three Years April 2002–March 2005*. London: Quaker Communications.

Thirlaway, K. J. and Hegg, D. A. (2005) Interpreting risk messages: women's responses to a health story, *Health, Risk and Society*, 7: 107–21.

Thomas, T. (2004a) When public protection becomes punishment? The UK use of civil measures to contain the sex offender, *European Journal on Criminal Policy and Research*, 10(4): 337–51.

Thomas, T. (2004b) Sex offender registers and monitoring, in H. Kemshall and G. McIvor (eds), *Managing Sex Offender Risk*, Research Highlights 46. London: Jessica Kingsley, pp. 225–48.

Thomas, T. (2005) *Sex Crime: Sex Offending and Society*. Cullompton: Willan.

Timmermans, S. and Gabe, J. (2003) *Partners in Health, Partners in Crime*. Oxford: Blackwell Publishing.

Trotter, C. (1993) *The Supervision of Offenders – What Works? A Study Undertaken in Community Based Corrections*. Melbourne, Victoria: Social Work Department, Monash University and the Victoria Department of Justice.

Trotter, C. (1999) *Working With Involuntary Clients: A Guide to Practice*. London: Sage.

Trotter, C. (2000) Social work education, pro-social modelling and effective probation practice, *Probation Journal*, 47: 256–61.

Trotter, C. (2007) Pro-social modelling, in G. McIvor and P. Raynor (eds), *Developments in Social Work with Offenders*, Research Highlights 48. London: Jessica Kingsley, pp. 212–33.

Tuddenham, R. (2000) Beyond defensible decision-making: towards reflexive assessment of risk and dangerousness, *Probation Journal*, 47: 173–83.

Tulloch, J. and Lupton, D. (2001) Risk, the mass media and personal biography, *European Journal of Cultural Studies*, 4(1): 5–27.

Tulloch, J. and Lupton, D. (2003) *Risk and Everyday Life*. London: Sage.

Turner, T. and Columbo, A. (2004) Risky business: the problem with MAPPs, *Criminal Justice Matters*, Autumn, 61(34–5): 40.

USSR State Committee on the Utilization of Atomic Energy (1986) The accident at Chernobyl Nuclear Power Plant and its consequences, information compiled for the IAEA Experts' Meeting, Vienna, 25–29 August.

Van Swaaningen, R. (1997) *Critical Criminology: Visitors from Europe*. London: Sage.

Van Swaaningen, R. (2000) Dutch crime prevention politics and the possibilities of a replacement discourse, paper delivered to the symposium on Rethinking Crime Prevention and Community Safety, The Open University, Milton Keynes, 29 June.

Villeneuve, D. B. and Quinsey, V. L. (1995) Predictors of general and violent recidivism among mentally disordered offenders, *Criminal Justice and Behaviour*, 22(4): 397–410.

Vivian-Byrne, S. (2004) Changing people's minds, *Journal of Sexual Aggression*, 10(2): 181–92.

Vollum, S. and Hale, C. (2002) Electronic monitoring: a research view, *Corrections Compendium*, 27(7): 1–26.

Von Hirsch, A. and Ashworth, A. (1996) Protective sentencing under Section 2(2)(b): the criteria for dangerousness, *Criminal Law Review*, pp. 175–83.

Walker, J., Golden, J. and VanHouten, A. (2001) The geographic link between sex offenders and potential victims: a routine activities approach, *Justice Research and Policy*, 3(2): 15–33.

Walklate, S. (1997) Risk and criminal victimisation, *British Journal of Criminology*, 37(1): 35–45.

Walklate, S. (1998) *Understanding Criminology*. Buckingham: Open University Press.

Wang, E. W., Owens, R. M., Long, S. A., Diamond, P. M., and Smith, J. L. (2000) The effectiveness of rehabilitation with persistently violent male prisoners, *International Journal of Offender Therapy and Comparative Criminology*, 44(4): 505–14.

Warburton, A. L. and Shepherd, J. P. (2004) Development, utilisation and importance of accident and emergency-derived assault data in violence management, *Emergency Medicine Journal*, 21: 473–7.

Warburton, A. L. and Shepherd, J. P. (2006) Tackling alcohol related violence in city centres: effect of emergency medicine and police intervention, *Emergency Medicine Journal*, 23: 12–17.

Ward, T. (2000) Sexual offenders' cognitive distortions as implicit theories, *Aggression and Violent Behaviour: A Review Journal*, 7: 513–28.

Ward, T. and Hudson, S. M. (1996) Relapse prevention: a critical analysis, *Sexual Abuse: A Journal of Research and Treatment*, 8: 177–200.

Ward, T. and Hudson, S.M. (2000) A self-regulation model of relapse prevention, in D. R. Laws, S. M. Hudson and T. Ward (eds), *Remaking Relapse Prevention with Sex Offenders: A Source Book*. Newbury Park, CA: Sage.

Ward, T. and Marshall, W. L. (2004) Good lives, aetiology and the rehabilitation of sex offenders: a bridging theory, *Journal of Sexual Aggression*, 10(2): 153–70.

Ward, T. and Maruna, S. (2007) *Rehabilitation*. London: Routledge.

Ward, T. and Stewart, C. (2003a) Criminogenic needs and human needs: a theoretical model, *Psychology, Crime and Law*, 31(3): 282–305.

Ward, T. and Stewart, C. (2003b) The treatment of sex offenders: risk management and good lives, *Professional Psychology: Research and Practice*, 34(4): 353–60.

Ward, T., Purvis, M. and Devilly, G. (2004) Relapse prevention: theory and practice, in H. Kemshall and G. McIvor (eds), *Managing Sex Offender Risk*. London: Jessica Kingsley.

Wasik, M. and Taylor, R. D. (1991) *Blackstone's Guide to the Criminal Justice Act 1991*. Oxford: Blackstone Press.

Watt, K. and Shepherd, J. (2005) *A Randomised Controlled Trial of Alcohol Brief Intervention for Violent Offenders in a Magistrates' Court*. Cardiff: Wales Office for Research in Health and Social Care.

Webster, C. and Hucker, S. J. (2007) *Violence Risk: Assessment and Management*. Chichester: John Wiley and Sons.

Webster, C., Akhtar, S., Bower, L. et al. (2004) The impact of the prison service sex offender treatment programme on minority ethnic offenders: a preliminary study, *Psychology, Crime and Law*, 10(2): 113–24.

Welch, M., Fenwick, M. and Roberts, M. (1997) Primary definitions of crime and moral panics: a content analysis of experts' quotes in feature newspaper articles on crime, *Journal of Research on Crime, and Delinquency*, 34: 474–94.

Whitehead, P. R., Ward, T. and Collie, R. M. (2007) Time for a change: applying the Good Lives model of rehabilitation to a high-risk offender, *International Journal of Offender Therapy and Comparative Criminology*, 51(5): 578–98.

Whitty, N. (2007) Risk, human rights and the management of a serious sex offender, *The German Journal of Law and Society (Zeitschrift fur Rechtssoziologies)*, 28(2): 265–76.

Wilczynski, A. and Sinclair, K. (1999) Moral tales: representations of child abuse in the quality and tabloid media, *Australian and New Zealand Journal of Criminology*, 32(3): 262–83.

Wilkinson, B. (2006) Best practice in the avoidance of errors, in H. Kemshall, G. Mackenzie, B. Wilkinson and J. Miller (2006) *The Assessment and Management of the Risk of Harm: Guidance and Training CD-rom for NOMS*. Leicester: DeMontfort University with Home Office Public Protection Unit/NOMS.

Wilson, D. (2006) *The Prison Trick*. Available at: www.guardian.co.uk/comment/story/o,,1799618.00.html (accessed 13 March 2007).

Wilson, R. J. (2003) Risk, reintegration and registration: a Canadian perspective on community sex offender risk management, *ATSA Forum, 15*.

Wilson, R. J. (2007) Out in the open, *Community Care*, 19–25 April, pp. 36–7.

Wilson, R. J. and Picheca, J. E. (2005) Circles of Support and Accountability: engaging the community in sexual offender risk management, in B. K. Schwartz (ed.), *The Sexual Offender, vol. 5*. New York: Civic Research Institute.

Wilson, R., Stewart, L., Stirpe, T., Barrett, M. and Cripps, J. E. (2000) Community based sexual offender management: combining parole supervision and treatment to reduce recidivism, *Canadian Journal of Criminology*, 42: 177–88.

Wilson, R. J., Huculak, B. and McWhinnie, A. (2002) Restorative justice innovations in Canada, *Behavioural Sciences and Law*, 20: 363–80.

Wilson, R. J., Picheca, J. E. and Prinzo, M. (2005) *Circles of Support and Accountability: An Evaluation of the Pilot Project in South-Central Ontario*, Research Report R-168. Ottawa, ON: Correctional Service of Canada.

Wilson, R. J., Picheca, J. E. and Prinzo, M. (2007a) Evaluating the effectiveness of professionally-facilitated volunteerism in the community based management of high-risk sexual offenders: part one – effects on participants and stakeholders, *Howard Journal*, 46(3): 289–302.

Wilson, R., Picheca, J. and Prinzo, M. (2007b) Evaluating the effectiveness of professionally-facilitated volunteerism in the community management of high-risk sexual offenders: part two – a comparison of recidivism rates, *Howard Journal*, 46(4): 327–37.

Winlow, S. and Hall, S. (2005) *Violent Night: Night-time Leisure and Contemporary Culture*. Oxford: Berg.

Wood, D. (ed.) (2006) *A Report on the Surveillance Society*. London: The Information Commissioner.

Wood, J. (2006) Profiling high-risk offenders: a review of 136 cases, *The Howard Journal*, 45(3): 307–20.

Wood, J. and Kemshall, H. (2008) Accountability and partnerships in criminal justice: the case of Multi-Agency Public Protection Arrangements (MAPPA), in B. Stout, J. Yates, B. Williams (eds), *Applied Criminology*. London: Sage.

Wood, J. and Kemshall, H. with Maguire, M., Hudson, K. and Mackenzie, G. (2007) *The Operation and Experience of Multi-Agency Public Protection Arrangements (MAPPA)*. London: Home Office, Research and Statistics Department. Available at: www.homeoffice.gov.uk/rds/pubintro1.html (online report 12/07).

Worrall, A. (1997) *Punishment in the Community: The Future of Criminal Justice*. London: Longman.

Worth, R. (2005) Questions about legality and effectiveness, *New York Times*, 3 October, p. 1.

Wynne, B. (1982) *Rationality and Ritual: The Windscale Inquiry and Nuclear Decisions in Britain*. Chalfont St Giles: The British Society for the History of Science.

Young, J. (1999) *The Exclusive Society: Social Exclusion, Crime and Difference in Late Modernity*. London: Sage.

Zevitz, R. G. and Farkas, M. A. (2000a) The impact of sex offender community notification on probation/parole in Wisconsin, *International Journal of Offender Therapy and Comparative Criminology*, 44: 8–21.

Zevitz, R. G. and Farkas, M. A. (2000b) Sex offender community notification: managing high risk criminals or exacting further vengeance? *Behavioral Sciences and the Law*, 10: 375–91.

Useful websites

www.crimestoppers-uk.org/ceop/ (accessed 20 November 2006).
www.dca.gov.uk/speeches/2007/sp070209.htm (accessed 23 November 2007).
www.derwentinitiative.org (accessed October 2007).
www.klaaskids.org (accessed 22 November 2007).

Index

Related books from Open University Press

Purchase from www.openup.co.uk or order through your local bookseller

---

RESEARCHING CRIMINOLOGY

Iain Crow and Natasha Semmens

> . . . what makes the book stand out is the inclusion of real research into various criminal justice institutions that have actually been undertaken by the authors. In doing so, what is produced is a book that stimulates interest and injects research passion, as well as offering research 'know how' into what can often be a difficult and sometimes dry area of research.
> *Tina Patel, Liverpool John Moores University*

> This book provides an essential tool for undergraduate students embarking upon their own research projects in Criminology. It provides clear and informative guidance on a range of research methods and designs to assist students in their own criminological endeavours.
> *Jacki Tapley, University of Portsmouth*

- How do criminologists go about studying crime and its consequences?
- How are programmes for offenders and communities evaluated?
- How can you collect and analyse criminological material?

Research on crime and criminality is often referred to by the media, policy makers and practitioners, but where does this research come from and how reliable is it?

Designed especially for students on criminology and criminal justice courses, and professionals working in the field, *Researching Criminology* emphasises the importance of research as an integrated process. It looks at the ways in which a mixture of investigative methods can be used to analyze a criminological question.

Written by two experienced researchers and lecturers *Researching Criminology* is a comprehensive introduction to the aims, principles and methods of doing criminological research. The book covers all the key topics that you will encounter when researching crime. Individual chapters include material on:

- The research process
- Principles of researching criminology
- How to design criminological research
- Evaluation research
- Researching ethically
- A glossary of essential key concepts

Structured in three parts, addressing the principles of criminological research, how to collect and analyse material and providing detailed examples of real world research, *Researching Criminology* will be of benefit to all students of criminology and criminal justice, for practitioners interested in criminological research, and for those undertaking criminological research for the first time.

Contents
Part one: The principles of criminological research – *The research process* – *The principles of researching criminology* – *Designing criminological research* – *Criminological evaluation* – **Part two: Collecting and analysing material** – *Researching by reading* – *Researching by looking* – *Researching by asking and listening* – *Analysing criminological research* – **Part three: Real world research** – *Researching offenders and employment* – *Researching the youth court* – *Researching a community safety programme* – *Researching the fear of crime.*

2007   312pp
978–0–335–22140–0 (Paperback)   978–0–335–22141–7 (Hardback)

THE SURVEILLANCE STUDIES READER

Sean P. Hier and Josh Greenberg

From the horrific images of James Bulger's abduction at the Strand Shopping Centre in Bootle, through to the frighteningly mundane pictures of the July 7th bombers at Luton Station, surveillance is a key part of our everyday lives.

In this topical reader Sean Hier and Josh Greenberg bring together extracts from some of the most influential readings on surveillance studies. The reader examines thoughts about self-surveillance, scrutiny of specific parts of society, sophisticated data gathering techniques and the ubiquity of CCTV. While surveillance is an intrinsic feature of human social relationships, it is only in the past few years that information and data-gathering techniques have emerged as a sustained multi-disciplinary topic of investigation and theorization.

Surveillance studies, now a rapidly growing area of academic study, has begun documenting the changing character and consequences of surveillance techniques throughout the world. The readings presented in this book represent one more step towards developing a coherent statement on surveillance studies.

The readings are organised into distinct sections:

- Surveillance, the nation-state and social control
- Computers, simulations and assemblages
- Surveillance in everyday life
- Surveillance, politics and social inequality
- Surveillance and public opinion
- Ethics, privacy and resistance

The Surveillance Studies Reader is key reading for students of sociology, politics, social policy, media and communications studies, social psychology and criminology.

Essays by: Charles Barker, Colin Bennett, William Bogard, Roy Coleman, Christopher Dandeker, Richard Eriscson, Michel Foucault, Oscar H. Gandy, Anthony Giddens, John Gilliom, Stephen Graham, Kevin Haggerty, Susan Hansen, Sean P. Hier, David Lyon, Gary Marx, Dawn Moore, Mike Nellis, Charles Raab, Alasdair Roberts, James Rule, Graham Sewell, Mimi Sheller, John Torpey, John Urry, Kevin Walby, David Wood.

Contents

2007   408pp
978–0–335–22026–7 (Paperback)   978–0–335–22027–4 (Hardback)